Joyce's Metamorphosis

*The Florida James Joyce Series*

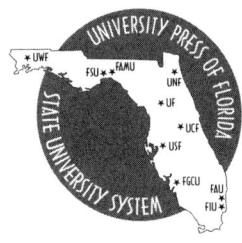

Florida A&M University, Tallahassee
Florida Atlantic University, Boca Raton
Florida Gulf Coast University, Ft. Myers
Florida International University, Miami
Florida State University, Tallahassee
University of Central Florida, Orlando
University of Florida, Gainesville
University of North Florida, Jacksonville
University of South Florida, Tampa
University of West Florida, Pensacola

The Florida James Joyce Series
Edited by Zack Bowen

*The Autobiographical Novel of Co-Consciousness: Goncharov, Woolf, and Joyce,* by Galya Diment (1994)
*Bloom's Old Sweet Song: Essays on Joyce and Music,* by Zack Bowen (1995)
*Joyce's Iritis and the Irritated Text: The Dis-lexic "Ulysses,"* by Roy Gottfried (1995)
*Joyce, Milton, and the Theory of Influence,* by Patrick Colm Hogan (1995)
*Reauthorizing Joyce,* by Vicki Mahaffey (paperback edition, 1995)
*Shaw and Joyce: "The Last Word in Stolentelling,"* by Martha Fodaski Black (1995)
*Bely, Joyce, Döblin: Peripatetics in the City Novel,* by Peter I. Barta (1996)
*Jocoserious Joyce: The Fate of Folly in "Ulysses,"* by Robert H. Bell (paperback edition, 1996)
*Joyce and Popular Culture,* edited by R. B. Kershner (1996)
*Joyce and the Jews: Culture and Texts,* by Ira B. Nadel (paperback edition, 1996)
*Narrative Design in "Finnegans Wake": The Wake Lock Picked,* by Harry Burrell (1996)
*Gender in Joyce,* edited by Jolanta W. Wawrzycka and Marlena G. Corcoran (1997)
*Latin and Roman Culture in Joyce,* by R. J. Schork (1997)
*Reading Joyce Politically,* by Trevor L. Williams (1997)
*Advertising and Commodity Culture in Joyce,* by Garry Leonard (1998)
*Greek and Hellenic Culture in Joyce,* by R. J. Schork (1998)
*Joyce, Joyceans, and the Rhetoric of Citation,* by Eloise Knowlton (1998)
*Joyce's Music and Noise: Theme and Variation in His Writings,* by Jack W. Weaver (1998)
*Reading Derrida Reading Joyce,* by Alan Roughley (1999)
*Joyce through the Ages: A Nonlinear View,* edited by Michael Patrick Gillespie (1999)
*Chaos Theory and James Joyce's Everyman,* by Peter Francis Mackey (1999)
*Joyce's Comic Portrait,* by Roy Gottfried (2000)
*Joyce and Hagiography: Saints Above!* by R. J. Schork (2000)
*Voices and Values in Joyce's "Ulysses,"* by Weldon Thornton (2000)
*The Dublin Helix: The Life of Language in Joyce's "Ulysses,"* by Sebastian D. G. Knowles (2001)
*Joyce Beyond Marx: History and Desire in "Ulysses" and "Finnegans Wake,"* by Patrick McGee (2001)
*Joyce's Metamorphosis,* by Stanley Sultan (2001)

# Joyce's Metamorphosis

Stanley Sultan

University Press of Florida
Gainesville · Tallahassee · Tampa · Boca Raton
Pensacola · Orlando · Miami · Jacksonville · Ft. Myers

Copyright 2001 by Stanley Sultan
Printed in the United States of America on acid-free paper
All rights reserved

05 04 03 02 01 00  6 5 4 3 2 1

Library of Congress Cataloging-in-Publication Data
Sultan, Stanley.
Joyce's metamorphosis / Stanley Sultan.
p. cm.—(The Florida James Joyce series)
Includes bibliographical references and index.
ISBN 0-8130-2105-7 (acid-free paper)
1. Joyce, James, 1882-1941—Criticism and interpretation. I. Title. II. Series.
PR6019.O9 Z824 2001
823'.912—dc21    2001027587

The University Press of Florida is the scholarly publishing agency for the State University System of Florida, comprising Florida A&M University, Florida Atlantic University, Florida Gulf Coast University, Florida International University, Florida State University, University of Central Florida, University of Florida, University of North Florida, University of South Florida, and University of West Florida.

University Press of Florida
15 Northwest 15th Street
Gainesville, FL 32611-2079
http://www.upf.com

To Rosemarie and Gabriel, Kendall and Jasmine

# Contents

Foreword by Zack Bowen   ix

Preface   xi

List of Abbreviated Titles   xiii

Introduction: Joyce/Lawrence   1

1. The Mature Autobiographer   14

2. A Young Writer   41

3. James Joyce and "I"   47

4. "Stories of My Childhood"   61

5. Transforming "The Sisters"   88

6. A Poetics of Autobiography   130

Appendix: Lawrence and Autobiography   155

Notes   181

Bibliography   193

Index   197

# Foreword

Stanley Sultan extensively reexamines the structure and meaning of a significant number of the *Dubliners* stories, especially in the light of earlier versions, editions, and surrounding documentation such as Joyce's correspondence. The archival research and detailed reading of the texts of these selected stories and *Portrait* passages are always thorough and very often brilliant. The idea is certainly not new, but the applications it has to narrative techniques and voice, and the subtleties and nuances involved are hardly as simplistic as the project itself sounds.

Sultan is and always was one of the best close readers in the business, and he painstakingly deconstructs the texts of the stories in *Dubliners* which are closest to Joyce's own personal life, and brilliantly delineates the changes made in Joyce's revisions from the earlier drafts and printed versions of those stories examined to the final versions we now have. He carefully dates the chronological relations among the actual dates of historical events in the stories, the dates of their original composition and revision, and the growth of Joyce's idea of making a version of himself the subject of his own fiction. That constitutes real news.

Sultan does not need to belabor the obvious connections between the Stephen Dedalus of *Portrait* and *Ulysses* and Joyce himself, but wisely concentrates on the earlier incarnations of a young Dedalus figure in the mature narrator who writes of his own boyhood experiences in the first three stories especially. Where Joyce's technique finally led him in *Ulysses* and the *Wake* is mostly summarized in the concluding chapter, but alluded to whenever germane during the course of the lengthy discussion of *Dubliners*.

Zack Bowen
Series Editor

# Preface

This is a biography of the writer when young, and strictly as writer: for example, important documentary evidence can take the form of radical revisions he made to writings as he matured. *Joyce's Metamorphosis* delineates the development of James Joyce out of his early fiction, marked by what I call a poetics of autobiography that evolved to its final stage in *Finnegans Wake*. The method can be described as philological biography. The book not only traces the young writer's development to maturity—the process of change that was the eminent Joyce's becoming—but proceeds chiefly from the history of his writing, intertextually as much as possible and almost always paratextually.

The introduction delineates, for its light on Joyce's development, the almost simultaneous, parallel, and contrary early development of D. H. Lawrence as a writer of fiction that involves the author's personal history. Six chapters and an appendix follow. The first chapter reveals the covert and elegant ways the mature Joyce inscribed himself in his art. The second briefly reviews the young writer's activity. The third demonstrates the distance from Joyce of the boys-and-narrators of the three "boyhood" stories that begin *Dubliners*. The next two discuss the evidence of young Joyce's development provided by the radical revisions he made, especially to the first (and his first published) story, "The Sisters." The final chapter traces through his career the evolution of the "poetics of autobiography" begun when young Joyce began to develop. And the appendix presents the evidence for my characterization in the introduction of Lawrence's early development.

In my acknowledgments of indebtedness, I would like to mention first my old friend Zack Bowen, for his invaluable advice about the organization of the book. My former student Jennifer Plante did with consummate skill most of the work on the index and bibliography. For advice and information I am indebted to a number of colleagues and friends: Sun Hee Kim Gertz; Morton P. Levitt; the late Augustine Martin and his colleague at University College, Dublin, the Reverend Professor Michael Nolan; Paul Schwaber; Thomas F. Staley; Robert A. Stein; William J. Sullivan; and Stephen E. Whittaker. Other assistance was generously given by Edith C. Mathis and Terri R. Rutkiewicz of the English Department, by James F. Hilow of the Office of Information Systems, and by Mary M. Hartman,

Irene W. Walch, and Edward J. McDermott of the Robert H. Goddard Library, of Clark University.

My final expression of gratitude is to my friend and former colleague, the novelist and independent scholar Anne Few Goble. For some reason, which I believe was not just striding senectitude, I found this book difficult to write. Indispensable to whatever I may have achieved in it was her generous granting to each draft chapter in turn the benefit of her erudition and her literary astuteness.

# List of Abbreviated Titles

*Argument*—Stanley Sultan, *The Argument of "Ulysses."*

"Benstock Principle"—Shari Benstock and Bernard Benstock, "The Benstock Principle," in *The Seventh of Joyce,* ed. Bernard Benstock.

*Berlin*—Isaiah Berlin, *The Hedgehog and the Fox: An Essay on Tolstoy's View of History.*

*Calendar*—Keith Sagar, *D. H. Lawrence: A Calendar of His Works.*

*Composite Biography*—Edward Nehls, ed., *D. H. Lawrence: A Composite Biography,* vol. 3.

*Croydon Years*—Helen Corke, *D. H. Lawrence: The Croydon Years.*

*Dual Voice*—Roy Pascal, *The Dual Voice.*

*Dubliners*—James Joyce, *Dubliners,* eds. Robert Scholes and A. Walton Litz.

*Early Years*—John Worthen, *D. H. Lawrence: The Early Years, 1885–1912.*

*Eliot*—T. S. Eliot, *After Strange Gods.*

*Eliot, Joyce, and Company*—Stanley Sultan, *Eliot, Joyce, and Company.*

*First-Draft Version*—David Hayman, *A First-Draft Version of "Finnegans Wake."*

Ford—Ford Madox Ford, *Return to Yesterday.*

*Forum*—D. H. Lawrence, "The Soiled Rose," *Forum* 43 (1913): 324–40.

Gabler, "Introduction"—Hans Walter Gabler, introduction to *Dubliners.*

*Hibernian Metropolis*—Paul Delany, "'A Would-Be-Dirty Mind': D. H. Lawrence as an Enemy of Joyce," in *Joyce in the Hibernian Metropolis: Essays,* eds. Morris Beja and David Norris.

*History, Ideology, and Fiction*—Graham Holderness, *D. H. Lawrence: History, Ideology, and Fiction.*

*In Search of James Joyce*—Robert Scholes, *In Search of James Joyce.*

*Irish Identity and the Literary Revival*—G. J. Watson, *Irish Identity and the Literary Revival: Synge, Yeats, Joyce, and O'Casey.*

*James Joyce*—Richard Ellmann, *James Joyce.*

*James Joyce's "Dubliners"*—John Wyse Jackson and Bernard McGinley, eds., *James Joyce's "Dubliners": An Annotated Edition.*

*Joyce-Again's Wake*—Bernard Benstock, *Joyce-Again's Wake: An Analysis of "Finnegans Wake."*

*Joyce Annotated*—Don Gifford, *Joyce Annotated.*

*Joyce, Bakhtin, and Popular Literature*—R. B. Kershner, *Joyce, Bakhtin, and Popular Literature: Chronicles of Disorder.*

*Joyce's "Dubliners"*—Warren Beck, *Joyce's "Dubliners": Substance, Vision, and Art.*

*Joyce's Voices*—Hugh Kenner, *Joyce's Voices.*

*Joyce We Knew, The*—Ulick O'Connor, ed. *The Joyce We Knew.*

*Kangaroo*—D. H. Lawrence, *Kangaroo.*

Kenner—Hugh Kenner, *Dublin's Joyce.*

*L'homme*—Emile Delavenay, *D. H. Lawrence: L'homme et la genèse de son oeuvre,* 2 vols.

Leavis—F. R. Leavis, *D. H. Lawrence: Novelist.*

*Letters* (Joyce)—James Joyce, *Letters of James Joyce,* 3 vols., eds. Stuart Gilbert and Richard Ellmann.

*Letters* (Lawrence)—D. H. Lawrence, *The Letters of D. H. Lawrence,* 7 vols.

*Life and Works*—Harry T. Moore, *D. H. Lawrence: His Life and Works.*

*Life into Art*—Keith Sagar, *D. H. Lawrence: Life into Art.*

*Literary Life*—Morris Beja, *James Joyce: A Literary Life.*

*Mimesis*—Erich Auerbach, *Mimesis: The Representation of Reality in Western Literature.*

*Mr Noon*—D. H. Lawrence, *Mr Noon,* ed. Lindeth Vasey.

*My Brother's Keeper*—Stanislaus Joyce, *My Brother's Keeper.*

*Personal Record*—Jessie Chambers ("E.T."), *D. H. Lawrence: A Personal Record.*

*Portrait*—James Joyce, *A Portrait of the Artist as a Young Man,* ed. Chester G. Anderson.

*Reader's Guide to "Finnegans Wake"*—William York Tindall, *A Reader's Guide to "Finnegans Wake."*

*Selected Essays*—T. S. Eliot, *Selected Essays: 1917–1932.*

*Selected Letters*—James Joyce, *Selected Letters of James Joyce,* ed. Richard Ellmann.

Shaw—George Bernard Shaw, *Man and Superman.*

*Short Fiction*—Janice Hubbard Harris, *The Short Fiction of D. H. Lawrence.*

*Stephen Hero*—James Joyce, *Stephen Hero,* ed. Theodore Spencer.

*Stories*—D. H. Lawrence, *The Complete Short Stories of D. H. Lawrence,* vol. 1.

*Third Census*—Adaline Glasheen, *Third Census of "Finnegans Wake."*

*Time of Apprenticeship*—Marvin Magalaner, *Time of Apprenticeship: The Fiction of Young James Joyce.*

Torchiana—Donald T. Torchiana, *Backgrounds for Joyce's "Dubliners."*

*Triumph to Exile*—Mark Kinkead-Weekes, *D. H. Lawrence: Triumph to Exile, 1912–1922.*

*Ulysses*—James Joyce, *Ulysses: The Corrected Text,* ed. Hans Walter Gabler.

Walzl—Florence L. Walzl, "Joyce's 'The Sisters': A Development," *James Joyce Quarterly* 10 (1973): 375–421.

*White Peacock, The*—D. H. Lawrence, *The White Peacock,* ed. Alan Newton.

*Workshop of Daedalus*—Robert Scholes and Richard M. Kain, eds., *The Workshop of Daedalus: James Joyce and the Raw Materials for "A Portrait of the Artist as a Young Man."*

*Years of Growth*—Peter Costello, *James Joyce: The Years of Growth, 1882–1915.*

# Introduction

Joyce/Lawrence

James Joyce and D. H. Lawrence were among the numerous post-Romantic writers of English fiction who put their own life experience and historical facts about themselves into their work. I propose that the initial stages of Joyce's evolving practice in this respect were crucial to his artistic development—to what I call Joyce's metamorphosis. Regarding Lawrence: although it is a critical commonplace that most of his early fiction is radically autobiographical, I propose that in fact he developed, almost at the beginning of his career, a very different relationship between his fiction and his personal history; and the development young Lawrence achieved seems to me an especially appropriate context for examining young Joyce's evolving practice.

The two of them are probably the most eminent writers of English fiction which draws extensively on the author's own personal history since Charlotte Brontë and early Melville. But Lawrence's development seems appropriate to me for at least three more particular reasons: (1) their early histories have many similarities, some of them singular; (2) they were absolutely hostile to each other's fiction; (3) correspondingly, their fiction documents precisely contrary views of the relationship between a writer's art and his or her life. This last particular connection between specifically those two writers is the most important one for my book; but the other two also need to be demonstrated if I am to invoke this other writer to introduce a study of Joyce.

\* \* \*

A unique similarity between the mature Joyce and Lawrence is that they were, in the words of one critic, "the two most notorious banned authors in English."[1] A similarity when mature also is revealing about them because although they were not unique it was uncommon: the outspoken opposition of both writers to the so-called Great War. Some of the similarities between them when young are of the latter sort. Both became teachers to support themselves, were reported to be good at it, and disliked it greatly. Both attacked their inherited religions. Both were democratic socialists, Lawrence briefly, Joyce for a decade or more. Both were absolutely convinced of their literary genius and went around declaring it prospectively. Both first achieved publication: in a local city newspaper; of a short story; and soon after reaching the age of twenty-two (Dublin, five months; Nottingham, two months).

Even more uncommon were their similar relations to their youthful environments. Both exiled themselves from home, yet Antaeus-like derived the matter of their art for the rest of their lives exclusively or predominantly from their home ground (Dublin and Nottinghamshire). And before their self-exiles both were graced with, and the acknowledged centers of, unusually stimulating intellectual environments.

Joyce's circle during high school and college included not only accomplished writers like "Seumas O'Sullivan," Padraic Colum, and Yeats's future doctor, future senator Oliver Gogarty, but also future judges (one of them the chief justice of Ireland), a Lord Mayor, a member of Parliament before Irish independence, and a number of prominent nationalist figures; some of these also wrote and published.

Young Lawrence's circle enjoyed less later distinction. Most were fellow prospective teachers, some also writers. (Jessie Chambers, the young woman with whom he was intellectually and emotionally involved for almost a decade, is the most well known—ironically, because of the book she wrote about their relationship, *D. H. Lawrence: A Personal Record.*) In a letter, he wrote of the "Pagans," as his circle called themselves, "Our set is a bit astonishing"; F. R. Leavis described "the extraordinarily active intellectual life enjoyed by that group of young people of which Lawrence was the centre"; and Ford Madox Hueffer/Ford wrote of "The Eastwood Intelligentsia" (in the phrase of one critic), "I have never anywhere found so educated a society," and described them at Lawrence's family home, "talking about Nietzsche and Wagner and Leopardi and Flaubert and Karl Marx and Darwin and occasionally the father would interrupt his counting to contradict them. And they would discuss the French Impressionists and the primitive Italians and play Chopin or Debussy on the piano."[2] According to their daughter, young Lawrence's older socialist and agnostic friend "Willie" Hopkin and his wife "Sallie" had guests like the Webbs, Ramsay MacDonald, Keir Hardy, and the Pankhursts (*Early Years*, pp. 116, 118).

Most striking in the similar early histories of Joyce and Lawrence is the unique complex of circumstances culminating in the self-exile of each. These similar complexes began with the death from abdominal cancer of a beloved mother; of course Lawrence, as he put it, "*loved* her, like a lover."³ Lawrence's consequent state of mind is recorded in his "mother poems" and in the state of his facsimile Paul Morel during the final chapters of *Sons and Lovers*. Joyce's is made a central element of the story of his facsimile Stephen Dedalus in *Ulysses*.⁴

The next occurrence in both complexes was unprecedented love for a woman who seemed totally inappropriate; and the consequence of that was a radical swerve by both writers into elopement which was simultaneously voluntary exile from their native homes. Of course, Joyce's rash precipitate involvement with the Galway-bred hotel maid, and Lawrence's with the daughter of a German baron and married mother of three—who had intended only an assignation on the Continent—turned out to be lifelong: Stephen's famous statement in *Ulysses,* "A man of genius makes no mistakes. His errors are . . . the portals of discovery," concerns Shakespeare's youthful marriage to Ann Hathaway. In any case, their self-exiles were simultaneously what seem to be the two most well known instances of an artist's elopement in this century. The time elapsed from their mothers' deaths, like their ages when first published, differed by three months.⁵

In isolation, this array of similarities in the early lives of Joyce and Lawrence may be more amusing than probative. But they are not isolated. Also confirming Lawrence's pertinence is the negative similarity of the mature writers' hostility to each other's fiction: although both criticized many writers, each singled out the other for special disapproval. Apparently, no two major writers in Western literature were more antipathetic to each other's art than James Augustine Joyce and David Herbert Lawrence. In the essay with the subtitle "D. H. Lawrence as an Enemy of Joyce," cited above, Paul Delany writes that they "must be counted among the great pairs of literary enemies" and declares, "It would need a book to do justice to the rivalry between" them.⁶

Their reciprocal animadversions focused on two of their banned books, *Ulysses* and *Lady Chatterley's Lover*. Joyce considered *Chatterley* pornography—that was not "effectively done"; he claimed to have read only "the first 2 pages of the usual sloppy English," in the famous sentence calling it "a piece of propaganda in favour of something which, outside of D.H.L.'s country at any rate, makes all the propaganda for itself."⁷ Lawrence reciprocated Joyce's compound compliment with the source of Delany's main title, "a would-be-dirty mind" (*Letters* VI, p. 507); but he was, characteristically, more involved and less contemptuous. Returning a borrowed copy of the recently published *Ulysses* on November 14, 1922, he wrote, "I am sorry, but I am one of the people who can't read *Ulysses*. Only bits. But I am glad I have seen the book, since in Europe they usually mention us together—James Joyce and D. H. Lawrence. . . . I guess Joyce would look as much askance on me as I on him" (*Letters* IV, p. 340).

And he had "seen" enough to make it central to "Surgery for the Novel—or a Bomb." He completed his attack on contemporary writers who, in Virginia Woolf's famous phrase in "Modern Fiction," "record[ed] the atoms as they fall upon the mind," by the end of January 1923.[8]

It is significant for Lawrence's relevance to Joyce that, according to their testimony, each of these superb readers misread the other; I shall propose below that the commitment to his own kind of art by each caused an antipathy to the mature fiction of the other that made it inaccessible. And the devotees of each usually followed suit.[9] A pair of distinguished examples are F. R. Leavis and a critic no less accomplished (and influential), who as a poet had been with Lawrence the other eminent English writer of the century to have his reputation established with Leavis's help: T. S. Eliot.

Agreeing in part with Joyce, Eliot wrote, in a passage Leavis quoted in *D. H. Lawrence: Novelist*, that Lawrence "often" wrote "very badly," though it was "in order to write sometimes well" (p. 304). But the quality of Lawrence's prose was irrelevant to Eliot's persistent criticism of him, which was moral and cultural, which is to say, ideological. (The outrage the anti-Christian sensualist engendered in the neo-Tractarian ascetic is at least partly amusing.) It is well known that Eliot was an ardent admirer, and one of the crucial early advocates (with Ezra Pound and Valery Larbaud), of *Ulysses*. And he contrasted precisely Lawrence with Joyce when, on the occasion of his politically notorious (and never republished) series of lectures, *After Strange Gods* (New York: Harcourt, 1934), he astutely juxtaposed two stories with similar situations, "The Shadow in the Rose Garden" and "The Dead." Lawrence's characters are "cruel" because "unfurnished with" any "moral or social sense" (p. 39); Joyce's treatment of his makes him "the most ethically orthodox of the more eminent writers of my time" (p. 41). (The asymmetry between Joyce's longest and most ambitious story and an unexceptional one by Lawrence aside, Eliot's simplistic grid ignores the fact that Lawrence's newly married couple may lack "social sense," but their unpleasant reciprocal frankness is by nature moral if honesty is moral.)

Leavis's juxtaposition of again precisely Joyce and Lawrence in *D. H. Lawrence: Novelist* is no more equivocal. He admonishes Eliot for "find[ing] the creative originality that really matters in the contrivances of Joyce, where insistent will and ingenuity so largely confess the failure of creative life" (p. 27), after declaring that Lawrence "would repay endless frequentation as Joyce would not. (Those two, it seems to me, were preeminently the testing, the crucial authors: if you took Joyce for a major creative writer, then . . . you had no use for Lawrence, and if you judged Lawrence a great writer, then you could hardly take a sustained interest in Joyce.)" (p. 10). The words in the ellipsis are "like Mr Eliot"; and Leavis's subject during much of the "Introduction," all of the "Appendix: Mr Eliot and Lawrence," and many passages between, in his book on "the great writer of our own phase of civilization" (p. 9), is Eliot's negative criticism of "the great creative genius of our age, and one of the greatest figures in English literature" (p. 303).[10]

Both my matched pair of examples are cultural and implicitly political in approach.[11] And the extremely partisan critics' juxtaposition of Joyce and Lawrence they exemplify, on grounds similar to theirs, was the rule before most recent considerations of the writers together, which have refused to take sides in the general dispute and, understandably, been appreciative of both.[12]

But something more important than that Lawrence was a "man [who] writes really too poorly" must have motivated Joyce's refusal to meet him in 1929, when both had become world-famous.[13] I have suggested that the antipathy of each writer to the fiction of the other derived from commitment to his own contrary type of art. The contrariety of their art can be approached by way of the fundamental opposition which "divide[s] writers and thinkers" set out by the late Isaiah Berlin in the opening pages of *The Hedgehog and the Fox: An Essay on Tolstoy's View of History* (New York: Mentor, 1957). "Dante belongs to the first category, Shakespeare to the second," he writes. A diachronic catalogue that begins with "Herodotus, Aristotle" ends with "Joyce"; and like Shakespeare, they "are foxes," who "seiz[e] on the essence of a vast variety of experiences and objects for what they are in themselves." Berlin does not mention Lawrence, but he can be recognized in the hedgehog, possessing (and possessed by) "one unchanging, all-embracing . . . at times fanatical, unitary inner vision" (pp. 7–8).

The relevance for literature of Berlin's distinction is elucidated in George Bernard Shaw's "Epistle Dedicatory" to his *Man and Superman* (1903; Baltimore: Penguin, 1952). His making exemplary (with Dickens) Berlin's exemplary fox recalls Shaw's self-serving comparisons of his own drama with Shakespeare's; but Shaw's scope here is broader:

> the artist-philosophers are the only sort of artists I take quite seriously. . . . Bunyan, Blake . . . Goethe, Shelley . . . are among the

writers whose peculiar sense of the world I recognize as more or less akin to my own.... I read Dickens and Shakespear without shame or stint; but their pregnant observations and demonstrations of life are not co-ordinated into any philosophy or religion.... They ... combin[e] sound moral judgment with light-hearted good humor. But they are concerned with the diversities of the world instead of with its unities: they ... have no constructive ideas: they regard those who have them as dangerous fanatics.... The truth is, the world was to Shakespear a great "stage of fools" ... and Dickens ... [took] the world for granted and bus[ied] himself with its details. Now you cannot say this of the works of the artist-philosophers. (pp. xxix–xxxi)

Shaw's dichotomy is Procrustean: his own work is full of good humor and the diversity of life; Shakespeare's embodies assertions (philosophy) about human beings and about their reality. But his distinction between writers fundamentally concerned to convey their ("hedgehog's") Truth, and writers who like Berlin's fox present "what [things] are in themselves," survives Shaw's rhetoric. This binary conception by which he juxtaposes doctrinal/didactic writers like himself and Shelley against eclectic/affirmant writers like Shakespeare and Dickens, expounded the year before the elder of Joyce and Lawrence published his first story, nicely assimilates as Shaw's own kind the younger, Lawrence, who called the author of *Ulysses* "like a schoolmaster with dirt and stuff in his head" (*Letters* IV, p. 345), and as the contrary kind Joyce, who dismissed *Chatterley* as "propaganda."[14]

Each of them also combines his one of Shaw's opposed fundamental conceptions with, for example, the increasingly recognized ideology and ethics in Joyce's work, and Lawrence's assertion on the third page of *Studies in Classic American Literature* (the last part of which often is cited), that "The artist usually sets out to point a moral.... The tale, however, points the other way. Never trust the artist. Trust the tale." But their prevailing attitudes remain—and can be shown to connect to their equally contrary attitudes toward the relationship of a writer's life and fiction.

The final element of my brief for young Lawrence's pertinence to this study of young Joyce concerns their part in a European legacy of Romanticism: the novel about the forming/educating (*Bildung*) of a young person whose name is different from the author's, whose life experience closely duplicates the author's, and who adopts the vocation of artist. Lawrence's *Sons and Lovers* was published (in 1913) while Joyce's *A Portrait of the*

*Artist as a Young Man* was being written (serial publication began February 2, 1914). Their novels are similar as the two most prominent autobiographical *Künstlerromanen* of the century, among many.[15] They are similar because each of those two (the beset theological metaphor seems warranted) canonical twentieth-century novels began its author's fame. (It then was helped to canonical status as compulsory reading because it was about the *Bildung* of its famous author.) They are similar because both avoid closure: *Sons and Lovers* gestures toward a life accepted in its final words ("He walked towards the faintly humming, glowing town, quickly"); the *Portrait* is ended triumphantly—but by the protagonist, whose triumph has been subverted, and is to be mocked (even by him) in a sequel. Finally, those paired novels are similar in the relation of each to the first major artistic undertaking of its author. The undertaking of Joyce, his abandoned novel *Stephen Hero*, whose autobiographical character is the protagonist, is the functional antecedent to the *Portrait;* that of Lawrence, his published novel *The White Peacock*, whose autobiographical character is the witness-narrator, is the functional antecedent to *Sons and Lovers*.

A point must be made about the nature of the autobiographical *Künstlerroman*, popular in this century. The novel about a young potential artist whose subject character is the facsimile of its creator is a distinct subgenre that, like other genres, is best conceived of rhetorically. And the necessary point is rhetorical.

It seems reasonable—certainly is understandable—to regard the authors of the two most prominent novels in the subgenre, Joyce and Lawrence, as two of the four preeminent modernist writers of English fiction during the first half of the century, and Woolf and Faulkner as the other two. Both those writers also wrote novels incorporating extensive autobiographical material. However, while in *To the Lighthouse* (1927) the mother-son relationship is an important element, as in the two novels by Joyce and Lawrence, and is Oedipal, as in Lawrence's, Mrs. Ramsay's "bundle of sensitiveness" in her phrase, her little boy James, does not represent young Virginia Stephen. And his sister Cam, who does represent her, is no more important in the novel than James. Cam's experiencing consciousness is rendered, but so is James's; she is a secondary character (Lily Briscoe, the gifted spinster painter, can be identified with the adult Woolf typologically). Even children of Julia and Sir Leslie Stephen who died figure in *To the Lighthouse*, for it is the story of the Stephen—alias Ramsay—parents *en famille*.[16]

Woolf's novel portraying her own family life while she was growing up has in common with Faulkner's *The Reivers* (1962) a fundamental difference from *Sons and Lovers* and the *Portrait* (and respecting Stephen, *Ulysses*).[17] In the affecting valedictory to his fictional world Faulkner wrote just before his death, the boy facsimile of the author (its full title is *The Reivers: A Reminiscence*) narrates a story about his family and his companions on an adventure. A common difference from the novels portraying themselves when young by Joyce and Lawrence is that in those by Woolf and Faulkner neither young person is a postulant artist; but the fundamental common difference is that the author's facsimile is not the subject: *To the Lighthouse* is not about Cam Ramsay or *The Reivers* about Lucius Priest.

For that reason, the term *autobiographical* describes Woolf's and Faulkner's novels only historically—as specifying the provenance of their material—not functionally. Writers of fiction usually draw on experience they know about, including their own, when making their *mimeses* of human experience. Sometimes, as in Woolf's and Faulkner's cases here, their material comes from their early lives, and their use of it is not disinterested: then the historical fact of emotional involvement can have artistic consequences, and so critical significance. But emotional involvement with one's personal history is not what one has done with that history. There is a stubborn fundamental distinction between the genetic fact that the author's own early life experience is the historical source of his or her novel, and the *rhetorical* consideration of the status the author has assigned to that life experience in it. My necessary rhetorical point is that either the essential subject of the novel is the experiencer of that experience, the implicit chrysalis of the writer her- or himself (the novel is a *Künstlerroman*), or the personal experience is material the writer used toward other ends. This distinction between the writer as strictly source of material and as also implicit essential subject helps constitute the relevance of Lawrence's development to that of Joyce.

Another consideration respecting autobiography and the fiction of Joyce and Lawrence is that too often autobiographical inference about even the material of a writer's work is based not in fact, but in error: it seems no more likely that the intimate impassioned lyric "To His Coy Mistress" was drawn from the life experience of the Puritan divine who wrote it, than that Marvell set himself a seduction poem as a creative endeavor, and showed a gifted poet's capacity for invention. My final similarity between Joyce and Lawrence is that both seem in some respects to practice a parsimony of precisely invention. Joyce's case will be discussed below; Lawrence used again and again experiences he had had—

autobiographical material in the historical, genetic, sense. However, he also extrapolated unrecognizably from his experience, and then recycled those in essence imagined—invented—elements of stories and novels in subsequent work. Two familiar examples of this practice are gamekeepers, and coarse brothers of the major female character, assembled in the family kitchen; each can be related to an experience of Lawrence's totally different from it.

The relationship Lawrence evolved between a writer's life and art is described briefly in this introduction and documented in the appendix. The foregoing combination of similarities and contrariety between Joyce and Lawrence is offered as context for that relationship, relevant to the relationship evolved by my subject because its exact contrary.

\* \* \*

Although Shakespeare has almost always been the most written about English author by a wide margin, in recent years Joyce has been the second-most. Yet the attention he has received from biographers is strikingly modest. During the first century since his birth there were only four formal biographies of him. Recently (in 1992) they were joined by another, and an expansion of the portion of an earlier one that takes him to his middle years; more recently (in 1999) by a sixth. Related books are: five memoir-biographies (by his brother and friends), one of which also is a helpful introduction to *Ulysses;* a (slim) volume of reminiscences of him when young in Ireland; another when on the Continent; and a slim volume recording its author's conversations with him. (Prompted by the critical attention to him, there also are two recent biographies of his wife and one of his father, books of photographs, and books about the Irish background and Joyce in different places.)

Lawrence appears to have been the subject of more biographical writing than any other English author of the twentieth century. (That is, in addition to three biographies of his wife, two more of them as a couple, one of his first lover, many books of photographs, and even more books about his background and Lawrence in different places, including two in Italy and six in Mexico and New Mexico.) While only one of the six biographies of Joyce is more than 400 pages long, the most recent biography (completed in 1997), three volumes by different authors, comprises almost 2,400 pages. The three-volume "Composite Biography" comprises with some previously published material almost 2,000 pages. At least twenty-two single-volume formal biographies of Lawrence and young Lawrence also have been published. There is a two-volume set of "Recollections." And in addition to dozens of shorter pieces, full-length biography-memoirs have been published by at least eleven friends and fellow-writers (John Middleton Murry wrote two), and by his sister (with a collaborator), his wife, and two women with whom he had been involved when young; he also figures extensively in a number of personal memoirs, such as Lady Ottoline Morrell's two volumes. This latter activity prompted James Thurber to write "My Memories of D. H. Lawrence," about an encounter which turned out to be with a Fitchburg, Massachusetts, businessman; it concludes "I am trying to forget D. H. Lawrence, which makes me about the only writer in the world who is. It is a distinction of sorts."[18]

The value of this small library of biographical material for a study of Lawrence and autobiography is apparent; but two points about it need to be made. Although the facts of Lawrence's life are generally accepted in the formal biographies, a few originate in the testimony of a single witness. And all who mention his early fiction consider it to be basically autobiographical not merely in the genetic but also in the rhetorical sense: to be about himself. Taking the most recent and ambitious biography as example: the index of the first volume, John Worthen's *Early Years,* has under *Sons and Lovers* half a column page of "Significant fictional *alterations* of real life" (p. 609; my emphasis). And for the protagonists of the two stories of special importance for my subject, "A Modern Lover" and "The Shades of Spring," the index has respectively the entries "Cyril Mersham as autobiographical hero" (p. 606) and "John Adderley Syson as autobiographical hero" (p. 607). Worthen's "Introduction" to the recent edition of *The White Peacock* (ed. Alan Newton [1911; Hammondsworth: Penguin, 1982]), calls them and other Lawrence protagonists "a series of fictional characters who are . . . clearly versions of Lawrence's continual rewriting of his autobiography" (p. 27).

The presumption is a familiar one among biographers of writers, and can be set aside. But (as my first paragraph mentioned) it is shared by Lawrence's critics when they consider his early life. Two suitable examples are the first preeminent Lawrence scholar, Harry T. Moore, and his successor in recent years, Keith Sagar. The most well known of Moore's many publications are an edition of Lawrence's letters, a travel record, and original and revised or expanded versions of both a biography and a critical study. In the last, *D. H. Lawrence: His Life and Works* (1951; rev. ed. New York: Twayne, 1964), Moore writes of "The Shades of Spring" that it is one of two stories "concerned with *White Peacock* and *Sons and Lovers* material: 'Second Best' and 'The Shades of Spring.' Both of them deal with a Midlands girl who has been dropped by the young man she loves. In each story he is a cultivated, educated young man, and in each of them the girl takes a somewhat cruder successor." Moore concludes, referring to the "girl," "This recapitulates Jessie Chambers's experience with Lawrence" (pp. 97–98). Later, he relates briefly the situation in "A Modern Lover" (105).

Sagar has written principally a formalist study of Lawrence's work that emphasizes his novels, the *Calendar* cited earlier, a biography, and an ambitious work whose title, *D. H. Lawrence: Life into Art* (New York: Viking, 1985), indicates its subject. It is a subtle and enlightening discussion of "the genesis of the art in the life," in a phrase in his introduction (p. ix); but it too identifies the early Lawrence with his protagonists in a "continual rewriting of his autobiography." The attitude is exemplified in *The Life of D. H. Lawrence* (New York: Pantheon, 1980), when Sagar quotes from Cyril Mersham on himself in a caption to a photograph of young Lawrence (p. 29).

I rely extensively on the work done by Moore, Sagar, and other scholars concerning Lawrence's incorporating facts of his life, and elements of his consciousness, in his early fiction. Nonetheless, I disagree with the critical consensus about the nature of Lawrence's practice, and therefore about what his practice signifies for his art.

The appendix demonstrates that his development as a creator of fiction out of his personal history can be traced in a striking documentary record. It comprises different works that share a recurrent story pattern. The pattern has two elements. One is an invented episode near the end of his first novel, *The White Peacock*, whose narrator and central consciousness is confronted on a visit home by the fiancé of his youthful sweetheart. (He is as uncomplicatedly autobiographical as Stephen Daedalus of an equally youthful Joyce's *Stephen Hero*.) The other element is derived from a visit Lawrence made from London to Jessie Chambers on her family's farm, in which he proposed that their relationship become sexual.

This story pattern explains Moore's statement about "*White Peacock* and *Sons and Lovers* material" that occurs in two stories. His second, "The Shades of Spring," is the later of the two mentioned as of special importance for my subject, the earlier being "A Modern Lover." The protagonist of each is portrayed visiting a former sweetheart from London. Cyril Mersham bests a suitor, then asks the woman to initiate a sexual relationship with him; John Adderley Syson is shocked to discover that the woman has a lover.

The appendix documents that the "modern lover" Mersham is portrayed subtly as snobbish, egotistical, emotionally and vitally parasitic, and ignorant about life and about love—most dramatically respecting himself. The most striking of the many negative traits Lawrence gave this "autobiographical hero" is ignorance of his sexual preference. On what grounds can it be proposed that the author of "A Modern Lover" is implicitly invoking himself in such a reprehensible and ultimately pathetic character? Lawrence's calumny against himself would include charging himself with unawareness of things about himself he points out.

Even as literary history, Mersham's source in his creator's life experience is significant mostly for establishing how far Lawrence removed the fictional person he created from the autobiographical material he drew on in creating him. It does not follow that Lawrence's character is the vehicle for an attack on homosexual love; that doctrinal construction of "A Modern Lover" no more adequately comprehends it than regarding Mersham as a surrogate for the author. The subject of Lawrence's harsh satire is faulted not for his sexual preference, but for adding to his considerable other faults a profound self-ignorance.

John Adderley Syson, the London intellectual of Lawrence's story pattern in "The Shades of Spring" and its earlier version, "The Soiled Rose," is mature and married; and his interest in his youthful sweetheart is platonic: he is a totally different character from the miscreant Cyril Mersham. Syson also is—as Mersham is—very different from Lawrence himself.

Moreover, Lawrence magnified the difference between Chambers and his fictional Hilda Millership in his revision of "The Soiled Rose," so that she becomes the most impressive character and the dominant figure of "The Shades of Spring." Hence, he increased the remoteness of his story about Syson from his own life experience involving Chambers. But even before he magnified it, the difference between his character and the real woman combines with the married self-deluding mature businessman's age, attitudes, and circumstances, to make Syson, like Mersham—but not in the same way as Mersham—a very unlikely agent of implicit self-representation by the author.

In creating his ostensible "autobiographical hero[es]," Lawrence used elements of his own life experience, radically extrapolated in different directions, for the making of fiction whose male protagonist is distinctly not a surrogate of the author. The appendix will make clear that the young D. H. Lawrence rapidly developed this wholly pragmatic attitude toward his personal history: that he used it as material for creating stories and their characters, not as the matter of implicit autobiography.

*   *   *

Another similarity between Joyce and Lawrence is the similar emphasis on autobiography in Joyce criticism. In Joyce criticism also, this emphasis often is misplaced; nevertheless, Lawrence's development as a writer of fiction is heuristic because young Joyce developed in the opposite direction: to doing fictional autobiography in the full rhetorical sense. Moreover, the practice of both writers was beyond the parameters of conventional autobiographical fiction: Lawrence created a relationship between his fiction and his life at one extreme limit; the relationship Joyce created is at the other.

After doing three drafts of his more or less naively autobiographical first novel over a period of four years, Lawrence began to use his life experience in his fiction pragmatically—even in the novel in which his young life was the subject.[19] Moreover, he used his autobiography as material in only a few of his scores of novels and long and short stories. For another contrast between the two writers is that of Lawrence's extensive and Joyce's intensive production. In a period of nineteen years Lawrence wrote more than forty books and more than a dozen separately published monographs and plays, as well as seven thick volumes of letters, and two of miscellaneous writings that comprise almost 1,500 pages. While Lawrence could draft well over 3,000 words of a novel in a day, Joyce famously spent a day arranging the already-chosen words of one sentence in *Ulysses*.

In reading them, one recognizes such similarities between the mature writers of fiction as the parsimonious husbanding of material by both. But the similarities are minor and the contrasts major. Lawrence evolved from poor Mersham to creating powerful radical types of the emotional parasite and unaware homosexual, in the destructive title characters of "The Lovely Lady" and "The Prussian Officer": the hedgehog, or artist-philosopher, selected from and schematized reality to propagate his "unitary inner vision" (Berlin) and/or "constructive ideas" (Shaw). In contrast, Joyce the fox, or mere artist, portrayed "the diversities of the world" (Shaw) "for what they are in themselves" (Berlin). And related to this contrast is the one between them that motivates the present introduction. It is between Lawrence's evolving as he matured a coolly pragmatic use in his fiction of (the reality of) his personal history, and Joyce's evolution into maturity in the opposite direction: his developing a commitment to including in his fiction (the reality of) the writer himself, fictionalized, as a subject. Moreover, as will be shown, at the end of the *Portrait* and in the very structure of *Ulysses*, Joyce made himself his subject with masterly elegance.

# The Mature Autobiographer

In his aptly titled compound biography–autobiography, *My Brother's Keeper* (London: Faber, 1958), Stanislaus Joyce frequently discloses direct connections between his brother's life and that of Stephen Dedalus. For example, its second page contains "Vance's elder daughter, Eileen, who comes into the early part of *A Portrait of the Artist*," its third page, "My brother liked [Vance], and introduces him by his right name into *A Portrait of the Artist*," and its fourth, "His first educator was ["Mrs. Conway"] who in *A Portrait of the Artist* is called Mrs. Riordan, and whom he, and the rest of us after him, called 'Dante'" (*Portrait*, pp. 28–30). Joyce's brother is here not so much inferring autobiographical elements in the *Portrait* as providing historical testimony. Other sources have shown that it usually is reliable; but see note 3 below.

Setting aside for the moment the matter of reliability, Stanislaus's testimony illustrates problems of inferring autobiography in Joyce's fiction. One is precise reading: both Vance parents (equally) are recalled as "Eileen's father and mother" by the child Stephen Dedalus. A more important problem is methodological: during the Christmas dinner, seeking to understand metaphor ("How could a woman ["the Blessed Virgin"] be a tower of ivory or a house of gold?"), Stephen recalls the experience "when playing tig" of Eileen's "hands over his eyes: long and white and thin and cold and soft," and decides that he understands the first metaphor.[1] No Vance is a character in Joyce's work of art: Vances are transitory elements of the child Stephen's consciousness; and even Eileen is remembered for the sake of his characteristic preoccupation with language.

Yet his brother's problematic inferences about the Vances in the *Portrait* do not alter the mature Joyce's practice: he could have given his child character's remembered neighbors names different from those of his own childhood neighbors. He named the Vances either because he liked Eileen or gratuitously: those are two ways in the complex of specific ways he implicated his own life in his mature fiction.

The practice Lawrence developed while young—to some extent common to all fiction writers—of pragmatically exploiting his experience in making art, can be invoked for comparison. For it is but one extreme in the range of the mature Joyce's ways. Its absolute—and rare—opposite, is dedicating his art to the subject James Augustine Joyce. An example of his exploiting his experience involves the historical Vances: in *Ulysses*, the birthday poem Bloom remembers sending Milly when a child is based on an insulting valentine Vance sent the child Joyce as from his playmate Eileen;[2] this example also illustrates the problem of reliability in biographical testimony.[3]

An example of the totally opposite way—dedicating his art to himself—occurs near the end of the *Portrait*. When he dated its last page "Dublin 1904/Trieste 1914," he was insisting on its continuity both with the "verbal vesture of an instant of emotion" he wrote in one day in January 1904 and could not get published, his Paterian story/essay "A Portrait of the Artist," and with his aborted autobiographical novel begun the next month, *Stephen Hero*, in whose twenty-five chapters "the artist prolong[ed] and brood[ed] upon himself as the centre of an epical event."

In the quoted phrases from the culminating paragraph of his aesthetic disquisition to Lynch in chapter V of the *Portrait*, Stephen is describing the first two of the three "forms" he says an artist's "handiwork" takes— "progressing from one to the next"—in the process of creation (pp. 186–87). Hence, Joyce caused its expounding protagonist also to recount the "progressing" of that very novel during those ten specified years, 1904 to 1914. And he made almost blatant the reflexive reference to itself of its protagonist's exposition, by having Stephen exemplify the interim "epical form," slightly inaccurately, with "that old English ballad *Turpin Hero*."[4] In Stephen's account to Lynch in the *Portrait* of how "creation is accomplished," Joyce constituted metafiction as esoteric autobiography, since the existence of both the "lyrical" and the "epical" predecessors of his "dramatic" novel was generally unknown; and his performance was elegant. Moreover, Stephen is not aware of what Joyce is saying through his mouth. In an intricate maneuver, Joyce is asserting his *auth*or*ity*, and simultaneously distinguishing himself from his facsimile of himself when young who, the *Portrait* makes plain, was not capable of writing the *Portrait*.

Also in common with (though not all, many) other fiction writers (hence the familiar phrase), the mature Joyce "put himself into" his protagonists other than Stephen and the both equally and differently autobiographical Shem the Penman. Significant congruences between aspects of his own life and the portrayed lives of, most conspicuously, H. C. Earwicker, Leopold Bloom, Richard Rowan of *Exiles,* and Gabriel Conroy of "The Dead" have been demonstrated by critics and biographers. Richard Ellmann first expounded one succinct example, "the root situation of jealousy for his wife's dead lover" (and specific autobiographical elements) in the case of Gabriel (*James Joyce,* p. 246). In these characters, Joyce breaches the distinction between pragmatically using one's experience to make art, and doing autobiography.

Yet these are not autobiographical characters *tout court.* For example, critics have proposed that in *Ulysses* Stephen represents the author when young, Bloom when mature.[5] That neat formulation is heuristic in a limited way: the novel identifies Stephen with Bloom in places, and that relates both characters to their author. But it oversimplifies. It ignores not only the other sources for Bloom (Alfred H. Hunter, Ettore Schmitz, et al.), but also the many radical dissimilarities from himself the mature creator created for his mature creature. The difference between Joyce's "putting himself into" these characters, and his dedicated and ambitious autobiographical facsimilizing in Stephen Dedalus, is one of kind, not degree.

Since from his very name Stephen is fictional, his autobiographical nature cannot be apodictic—in effect a hermeneutic fact, as when Joyce inscribed himself in the *Portrait* through Stephen's exposition of a "progress" through three "forms" of the artist's "handiwork." But discrepancies between the life-experience of the author and that of the character are exceptional, and usually dictated by artistic considerations: the man Joyce is the manifest subject of the character Stephen.

What follows is a catalogue—which does not claim to be exhaustive—of ways the mature writer implicated his life in the *Portrait* and *Ulysses* through the character and world of Stephen, between the two opposite extreme ways of using his experience pragmatically as material (exemplified by Bloom's birthday poem to Milly), and inscribing himself *in propria persona* (exemplified by Stephen's three "forms"). It begins at the non-autobiographical end of the range.

He portrayed a generic aspirant artist in a philistine turn-of-the-century Dublin. Because the aspirant artist is more than generic, Joyce's use of his experience for Stephen is not purely pragmatic. The relevant experience was derived largely from his youthful translation, admiration, and writing. Those provided models such as Hauptmann's Michael Kramer, romantic artists and young intellectuals in Ibsen, and the Dubliner James Clarence Mangan, as represented in Mangan's "Fragment of an Unpublished Autobiography"; and he had intimate knowledge of a young intellectual in his own family, Stanislaus.[6]

He incorporated, as exemplary for an aspirant artist in that Dublin, elements of the social reality he himself had experienced. A complicated instance is the letter of his fellow-students at University College protesting Yeats's *The Countess Cathleen;* he was criticized in print for his public refusal to sign it (see *James Joyce*, pp. 67, 90). The complication is that the incident in the *Portrait* also conveys his character Stephen's spirited commitment to art; and he had a corresponding commitment.

He introduced as characters historical figures he had known (wrote historical autobiographical fiction). Stephen's original auditors in Dublin's National Library depict real people who all held on June 16, 1904, the offices they are said in *Ulysses* to hold; furthermore, all four were scholars and men of letters active in the Irish literary movement, one at least (George Russell) not only prominent in Dublin but (as AE) internationally known.[7]

He gave real people he had been more involved with pseudonyms (wrote autobiographical *romans à clef*), often meaningful ones. The name of the late arrival to Stephen's lecture, Malachi Mulligan, is a double dactyl like that of his real original; Simon is to Stephen as John is to James; Vincent Cosgrave resented but apparently deserved the notorious (though a common Galway) name Lynch.

He assigned the names of real people to antipathetic characters to discharge resentments. It is well known that two English antagonists during his English Players project in Zurich, Henry Carr and Sir Horace Rumbold ("Sir Whorearse Rumphole," *Selected Letters,* p. 239), provided the names for Private Carr, who knocks Stephen down in Nighttown, and H. Rumbold, Master Barber, the hangman who boasts of his "special nack of putting the noose" (*Ulysses* 12.427/p. 249) in the letter Alf Bergan passes around in Barney Kiernan's pub. (Less well known is that Rumbold was an impressive diplomat: as ambassador to Germany he understood Adolf Hitler's intentions early, and vainly warned the British government against appeasement at the very time Hitler took power.)

He named characters for real people because he liked the people. Alfred Bergan, his father's young friend and his own occasional companion (Costello has Bergan only two years older than him—*Years of Growth*, p. 151), was a sheriff's assistant in life and had shown a letter in which an English hangman boasted of his skill in making nooses (*James Joyce*, p. 43).

He incorporated gratuitous (nonfunctional, irrelevant) details of his life. Costello's *Years of Growth* identifies many Dubliners named in passing in his work. It cannot be known if he named the Vances because he liked Eileen, or for no good reason. However, when Stephen lists his debts near the beginning of *Ulysses* (2.255–59/pp. 25–26), the question does not arise. Some debts are owed to characters in the *Portrait* and *Ulysses* based on real people (Mulligan, McCann—here "MacCann," Temple); and one is to a character representing a real person (Russell/Æ). One name, "Bob Reynolds," has not been traced. Possibly, in that single case Joyce created a fictional identity: for the remaining names on Stephen's list are, gratuitously, those of real Dublin residents who do not appear—nor do their names ever otherwise occur—in Joyce's work, and from most of whom James Joyce is known to have borrowed money during the period of *Ulysses*. The list ends, "Mrs MacKernan, five weeks' board," and the McKernans (*sic*) had asked Joyce to leave his lodgings with them on June 15, 1904, until he could pay his back rent; he went that day to James and Gretta Cousins ("Cousins, ten shillings") "and asked them to take him in"; his stay at the Martello tower was not until about September 9 to 15 (*James Joyce*, pp. 155, 171, 175, and *Letters* II, p. 53).

In this catalogue of ways Joyce implicated his life in his mature fiction that are intermediate to the two extreme ways of use as material and celebration of himself, the last corresponds to the penultimate way at the other end of the range: he portrayed, in a philistine turn-of-the-century Dublin, a most particular aspirant artist. In life, John Eglinton (W. K. Magee) was the coeditor of the new periodical *Dana*, which had rejected Joyce's "Portrait" story/essay (*Literary Life,* p. 40). When in *Ulysses* Russell rises to leave the group at the National Library, Eglinton, who "holds my follies hostage," Stephen has said at the beginning of the chapter (9.35/p. 152), asks "Shall we see you at [George] Moore's tonight?" (273–74/p. 157); and Stephen mocks an expected guest and Russell. Then Lyster the Librarian mentions a collection of poems by younger poets Russell is preparing (289–91). Immediately "Anxiously [Stephen] glanced at" the faces of his three still-seated auditors, and tells himself "See this. Remember," then "Listen" while the seated men discuss with the departing Russell his anthology and Moore's party. Stephen learns that Moore has invited Mulligan and asked him to bring (only) Haines, and thinks "Cordelia. *Cordoglio* [Ital.: anguish]. Lir's loneliest daughter," and the archaic topographical "Nookshotten" ([here, being] run into corners) (292–315). Apparently the young Joyce was snubbed by George Moore as Stephen is in *Ulysses* (see *James Joyce*, p. 135); but George Russell in fact helped him in many ways, and about a fortnight after the date of the scene in the National Library extended the invitation to write a story for the *Irish Homestead* that precipitated *Dubliners*.[8] But Russell's slender anthology (56 pages) *New Songs, A Lyric Selection* (which actually had been published in Dublin by June 16) did not include poems by James Joyce, some of which Russell had seen and praised to a correspondent for "perfect art."[9]

In general, Stephen's scant poetic activity in the *Portrait* and *Ulysses* does not warrant his "anxious" reaction to mention of the anthology, while young Joyce's own activity does. To judge from his correspondence and *My Brother's Keeper*, beginning in his midteens he had written volumes of poetry, and as well prose sketches and an Ibsenite play, and translated poetry and plays (little of this has survived); moreover, *Chamber Music* was completed, and in September would be submitted to Grant Richards.[10] The autobiographical significance of Stephen's portrayed embarrassment when the anthology is mentioned, and subsequent sense of rejection and isolation, is historically documented in Joyce's simultaneous portrayal of himself, in his Juvenalian broadside, "The Holy Office," as "Unfellowed, friendless and alone" in literary Dublin; both his bravado in the poem and his unfairness ("distantly I turn to view / The shamblings of that motley crew") confirm his feelings.[11] *Ulysses* represents both the respectful attention young Joyce actually received from Dublin literary men (those in the National Library attend critically to Stephen's expatiation on Shakespeare) and journalists at the time of the novel, and his no less actual feelings of rejection and isolation. The combination affirms the good faith of the autobiographer.

In addition to the common writer's practice of pragmatic exploitation of his or her experience (at one extremity of the range), my catalogue of ways the mature Joyce implicated his life in his fiction includes discharging of resentments, and incorporating details gratuitously; every other way he implicated it serves his making autobiographical art out of the story of his aspirant artist Stephen Dedalus.

Of course, he did not always implicate his life: like other artists, he invented. However, "the web of memory and invention" Eliot called his autobiographical fiction (in the preface to *My Brother's Keeper*, p. 12) in fact has less of either than meets the eye. He supplemented his memory; and although his fiction is by one of the greatest *formal* and *verbal* inventors in literary history, he seems to have invented the matter of fiction (Aristotle's aspirated alpha: "what") in it—characters, incidents, places, and things—reluctantly.

Both his supplementing memory and parsimonious inventing can be illustrated by his use more than a decade later of two adjacent entries in the "Pappie" section of his Trieste notebook; he used them a few pages apart in the Nighttown chapter of *Ulysses*.[12] In the first use, "His Eminence Simon Stephen cardinal Dedalus" recites the self-pitying "verses" John Joyce "quotes most" (15.2663–67/p. 427). In the other, Bloom's fantasized Bello, a quasi-invention out of the brothel-keeper "Mrs. Cohen [who] . . . by 1904 had either retired or died" (*James Joyce,* p. 368), says that when tormenting Bloom "he" will "suck my thumping good Stock Exchange cigar while I read the *Licensed Victualler's Gazette*" (15.2897–98/p. 434), the specialized actual periodical Joyce had noted (correctly as "*Victuallers'*") "He read."

In the dramatized daymares of Nighttown, one of the most striking innovations in a book more innovative than almost any except his own next and last book, Joyce not only supplemented with notes his memory of his "pappie" in portraying Stephen's father, but used his notation of his father's exotic reading for Bloom's fantasized tormentor. The preface to *James Joyce: A Literary Life* is entitled "Imagination as Memory," and quotes Frank Budgen's report that Joyce dismissed Budgen's talk of imagination with "the assertion that imagination was memory" (p. ix). With most writers of autobiographical fiction, it is at least as likely that ostensible memory is imagination (invention): even in strict autobiography, which lacks the license of fiction, the specific historical facts of the autobiographer's experience, what one called "the undeniably real," may be condensed, rearranged, or misrepresented in the service of a conceived general truth.[13]

Despite that license, Joyce adhered to specific facts inordinately when composing the matter of his fiction. If judged from "*Licensed Victualler's Gazette,*" his practice was at least a habit of dependence, if not poverty of invention; but the diligent historical preciseness that caused close questions in letters back to Dublin suggests respect for "the undeniably real" more than habit or need. Although it was three months after the night before *Ulysses,* he had stayed—and undergone Stephen's nighttime experience—at the Martello tower in Sandycove: as he, so his autobiographical character. It is true that contrary to his reported "assertion" he assisted his memory with notes; however, the very measure he took to supplement memory reaffirms the priority the radical formal and verbal inventor gave those characters, incidents, places, and things—the matter of fiction—he had experienced in reality.

On the other hand, a significant invention in *Ulysses* is that Stephen rented and has been residing at the Martello tower.[14] Moreover, this writer so reluctant to invent departed from veridical autobiography in ways that are more singular than invention. Three very different such departures, two when writing the *Portrait* and one when writing *Ulysses,* illustrate his adroitness as maker of autobiographical fiction.

A crucial revision of *Stephen Hero* was the mature Joyce's "dramatic" metamorphosis of the young Joyce's simple author-surrogate Stephen Daedalus into the partly generic character of the *Portrait,* object as well as subject (in his famous remark to Frank Budgen, "this young man," who also, he adds, is himself).[15] The young intellectual in his own family was mentioned as an available generic model for his aspirant artist. In the service of his art, Joyce departed from veridical autobiography far more radically than merely eliminating as superfluous the younger brother Maurice of *Stephen Hero*. Instead of his own temperament when young —gregarious, high-spirited, bibulous, athletic, tolerant of faults, and reluctant to offend and hurt—"Sunny Jim" gave Stephen Dedalus the temperament revealed in Stanislaus's autobiographical writings: solemn, abstinent, intolerant, loathing his father, attacking the Church without consideration for his parents' feelings, mortified by the family's poverty. When he "announced . . . that I would refuse to do my Easter duty," Stanislaus writes, "Jim made a half-hearted attempt to dissuade me," and "The painful conflict between my mother and my brother originated from my refusal." At one point Stanislaus recounts his embarrassment at a drunken public antic of his father's, remarks "I wish I could see now, or could have seen then, the funny side of such happenings, as my brother did," and points out that Stephen Dedalus's attitude is like his own, "but, of course, Stephen Dedalus is an imaginary, not a real, self-portrait and freely treated" (*My Brother's Keeper,* pp. 116, 118, 67).

A second kind of singular departure from veridical autobiography Joyce made is the inverse of pragmatically using his experience for characters other than Stephen. A blatant (and familiar) example of it is the source of the long scene in the *Portrait* in which Stephen converses with the dean of studies (pp. 162–66). Joyce's friend J. F. Byrne complained in his autobiography of the "conglomeration of piffle" Joyce made in the *Portrait* of a slight encounter Byrne had had with the dean of studies at University College, Father Joseph Darlington, after having rendered it "with approximate accuracy in fewer than two hundred words" in *Stephen Hero*.[16] In the first (fragmentary) extant chapter, XV, Father Butt kindles a fire "approximate[ly]" as Father Darlington had done, and in two brief remarks "returned . . . in kind" Stephen Daedalus's trump in conversation the day before (*Stephen Hero,* p. 28). The mature Joyce revised this brief description and exchange into the occasion for Stephen Dedalus's reflections on the English convert Jesuit dean, and on his own alien relation to the language he spoke and wrote—created a statement of the situation of the Anglo-Irish writer. In other words, he made not "piffle" but, as he was wont to do, the trivial quadrivial. Relevant here, however, is that this writer who gave his autobiographical character his own childhood neighbors by name and listed (some of) his own debts, also coolly violated historical verisimilitude to the extent of giving that character both someone else's personality and a different other person's life experience.

Both these departures from veridical autobiography are more singular than invention because they appropriate biography from other real people; and they are significantly different from invention in being derived from the autobiographer's real experience of those people. Joyce's third departure contrasts dramatically with them, being prodigious invention, of both character in and event throughout *Ulysses*. But he invented to serve his most radical autobiographical practice: inscribing himself in his art, *in propria persona*. Like Stephen's exposition of the three "forms" of art when James Joyce was unknown, it is both elegant and esoteric.[17] In setting *Ulysses* on—incorporating historical events of—the particular day in June 1904 now known as Bloomsday, he developed his autobiographical project using his facsimile Stephen Dedalus to a singular audacity.

### Joycesday

My interest is in Joyce's development as maker of art out of his life, not in biography (even critical biography) as such; but my point about *Ulysses* requires first establishing what he experienced during about three critical months, then connecting that to his portrayal of Stephen in it.

From its first chapters, Stephen is shown to be desperately troubled. He is eloquent, principled, dauntless, and near the end of his tether emotionally; Joyce succeeds in making his despair not only manifest, but affecting. And the evidence is that at the time of *Ulysses* young Joyce himself, the former "Sunny Jim" to his younger sisters and brothers at home, "Joacax" and "the Mad Hatter" in *St. Stephen's,* the University College student newspaper, was no less troubled. For example, an entry in his long diary by the architect of the Abbey Theatre and Dublin playgoer Joseph Holloway records a visit to Joyce's friends Gretta and James Cousins:

"Mrs. Cousins played a couple of classical pieces on the piano. Then Mr. J. Joyce, a strangely aloof, silent youth, with weird, penetrating, large eyes . . . sang some dainty old world ballads most artistically and pleasingly. . . . Later he sat in a corner and gazed at us all in turn in an uncomfortable way from under his brows and said little or nothing all the evening."[18] It is dated "June 8, 1904."

The day of *Ulysses* is the day (all evidence indicates) of the first evening its author spent with Nora Barnacle. The original edition of *James Joyce* (1959) first asserted he "set *Ulysses* on this date" in "tribute to Nora," through whom "he entered into relation with the world around him and left behind him the loneliness he had felt since his mother's death" (rev. ed., p. 156). Although he was shortly to terminate his "relation with th[at] world," and his letters reveal closeness to Stanislaus and a few friends, the importance for him of "his attachment to her" (p. 156) is clear. And unedifying; for citing that attachment to explain the date of *Ulysses* begs the question relevant to his art: What has she or/and it to do with the novel? Had he simply "set *Ulysses* on this date" in homage to his wife, as many believe, his undoubtedly gracious personal gesture would have created an autobiographical curiosity at best—a frivolous, and in the fullest sense a sentimental, imposition of ego on art.

His elegant achievement, the esoteric functional connection between autobiography and artwork in *Ulysses*, can be approached by way of his tribute to Nora usually rendered "You made me a man." The tribute often is cited as explaining his supposed personal gesture; and recently he was taken to mean she made him so the very day of *Ulysses*, on the grounds that a veteran of venereal disease who had been consorting with prostitutes from the age of sixteen paid her that tribute for having masturbated him spontaneously their first evening.[19]

His tribute seems to have been drawn (by Ellmann) from a paragraph in the first of the two letters he sent her during his first 1909 trip to Dublin (August 6 and 7), following Vincent Cosgrave's allegation that she had been romantically involved with him simultaneously in the summer of 1904: "O Nora! Nora! Nora! I am speaking now to the girl I loved, who had red-brown hair and sauntered over to me and took me so easily into her arms and made me a man."[20] Even were one to disregard the intrinsic unlikelihood that the masturbation incident—either his gratification or her sudden spontaneous act that caused it—had somehow immediately conferred manhood on one with Joyce's prior experience, and the additional unlikelihood that he would propose to her it did so, his language precludes so narrow an attribution for "and made me a man." "Saunter over to me" and "took me so easily into her arms" seem metaphors describing the advent of their relationship ("when you came sauntering to me first through those sweet summer evenings," p. 161). But even if literal, the phrases are part of a general statement: the former one does not describe the circumstances of, or the latter one her activity in, her erotic initiative.

He recounted the incident in detail in one of the series of "extraordinary" (p. 180) letters they sent each other, apparently sometimes daily, for three weeks (December 1–20) during his second 1909 Dublin visit, to facilitate masturbation.[21] That series, the two letters he had written her in August following Cosgrave's allegation, and letters exchanged "When I was courting you" (p. 165) in 1904 disclose that they spent evenings (usually from after eight-thirty to about eleven) together in a field near the Dodder River, for a time every other day (pp. 158, 159). They did not consummate their extralegal marriage before eloping (p. 158), but her initiative cannot have been the impecunious couple's only furtive erotic activity those many summer evenings.[22] Hence: at the end of a week she was addressing him as "My Precious Darling" (June 23; *Letters* II, p. 42); he cajoled her to stop wearing "that breastplate" in July (p. 22), then progressed to "that dragoon's stays" at the beginning of September (p. 28); and the first letter following Cosgrave's allegation includes "At the time when I used to . . . walk out with you and feel your hand touch me in the dark" (p. 158).

For the reasons given above, Joyce was not likely to have attributed Nora's "ma[king] me a man" simply to her initial spontaneous masturbating of him, so that it, and therefore its date, is not likely commemorated in the day of *Ulysses*. But the elementary historical point also should be made that although it probably happened earlier rather than later during the summer, and even may have happened their first evening together, June 16, 1904, there is no evidence it did happen that evening—or indeed what evening it happened.[23] His July letter with "*Please* leave off that breastplate" first calls her "Goodie-Brown-Shoes" and describes her glove, presumably a favor either taken or given, as "conduct[ing] itself very properly—like Nora." In the context of "Goodie-Brown-Shoes," "properly" does not seem ironic here.

But whatever its date, the incident must be situated in a burgeoning love relationship with a strong erotic component, that culminated in elopement in less than four months, and began a lifelong, if sometimes strained, commitment. Moreover, his letter in the 1909 series recounting the incident to her declares specifically that the erotic component of their love began with it (p. 182).

Thereafter, familiarity and involvement developed their erotic love throughout the summer, to the point of elopement. And to the point of ending, according to his testimony, his dichotomizing of women in the fashion of Stephen Dedalus (and most adolescent boys, especially in the era of the sexual double standard), as either (in his words) "virgin or madonna" or "shameless . . . and obscene" (pp. 166–67), in both cases preventing a true human love relationship; that, although twenty-two, the middle-class late-Victorian Catholic Dubliner may never before have been physically intimate with a girl or woman who was not a prostitute, supports his testimony.[24] He did not cease to consider the erotic "dirty," "filthy," "devilish" (recurrent words in his adult letters to her); but his erotic urge ceased to be irreconcilable with that for agape, "pray[ing] to the spirit of eternal beauty" (p. 181). His description of the spontaneous masturbation incident concludes "frigged me slowly until I came off through your fingers, all the time bending over me and gazing at me out of your quiet saintlike eyes" (p. 182).

His previous "extraordinary" letter, second and first extant one in the series, eloquently articulates his awareness that with her he had realized an integration of his erotic and idealizing or spiritual motives. That letter of December 2 frames, within a compound metaphor for her as a flower that recurs in the series, a long and physically explicit passage that begins "side by side and inside this spiritual love I have for you there is also a wild beast-like craving for every inch of your body . . . for every odour and act of it," and reiterates a total of six more times the same integration of the erotic and the ideal, concluding, "be my whore, my mistress, as much as you like (my little frigging mistress! my little fucking whore!) you are always my beautiful wild flower of the hedges, my dark-blue rain-drenched flower" (pp. 180–81). He makes the point in other letters to her, in that series (pp. 183, 187, 193), during his previous Dublin visit (pp. 163, 166–67, 169 [September 5 and 7]), and as early as the latter part of their first summer, in two letters that also refer to an unspecified singular event (August 29 and September 10; pp. 26, 29); in the second he reproaches her for "treating me as if I were ["that night"] simply a casual comrade in lust."

The sometimes egregiously explicit letters the couple exchanged for three weeks to stimulate masturbation when apart constitute an earnest of their devotion to each other at the time: certainly he, with his early experience, and travelling as he was through European and to different Irish cities, could have sought out alternatives. If, as the extant letters also assert repeatedly, she enabled him to integrate his erotic and idealizing drives, to commit himself to conjugal love and the consequent family, he was right that she made a man of a boy. Budgen's book reports he considered neither Hamlet nor Faust "a complete man": Hamlet "is a son only," and Faust "isn't a man at all. . . . Where are his home and family?" (p. 16).

Joyce's reason for "set[ting] *Ulysses* on this date," then, was not simply a gracious gesture to Nora, but more personal—more strictly autobiographical. *Ulysses* commemorates the day that inaugurated a development in himself of which she was the indispensable agent. That development, his integration of previously unreconciled yearnings, resulted in his becoming able to depart at last (and promptly) from Ireland, and to be committed to a wife and children.

The development also coincided with his first artistically successful writing, the three *Irish Homestead* stories of *Dubliners*. The eponymous Eveline of the second of them is in Nora's situation almost precisely, but lacks her authenticity and courage; the last of them, "After the Race," he turned in to the paper four days before taking her abroad (Gabler, "Introduction," p. 4).

This historical conjunction between the crucial development in young Joyce's life and the inauguration of his successful art is a clue that they are related, and so jointly implicated in his elegant and esoteric autobiographical achievement in *Ulysses;* for the coincidence is too striking to be dismissed as mere accident. I propose as the key to the clue a broader—more general, indeed metaphysical—integration that his relationship with his "little fucking whore" *cum* "beautiful wild flower" enabled him to achieve.[25] My thesis is that young Joyce's newly achieved integration of eros and agape endued the writer of fiction as well as the husband and father, because for him those inner contraries he had been unable previously to reconcile were particular expressions of, respectively, ens and idea: in Yeats's terms, Is and Ought, Reality and Justice. Not only the particular contraries of his own inner urges, but the general contraries of the human condition he shared—the metaphysical corollary to his contrary urges—had become for him integrated, benign; and that resolution of an agon both emotional and metaphysical enabled him to make fiction precisely about the human condition.

Moreover, the general/metaphysical dimension of the contraries James Joyce succeeded in integrating with the relationship begun the evening of June 16, 1904, which is the key to the historical conjunction between a crucial development in his life and one in his art, also establishes the esoteric functional connection between autobiography and artwork in *Ulysses*. For, as I must now take some space to demonstrate, that metaphysical dimension of young Joyce's new integration is what links the critically troubled Stephen of June 16 to the man and writer who that evening began to achieve those historically conjoint crucial developments in life and art.

Stephen's destructive personal dilemma in *Ulysses* is portrayed in precisely those general/metaphysical terms. He is unable to reconcile the reality of (his) life *as he conceives that reality* with justice—reconcile ens with idea. The death of his mother has brought his inability to do so to a crisis which includes, logically, hostility to the One responsible. She and he are subject to a *dio boia,* creator of the "Throb always without you and the throb always within," as he puts it on the street at midday; he would "Shatter them," but knows that God can "Shatter me": "Bawd and butcher were the words" (*Ulysses* 10.824–26/p. 199). He is the only one of the selected denizens of Dublin negotiating that city between two destructive Wandering Rocks in the tenth chapter to have two portrait miniatures devoted to him; both focus on his dilemma. In the other one Almidano Artifoni, motivated by solicitude, informs him that when young "*come Lei,*" he too was convinced "*che il mondo è una bestia*" (10.344–51/p. 188).

However, that Joyce shared Stephen's general/metaphysical dilemma before Nora Barnacle enabled the crucial development in his young life to begin the evening of June 16 remains to be demonstrated. For unlike Joyce's own case, neither erotic nor spiritual desire for women is prominent in Stephen's consciousness (the contrast with Bloom is striking) on the day of the novel. Hence, in the brothel he talks dirty in his intellectual fashion, and even pays the fee, but he shows no trace of Lynch's manifest intent (see, for example, 15.2290–92/p. 416, and 3568–75/pp. 454–55).

Stephen's predicament is dramatized *in extremis,* and in a novel occurring on a single day. But Joyce's meticulous portrayal of its development, in the younger Stephen of the *Portrait*, not only presents that Stephen as becoming beset by the conflict of ens and idea both in those inner urges absent from *Ulysses* and in an outer world, but also relates the personal precisely to the general/metaphysical. It is this meticulous portrayal of the conflict's developing in his autobiographical facsimile that establishes it was Joyce's own condition. And one of the richnesses of the *Portrait* is that Stephen's failure to cope with the dual condition of his own nature and his circumstances not only is carefully elucidated (Joyce seems to have understood the etiology of the condition he had overcome), but also is the chief subject of the ironies in the novel.

My sketch of the main elements of Joyce's portrayal begins with chapters II and III, which in tandem present the boy Stephen's condition and his persisting failure to cope with it, in a chiastic pattern that itself embodies both sympathetic exposition and irony. "His ["salubrious"] arbour, as [Uncle Charles] called the reeking outhouse" on the first page of chapter II (p. 63) is a tonal key to the pair of chapters. And on the fourth page Mercedes of *The Count of Monte Cristo* becomes the agent of an idealization that turns erotic ("as he brooded upon her image, a strange unrest crept into his blood"), yet remains ideal ("He wanted to meet in the real world the unsubstantial image which his soul so constantly beheld"); the ideal "would, without any overt act of his, encounter him" and "he would be transfigured" (pp. 66–67). The parodic fulfillment of Stephen's yearning in the familiar passage, that begins with the prostitute's "Good night, Willie dear!" occurs at the end of the chapter (pp. 95–96), after such things as his father's self-deluding posturings, a pattern of other instances of illusion and self-delusion in his Dublin, and the "pink enamel" with which he is able only partly to paint his room, during his failed effort, using his prize money, "to build a breakwater . . . against the sordid tide [compare "throb"] of life without him and . . . the tides within him" (pp. 93–94). Chapter III begins with "The whores" and reverses the trajectory through Father Arnall's sermon to his taking Communion. Yet his agon with eros and agape continues: two pages after Stephen in the stews at the beginning, "The glories of Mary held his soul captive" (p. 98); and, affirming the chiasmus that generates both sympathy and amusement, at the beginning of chapter IV his new dedicated spirituality is subverted by his response to the line in "the canticles" with its pun *"ubera"* (p. 136).

In these two chapters of the *Portrait* Joyce not only presents the course of the experienced conflict between ens and idea both in the growing boy's urges and in the world Stephen was born into; he also exemplifies the reconciling of the contraries he himself had not been able to achieve until the summer of 1904. He does so in chapter II, the first of them.

One element of the parodic relationship between Stephen's ideal woman and the prostitute is that his "transfigured" condition would result from his "fad[ing] into something impalpable under her eyes" (p. 67); and in the last paragraph of the chapter, "she bowed his head and joined her lips to his and he read the meaning of her movements in her frank uplifted eyes" (p. 96). The location of the eyes relative to Stephen in each case is part of the juxtaposition; and an instance of Joyce's use of his life in creating his character is that in his description to Nora of his first integrating erotic experience with her, her "quiet saintlike eyes" were "bending over me" while she "frigged me."

The example he provides in chapter II of a reconciling of the contraries is more appropriate to the growing boy Stephen; but female eyes figure in it. To prepare for this, he presents: one page after the "transfigur[ing]" eyes the boy expects above him (p. 67) a scene (pp. 68–69) in which he, his aunt, and his girl cousin are looking at the newspaper photograph of a popular entertainer, until his cousin's "eyes rested long upon those *demurely taunting* eyes" (my emphasis); and one page after that, the boy's first meeting (at the children's party) with E.C., whose "glances travelled to his corner, flattering, taunting, searching, exciting his heart" (p. 70). They travel home on the tram together, she repeatedly coming up to his step and sometimes "forgetting [!] to go down"; for his part, "He heard what her eyes said to him from beneath their cowl" and, on the other hand, "He saw her urge her vanities, her fine dress and sash and long black stockings, and knew that he had yielded to them a thousand times." He thinks of Eileen Vance, and "She too wants me to catch hold of her, he thought. That's why she came with me to the tram. . . . I could hold her and kiss her" (pp. 70–71).

Although E.C. seems to combine eros and agape with her "saintlike" eyes ("beneath their cowl") and her flirting and "vanities," Stephen does not attempt to reconcile the contraries here. "But he did neither" the brief next paragraph says; instead, he makes his first formal artistic effort in the novel, and his process of composition is described as follows: "During this process all those elements which he deemed common and insignificant fell out of the scene. There remained no trace of the tram itself nor of the trammen nor of the horses: nor did he and she appear vividly. The verses told only of the night and the balmy breeze" and so on until "the kiss, which had been withheld by one, was given by both" (p. 71). The boy's smothering of ens with idea in their general/metaphysical dimension when making his poem, his inability to deal as artist with (his) human reality, relates to the conjunction in 1904 between young Joyce's crucial development as a man and as a writer. It also relates to an older Stephen's laughing (in chapter IV) at how a neighboring gardener whom the Dedaluses "had nicknamed the man with the hat . . . worked, considering in turn the four points of the sky and then regretfully plunging his spade in the earth" (p. 144); the man with the hat recalls (and could have derived from) "The Poet" in Strindberg's *A Dream Play* (*Ett Drömspel*), who "is walking with his eyes fixed on the heavens, and he is carrying a bucket of mud"

(*Strindberg: Selected Plays and Prose,* ed. Robert Brustein [New York: Holt, 1964], p. 192).

Stephen makes his attempt in chapter II to reconcile the contraries during the episode of the Whitsuntide play, which begins just two pages after his idealizing poetic effort. Although two years have passed, he has not seen E.C.; but when friends recount her asking his father about his role in the play, he responds angrily to their teasing, for he appears already to know of her current "interest and regard":

> All day he had thought of nothing but their leavetaking on the steps of the tram at Harold's Cross . . . and the poem he had written about it. All day he had imagined a new meeting with her for he knew that she was to come to the play. The old restless moodiness had again filled his breast . . . but had not found an outlet in verse. The growth and knowledge of two years of boyhood stood between then and now, forbidding such an outlet. (p. 77)

When he is backstage at the play, this promising attitude is confirmed. He thinks with embarrassment of some of his lines, and then in his mind:

> He saw her serious alluring eyes [in contrast to the entertainer's "demurely taunting" eyes of fourteen pages before] watching him from among the audience and their image at once swept away his scruples, leaving his will compact. Another nature seemed to have been lent him. . . . For one rare moment he seemed to be clothed in the real apparel of boyhood: and . . . he shared the common mirth. (83)

If the words are to be believed, Stephen has achieved a "rare" state of mind that involves the interaction between his inner urges and his existence in the world: his self-consciousness, invoked by the lines he must speak in public, is "swept away" by the image of E.C.'s eyes; in a sense, "he [has] be[en] transfigured." That the metamorphosis also embraces his inner self is shown by the crucial fact that, for the very first time respecting a female—in fantasy or in life—he is not passive, seeking to be "encountered" (p. 66; "the holy encounter," p. 95): he leaves the stage and the theater "in haste, eager that some prey should not elude him." His family is waiting, and "In a glance he noted that every figure of the group was familiar and ran down the steps angrily." He makes his excuses and runs on, seeking her. Without success: circumstances, the world, defeat his unique effort in the novel to reconcile his contrary inner urges. "Pride and hope and desire" become "wounded pride and fallen hope and [above all] baffled desire"; "his anguished eyes" "burned," then gradually the familiar composed, alienated Stephen returns (pp. 83–84). Joyce's placement of this singular incident between Stephen's idealizing at the beginning of the chapter and his engaging a prostitute at the end is eloquent.

The pattern in the *Portrait* that represents Stephen's contrary-inner-urges-with-general/metaphysical-significance is completed in the six-page episode (pp. 188–94) of his second artistic endeavor in the novel, near its end. Don Gifford's *Joyce Annotated* (Berkeley: University of California Press, 1982) guardedly characterizes the villanelle it produces as "an evocation of the avant-garde aesthetic climate of the 1890s," and emphasizes Pater, Yeats, and D'Annunzio (pp. 257–61). In a spirited essay (pp. 71–81) in *In Search of James Joyce* (Urbana: University of Illinois Press, 1992), Robert Scholes concedes that "Its literary models are the poems of the nineties" (p. 79), but argues "The inspiration and the poem are both intended to be genuine," and "Stephen ceases to be an aesthete and becomes a poet" (p. 81). Scholes quotes from Joyce's Trieste notebook manifest sources of elements in the narrative of Stephen's creative process (pp. 80–81); and he points out that "Nightpiece," the ninth poem in *Pomes Penyeach,* shares some images with the villanelle. (The poems were written during the twenty-year period following the publication of *Chamber Music* in 1907; the last, "A Prayer," invokes a dominating female who is both ideal and erotic.) What Scholes calls "Joyce's explicatory narrative" (p. 74) in the episode is highly subjective, keyed by free indirect discourse: its second sentence is "O what sweet music!" So he may have been composing the episode in the Trieste notebook passages as much as drawing from them. Still, he seems not simply being dismissive of his character's villanelle: it is a technically skillful composition in a demanding form, and as such demonstrates Stephen's potentiality as a poet. But the episode near the end of the *Portrait* is not averring that Stephen has begun to realize his potentiality. *Ulysses* confirms he has not; and together the villanelle and the process of its composition indicate the reason why.

How the episode is to be taken is conditioned by the fact that it is connected explicitly to the earlier—and only other such—one in the novel: "He had written verses for her again after ten years" (p. 192). Joyce's combining the skillful later "verses for her" with an account of Stephen's writing them attests that the connection is made because the episode in chapter V is a more elaborate *ricorso* of his endeavor in chapter II. In other words, like his earlier poem (as described)—only more significantly, for Stephen is approaching graduation from the university and maturity—the villanelle is a functional instrument in fiction. It is akin to Hynes's bathetic elegy for Parnell (possibly the "Et Tu Healy" of a clever nine-year-old) in "Ivy Day in the Committee Room," and to Stephen's single poetic effort in *Ulysses,* the quatrain he begins on the beach (3.397–400/p. 40) that is presented in the newspaper office (7.522–25/p. 109), and is largely an unconscious plagiary from the last quatrain of "My Grief on the Sea," one of Douglas Hyde's translated *Love Songs of Connacht.* And as with his earlier "verses for her," the relation of Stephen's villanelle to the process of its composition is the source of its instrumentality.

In *My Brother's Keeper,* Stanislaus Joyce mentions "the poem he called 'The Villanelle of the Temptress'" as one in *Shine and Dark,* the second of two volumes of lyrics Joyce composed while at Belvedere College and the university (p. 100). His departure from his own impressive productivity as a young poet (as well as writer of prose sketches and the Ibsenite play "A Brilliant Career," and translator of Horace and Verlaine) functions to emphasize Stephen's apparent single endeavor "after ten years"; on the other hand, both extant evidence from his poetry and his portrayal in *Stephen Hero* of the closely autobiographical Stephen Daedalus when they were Stephen's age, help establish the connection between Stephen as portrayed in the episode and Joyce's own condition before the summer of 1904. Stephen Daedalus's "extravagant" proposal (proposition) to the middle-class Irish Catholic virgin Emma Clery that she take him into her bed and they never speak after, probably never happened; but it is worth recalling here as a hyperbolic trope, provided by a slightly older Joyce, of his own condition then.

Stanislaus reports that the villanelle in chapter V is Joyce's youthful poem in *Shine and Dark;* but the poem itself is not extant to serve as evidence. In the last full chapter of the *Stephen Hero* fragment (XXIV; XXV in the Spencer ed.), just before his brief aesthetic discourse to Cranly, Stephen Daedalus witnesses "a trivial incident [that] set him composing some ardent verses which he entitled a 'Vilanelle of the Temptress'"; it also "made him think of collecting many such moments together in a book of epiphanies" (p. 211). What he witnesses is a flirtatious conversation; but the misspelled "Vilanelle" inspired by the significant "trivial incident" is not presented.

However, in the first full chapter of the fragment (XVI), Stephen Daedalus is said to be writing, to a woman as yet "unknown," "verses" that "commemorate" an "evil dream of love"; the statement "He had abandoned his Madonna," and two quatrains addressed to "the unknown," are canceled. The first of these, "The dawn awakes with tremulous alarms, / How grey, how cold, how bare! / O, hold me still white arms, encircling arms! / And hide me, heavy hair!" (pp. 36–37), is usefully juxtaposed against an equally early Yeatsian passage from the same period in Joyce's life printed in *James Joyce:* "Wind thine arms round me, woman of sorcery, / While the lascivious music murmurs afar: / I will close mine eyes, and dream as I dance with thee" (p. 82). Stephen's villanelle is more elegant than the "verses" of either Stephen Daedalus or Joyce himself when both were slightly younger; he may have improved his own poem "of the Temptress" to establish Stephen's talent. But the kinship of poems—and poets—is plain.

Early in his aesthetic disquisition to Lynch, Stephen says, "When we come to the phenomena of artistic conception, artistic gestation and artistic reproduction I require a new terminology and a new personal experience" (p. 182). At its conclusion they join other students, "Lynch whispered to Stephen:—Your beloved is here," and he looks at and thinks about E.C., asking "And if he had judged her harshly? If her life were a simple rosary of hours . . . ? Her heart simple and wilful as a bird's heart?" An immediate break in the text is followed by, "Towards dawn he awoke. O what sweet music! His *soul* was *all dewy wet* . . . a morning inspiration. A spirit filled him" (pp. 187–88—my emphasis): Stephen's "new" [quasi-erotic] "personal experience" and "terminology" have begun his composition of his villanelle.

Two general points about the episode should be made. Stephen composes a prosodically complex lyric in finished form: Joyce is portraying a tour de force by an impressive young talent. And Stephen's poem is the product not of a single one, but of three distinct, creative impulses.

Stephen's initial "morning inspiration," the visitation he wakes to, produces the first three tercets. The five paragraphs describing it present as the same entity his *mind/soul/imagination/spirit/heart;* for example, the first paragraph declares, "His mind was waking slowly" and "his soul was waking slowly" (p. 188). His muse ("sweet music")—the instrumental other "spirit" that has "filled" the composite "him"—begins as "light," then becomes "An afterglow [that] deepened within his spirit," then "deepen[s] to a rose and ardent light. That . . . light was her [the other spirit's] strange wilful heart," which is also "that ardent roselike glow" (pp. 188–89). "She" is the inspiration—the breathing into—he awakes with, that has taken possession of him: her *spirit/heart* is "within" his, which changes gender metaphorically. The allusion to the Annunciation does not invoke the Virgin as Madonna/Temptress; the analogy Stephen is making is between Mary, a human vessel for divine creative power (the Holy Spirit), and himself now: "O! In the virgin womb of the imagination the word was made flesh."

"Gabriel the seraph" may not be among "the choirs of the seraphim" lured from heaven by the "roselike glow" that possesses him, because Gabriel (who "had come") had announced the visitation of his muse. But that a poet's inspiration should *lure* (the word is the most nineties part of a nineties idea) the highest angels into "falling from heaven," is not embodied in the memorable line it inspires, "Lure of the fallen seraphim": the phrase might signify Milton's Eve, except that "she" was "wilful from before the beginning of the world" (p. 189). No more is inspiration, one's muse, signified in the preceding line, and first of the villanelle, "Are you not weary of ardent ways." It is understandable that readers have been put in mind of a "Belle Dame Sans Merci," the Madonna, and so forth.

Nonetheless, true inspiration is at work in the process: "murmuring the verses [of the first tercet] over, he felt the rhythmic movement of a villanelle pass through them. The roselike glow sent forth its rays of rhyme." (p. 189). And the second tercet uses two of "the rays from the rose that was her [the inspirer's] wilful heart," in its new rhyme-words, "(a)blaze" and "him."

After the third tercet, precipitated by the thought of "Smoke, incense," association produces "a ball of incense, an ellipsoidal ball," recalling "His fellow student's rude humour" during the previous day's physics lecture (p. 168), and the inspiration ends. He surveys his real surroundings, tears open "a cigarette packet" to write down the three tercets, and then his "lumpy pillow," again by association, "reminded him of the lumps . . . in the sofa of her parlour" (p. 190). Thereupon, "He saw" himself and E.C. at a party at her house, where sometimes "her eyes seemed about to trust him" until "her eyes were a little averted," and they had a brief exchange in which he was abrasive. He expresses jealousy of the young priest with whom she is associated in the Irish language movement, and "Rude brutal anger routed the last lingering instant of ecstasy [his initial inspired state] from his soul" (p. 191). He thinks of other "figure[s] of the womanhood of her country" he had known, "distorted reflections of her image," then turns to "coarse [actually, snobbish] railing at her paramour," the young priest, whom she favors over "him, a priest of the eternal imagination, transmuting the daily bread of experience into the radiant body of everliving life" (p. 192). The famous metaphor (in it Joyce creates a complement to Stephen's first Christ-based metaphor—of the Annunciation) is his second creative impulse. A paragraph-break follows, and: "The radiant image of the eucharist united again in an instant his bitter and despairing thoughts, their cries arising unbroken in a hymn of thanksgiving." The final two tercets result, and he writes them down. The pairs of new lines in the tercets suggest not thanksgiving but a grudging tribute, to—the narrative has disclosed—the appeal the power to make art has for the artist.

Then, recalling "During this process all those elements which he deemed common and insignificant fell out of the scene" when he made his earlier poem (p. 71): "he knew that all around him life was about to awaken in common noises, hoarse voices, sleepy prayers. Shrinking from that life he . . . star[ed] at the great overblown scarlet flowers of the tattered wallpaper . . . imagining a roseway from where he lay upwards to heaven, all strewn with scarlet flowers." But the next words are "Weary! Weary! He too was weary of ardent ways." The ways ("roseway") seem to be both his yearning for E.C. and creative endeavor; and he looks forward to sleep. Then he thinks that "He had written verses for her again after ten years," remembers in detail their tram ride ("She came up to his step many times . . . once or twice . . . forgetting to go down"), and protests "Let be! Let be!" But the familiar pattern develops ("He began to feel that he had wronged her"), with an added element: "the strange humiliation of her nature" that has accompanied maturing, "the dark shame of womanhood" (p. 193). And he wonders if, during this period when "his soul had passed from ecstasy to languor," "her soul . . . had been conscious of his homage? It might be."

Following the thought that she menstruates and the highly unlikely speculation, he has his third creative impulse: "A glow of desire kindled again his soul and fired and fulfilled all his body. . . . Her eyes, dark and with a look of languor, were opening to his eyes. Her nakedness yielded to him, radiant, warm, odorous and lavishlimbed, enfolded him . . . : and . . . the liquid letters of speech, symbols of the element of mystery, flowed forth from his brain." The two segments of five tercets printed earlier are printed again, together with the new quatrain that completes his villanelle, and the episode ends. In the concluding quatrain not inspiration—his muse—itself, nor the artist's creative power, but a literal female individual is addressed, in language derived directly from his thoughts of E.C.: "And still you hold our longing gaze / With languorous look and lavish limb!" "Desire" for E.C. consummated in fantasy is his final creative impulse ("the liquid letters . . . flowed forth"); and that it both "kindled again his soul" and "fired . . . his body" ("Her eyes" being joined with "Her nakedness") is salutary.

Nevertheless, the episode demonstrates the crucial difference between

Stephen's art before the evening of June 16, 1904, and Joyce's own after it. Stephen's villanelle skilfully fulfills the demanding form of its prosodic contract; and it is as evocative as it is vague. But in portraying the process of its creation, with the meanings Stephen intended it to embody, Joyce is providing a gloss which therefore is a comment precisely on that vague evocativeness.

The "rays" of the "ardent roselike glow" from Stephen's "morning inspiration" are said to have "consumed the hearts of men and angels." That explains Stephen's intended meaning for "Lure of the fallen seraphim"; but the point has been made that the line itself remains at best a suggestive hyperbole. And the personification (in "Your *eyes* have set man's heart ablaze") of the "rays" from the "rose" that is the "wilful heart" of the muse is simply not supported in the poem, since the first three tercets do not identify the object of their apostrophe as the poet's muse/inspiration. In similar fashion, the addressee of the two remaining tercets, the artist's creative power, that divine mystery of "transmuting the daily bread of experience into the radiant body of everliving life," can no more be identified than the "thanksgiving" of his "thoughts" can be perceived, from Stephen's metaphorical use of the eucharist, "eucharistic hymn": even that it is not literally signified but a metaphor is unclear. Only in the two new lines of the concluding quatrain—"And still you hold our longing gaze / With languorous look and lavish limb!"—is the narrative Joyce provided of Stephen's process not the actual source of any meaning Stephen intends for his villanelle.

The creative impulse behind those two lines is his desire for E.C. Beginning with the abrupt juxtaposition of the episode and Stephen's sight of and thoughts about E.C. the previous day, Joyce makes clear her instrumental role in Stephen's process of composition. After his first creative impulse Stephen thinks of her and his yearning for her almost without interruption. Thought of her and the young priest invokes the eucharist metaphor. And before she becomes explicitly the source of his third creative impulse, he himself observes that "He had written verses for her again after ten years."

But even to ignore the two earlier specific sources of creative impulse, and regard the whole villanelle as inspired by E.C., would make it no more a coherent, and above all no more an articulate, expression of its creator's thoughts and feelings when creating it. The two refrain lines of the poem, "Are you not weary of ardent ways?" and "Tell no more of enchanted days," not only do not suit either of his first two creative impulses ("weary"?), but do not suit her ("Tell no more," "ardent ways"). The vagueness of the important refrain lines, and of the whole poem, can be contrasted with a successful villanelle, such as Dylan Thomas's "Do Not Go Gentle into That Good Night," in which each of the two refrain lines is fitted to two different kinds of "men" appropriate to it in the four inner stanzas.

What the subjective narrative in the villanelle episode discloses is that the episode is a *ricorso* of Stephen's other attempt to create art in the novel. Neither his real inner experience during the process, nor the real young woman who is its object, is any more manifest in Stephen's technically fulfilled apostrophe, to a hyperbolic but vague female addressee, than was the case with his tramcar experience or the young girl E.C. "Shrinking from that life" "all around him," turning "the great overblown scarlet flowers of the tattered wallpaper" into "a roseway . . . upwards to heaven," denying life experience—except in the two quoted new lines in the final quatrain—he fails precisely to "transmut[e] the daily bread of experience": Joyce has made Stephen's often-quoted metaphor for the proper work of the artist more suited to his case than he knows.

Most relevant here is that as Stephen had done in his boyhood poetic endeavor, Stephen the graduating university student persists in doing: he causes idea to smother ens when making art. He also is entering adulthood still unable to deal any more effectively with his corresponding inner urges; this is shown both by the nature of his thoughts about E.C. in the episode, and by her continual recurrence (eight times) in the journal entries with which the novel ends, until "O, give it up, old chap! Sleep it off!" on the last page (p. 218).

About half a year after his own graduation from University College and two months to the day before his twenty-first birthday, on December 2, 1902, young Joyce passed through London on his way to Paris. Yeats kindly met him at Euston Station at six in the morning (*James Joyce*, p. 111), then devoted the day to him, taking him to literary people who might be useful; Joyce wrote his family ("Dear Everybody") on December 6, "I breakfasted, lunched and dined with him and he paid all the hansoms and busses."[26] On December 18, Yeats wrote to him in Paris a long, encouraging letter whose immediate subject was a poem he had asked Yeats to place. "I think that the thought is a little thin," Yeats wrote, though when he had heard it earlier it derived "a certain richness from the general impression of all taken together and from your own beautiful reading." He also observed "Your technique in verse is very much better than the technique of any young Dublin man I have met during my time." The episode in chapter V of the *Portrait* devoted to the villanelle and the process of its composition makes about Stephen's poem both Yeats's points about the poem written by Stephen's creator when more or less the same age.

I have discussed certain details in the *Portrait* to demonstrate the connection between Stephen's predicament in *Ulysses* and Joyce's own on the historical day of *Ulysses,* as necessary to my point about his audacious autobiographical achievement in the novel. The title he took from painting (troping on *portrait*) helps define that connection between Stephen's predicament and his own.

When, "chewing and laughing," Buck Mulligan tells Haines Stephen "is going to write something in ten years" (10.1089–90/ p. 205), he is being disloyal but not inaccurate. His statement would be inaccurate for the diligent and productive, if not very successful, James Joyce on June 16, 1904: Stephen the would-be artist is not the facsimile of the young artist Joyce but of the young man. Among painters contemporaneous with Joyce the simpler *Self-Portrait* was the more common title (Whistler did five), but *(A) Portrait of the Artist* was used by many at least since Rembrandt, a few of whose dozens of self-portraits have that title; modernist painters who used it include Cézanne, Gauguin, van Gogh, Matisse, and Rousseau. However, although the qualifier *As a Young Man* exists, it is rare with either title, for the good reason that in the title of such a painting "man" would be redundant and even "young" self-evident.

Joyce is using the at-best-innocuous qualifying phrase precisely, slyly exploiting its redundant last word. The painter of a self-portrait may paint only her or his reflection in a mirror, or include a mirror-image, creating a pictorial analogue to the fictional name of an autobiographical character. But the painter is *constrained* to represent on the canvas, however abstractly, his or her (own) physical self, perhaps in painter's smock and even painting. The self-portrait of a young male painter is a pictorial representation of a young man who is identified, usually by his own title for it, as the painter (artist) himself. Since Joyce's (self-)portrait is not a physical representation of himself, but words (literature), "portrait" in his title for his novel is a metaphor. And since Joyce had the option to "portray" in his words not just the (physical) young man to which depiction the painter is restricted, but also (in fact, even exclusively if he chose) an artist, his metaphor enables his title to emphasize in its qualifying phrase the specific nature of his self-portrait: Stephen is "the Artist" himself, but "Portrayed" as only "a Young Man," although he could readily have been "portrayed" as also a young artist. Not constrained to create a physical (pictorial) young man, Joyce also was under no obligation to make Stephen, like himself, an active young writer.

Hence, Stephen is not. Despite his manifest talent, he seems to have created nothing but two failed poems in ten years: the *Portrait* makes this a blatant consequence of his clearly articulated inability to harmonize ens and idea in himself and in the world. As an artist, Stephen Dedalus is a purposefully exaggerated representation of his creator and subject—before Joyce's fateful evening with Nora Barnacle.

In *Ulysses,* Stephen is strictly the young man still: gifted, but only potentially an artist. And Joyce did not recapitulate for Stephen the apparently crucial development in himself—crucial for both his life and his art—inaugurated on June 16, 1904; but the development he caused his autobiographical character to experience the evening his own began represents it. Stephen (like Joyce himself) is enabled by the agency of a particular individual he comes to know on June 16 to effect (as Joyce did) a resolution of his dilemma, a reconciling of apparent contraries, that ends his self-destructive submission to the conditions (like Joyce's own) the novel presents. He sings—"Youth here has End" in Joyce's purposive mistranslation ("[you] made me a man") from Sweelinck; he converses —as distinct from debating, lecturing, entertaining; he sings some more, and recites an Irish valediction about "walk[ing] your way," "in safety" though "with care"; and he leaves *Ulysses* with the recurrent passage from the layman's prayer for the dead, which has accompanied his recalled dream of his mother from the novel's opening pages, now subtly altered to assert her salvation (17.1230–31/p. 578).

My point about Joyce's autobiographical achievement in *Ulysses* must now be apparent. By means of truly prodigious invention, he composed his novel embodying the interrelated stories of his facsimile Stephen and his consummate invention Leopold Bloom so that it moves to Bloom's fulfilling the evening of the very next day Stephen's dream of rescue, and so that an indispensable element of the plot of the work of fiction in which the fictional Leopold Bloom unknowingly resolves the fictional Stephen Dedalus's story one evening represented as June 16, 1904, is an actual (a historical) public event of the historical June 16, 1904: the horse race for the Gold Cup trophy run about 3 P.M. at the track on Ascot Heath near London.

Thus did Joyce dedicate the whole novel, in a sense (although in only one of many), to a significant occurrence in his life. The full extent of the change his relationship with Nora effected in him would explain his frenetic reaction in August 1909, when Cosgrave alleged erotic involvement with her in 1904. For during the summer of her alleged involvement with Cosgrave, he himself did not become committed to her for a time, and was interested in other women (see, for example, *James Joyce,* p. 161). His distress, as the letters of August 6 and 7, 1909, indicate, was not mere jealousy (of a defeated rival); it expressed disillusion. While that disillusion persisted, it threatened his achieved integration, the whole reconciliation of Is and Ought in both his inner urges and his general human condition, that enabled him to function both as a person and as a writer.

Joyce's audacious autobiographical achievement in *Ulysses* is esoteric not only because of the nature and significance of the development in him his novel celebrates, but also because Bloom is the analogue he invented for Nora. (A lesser artist would have given Stephen a savior directly equivalent to her. She was an inevitable source for traits of Molly Bloom, of course; but Molly is not the agent enabling the resolution of Stephen's predicament.) And his achievement is elegant because he composed the plot of *Ulysses* to make the day on which the development in his own young life was inaugurated, June 16, 1904, the historically indispensable day for the novel portraying the analogous development in the young life of his autobiographical facsimile.

There can be no greater contrast to Lawrence's pragmatic attitude toward his own life experience than the mature Joyce's radical self-presentations at the end of the *Portrait* and in the very design of *Ulysses*. Now I shall endeavor to trace his becoming the master artist–autobiographer.

# 2

# A Young Writer

> I have a clearer recollection of our next house[, Stanislaus Joyce says]. It was the house in North Richmond Street described in 'Araby.' ... The rest of the story of 'Araby' is purely imaginary. In the preface to the American edition of *Dubliners* [New York: Viking, 1925], Padraic Colum says that this story and 'The Sisters' are evidently recollections of childhood. This is a mistake. In fact, only two of the stories—'An Encounter' and 'A Mother' . . .—are based upon his actual personal experience. (*My Brother's Keeper,* pp. 78–79)

James Joyce's fellow young Dublin poet and later friend is here gently admonished for an early instance of a "bad habit" among Joyce biographers recently decried by Denis Donoghue: "assum[ing] that . . . if something is in the [fiction] it must have happened."[1] *My Brother's Keeper* earlier mentions in passing that "Araby" includes a "reminiscence" of fights with "urchins" the two brothers had when very young (p. 39). This only slightly qualifies Stanislaus's positive assertion ("in fact") pointedly denying Joyce's "personal experience" to most of "Araby" and any of "The Sisters."

But unlike his younger brother, Joyce himself seems precisely to encourage the bad habit. He called those two stories as well as "An Encounter" "stories of my childhood," in the familiar passage in his long letter of "About 24 September 1905" describing—to none other than the same monitory brother—"The order of the stories" (then twelve) in *Dubliners* as it neared completion. It "is as follows. *The Sisters, An Encounter* and another story which are stories of my childhood," and three more groups (of three stories each: "stories of adolescence," "of mature life" and "of public life in Dublin" [*Letters* II, p. 111]). "A Mother" is in the last group. Joyce describes neither that story nor the "stories of adolescence" as even related to "his actual personal experience"; he seems to insist the entire first group is autobiographical.

To insist that would be to flout Stanislaus's knowledge that one of its two extant stories ("Araby" probably was not yet written) lacks a biographical origin (despite the brothers' mother's Flynn aunts and uncles). Moreover, although Joyce employs the idiomatic singular pronoun, it is widely known that the only story of the three having a specific historical source in "my childhood" is based on an "actual personal experience" Stanislaus shared with him. The long letter begins with a series of questions of Dublin fact (like those he would send his aunt Josephine Murray while working on *Ulysses*); Stanislaus's letter answering the questions, dated October 10, 1905, goes on to discuss "An Encounter"—which he was sent with Joyce's previous letter on September 18 (*Letters* II, p. 108)—saying among other things, "The sensation of terror—you were afraid he might catch you by the ankles—is cleverly put in" (p. 115). "An Encounter" is, to adapt the older brother's locution, a story of both their childhoods.

The lionized author (and assiduous publicist) James Joyce lied readily, for example providing different "schemata" for *Ulysses* and lists of four "key words" in Molly's soliloquy. Moreover, he lied precisely about the extent of veridical autobiography in his work, by misrepresentations to his first biographer, Herbert Gorman. But his description of the first three stories of *Dubliners* as all "of my childhood"—in a letter also containing questions that exemplify his famous diligent historical preciseness—was addressed by an isolated and unknown twenty-three-year-old to the twenty-year-old brother who was also at the time his principal friend, confidant, critic, and helper. Their letters document this relationship. Stanislaus socialized with his brother's circle in Dublin. He served as conduit to members of the circle for completed sections of *Stephen Hero*, and as agent for *Dubliners* stories and for poems. The long letter putting questions and describing "The order of the stories" also asks, "Will you read some English 'realists' I see mentioned in the papers and see what they are like—Gissing, Arthur Morrison and a man named Keary" (p. 111; question mark omitted in original). Joyce sent Stanislaus for criticism each new story as drafted, and (to judge from the letters) respected his comments. *Dubliners* was to be dedicated to him (see *Letters* II, p. 83).

These powerful reasons for sincerity to Stanislaus about its first group of stories also are superfluous: when he could read the (mostly) "purely imaginary" third one, "Araby," Stanislaus would know two of the three were not historically authentic "stories of my childhood," which would have made misrepresentation in his brother's letter totally pointless. Moreover, Joyce's other extant account of the sequence of stories, to the publisher Grant Richards—a stranger who could not have known the truth—avoided making any autobiographical connection.[2]

Seen in this context, not only does Joyce's phrase "stories of my childhood" not encourage, it confounds the "bad habit" decried by Donoghue. For its very pointlessness were he to have been making a patently false historical (autobiographical) assertion to Stanislaus about the three stories argues that he had not been doing so: he must have been trying to convey to his brother something else about them.

"It is beyond dispute that few writers have been more intensely, intimately autobiographical," Hugh Kenner wrote, as he deplored "oversimple" "assertions . . . of tangency between life and work": the biographers' "bad habit."[3] My conclusion will address what with justice can be called the poetics of autobiography the mature Joyce had developed for Stephen Dedalus most prominently in the *Portrait* and *Ulysses*, and that informing predominantly Shem the Penman in *Finnegans Wake*; but those developments were out of his earliest practice. What the indisputably intense intimate autobiographer was trying to convey when a very young writer, by a brief phrase in a letter to his even younger brother, is worth understanding—and the exercise in historical criticism required to understand it is warranted—for two related reasons. The first reason is that what he meant by "stories of my childhood" constituted his understanding then of the relationship of his life and his art. The other reason is, I hope to show, that the three stories about which he wrote the phrase record—as he evolved them—the very young writer evolving the beginning of James Joyce's mastery of the making of art out of his life. The two reasons are related because a major component of his evolution as an artist was the poetics of autobiography he developed.

The period of evolution is almost exactly two years, from the first version of "The Sisters," written five months after he became twenty-two, to the third and final version, made five months after he became twenty-four; and the context of those two years is the whole of what may be considered the initial stage of his fiction writing, which began about his twenty-second birthday and was superseded half a year after his twenty-fifth. Many details of the following chronology are familiar, but the juxtaposition here of familiar data with less familiar is pertinent.[4]

On January 7, 1904, Joyce "wrote off in one day" (*James Joyce*, p. 144) the Paterian story/essay, "A Portrait of the Artist," which he promptly submitted to the Dublin magazine in preparation, *Dana*, to be rejected. For February 2, Joyce's twenty-second birthday, Stanislaus's diary entry declares that his brother "has decided to turn his paper into a novel" and "is beginning his novel . . . about himself" (*Diary*, pp. 11–12, and *James Joyce*, p. 147). Joyce finished the first chapter eight days later (*James Joyce*, p. 148). By June, he had written enough of "the marvellous novel" (his phrase) to show the manuscript to his friend Constantine Curran, and by July—with an added 102-page chapter—to George Russell (AE).

This information is in two short letters to Curran (*Letters* II, p. 55). The July letter also announces he had "written one" of "a series of epicleti—ten—for a paper"; Gabler dates it July 15 and proposes that a neologism, "epiclets," was misread.[5] The *Irish Homestead* accepted "The Sisters" on July 23 and published it on August 13; "Eveline" followed on September 10 and "After the Race" on December 10; the paper then rejected "Hallow Eve" ("[The] Clay"), written (in Pola) during January. By the end of a year, Joyce had drafted three more stories: "The Boarding House," "Counterparts," and "A Painful Case," and extensively revised the last.

By that second July he also had written all he was to write of *Stephen Hero*, 25 chapters of 914 autograph pages, "about half the book" (*Letters* II, p. 132). At the end of his first year of work on it, February 1905, he was writing chapter XVIII. On May 27 he sent Stanislaus a postcard from Trieste promising "in a fortnight the University College episode of eleven chapters" (chapters XV–XXV, the extant manuscript plus an unknown number of pages at the beginning of chapter XV and twelve pages at the end of chapter XXV). On June 7 a postcard announces "Have now finished Chapter XXIV. Will send the episode in about a week." He sent the eleven chapters soon after: in a long letter dated July 12 (it seems unconsciously revealing about Nora: *Letters* II, pp. 92–98), he boasts about his writing in the final "incident in Chap. XXIII."

While (it turned out) he abandoned *Stephen Hero* by July 1905, during the next four months he wrote the remaining five stories (almost half) of the original *Dubliners*: "Ivy Day in the Committee Room," "An Encounter" (sent Stanislaus on September 18), "A Mother," "Araby," and finally "Grace." The whole twelve-story volume, which had begun as a project of ten stories "for a paper," took him a little over fifteen months. And the latter two of the three "stories of my childhood" were written during the final six weeks.

Preparing the volume also involved revising some stories; for example, the questions of fact asked in his late September letter to Stanislaus are connected with four written stories, one of them "The Sisters." And his revision of the first story "of my childhood" was done, or at any rate completed, in the latter part of that final six-week period, after Stanislaus's response of October 10 caused him to change "in a brown habit" to "vested as for the altar," in describing the dead Father Flynn lying in state. (The detail substituted for the sake of historical accuracy would serve functionally the recast and expanded final version he was to make close to nine months later.) He wrote to Grant Richards on November 27 that he would submit *Dubliners* to him "tomorrow," and sent it on December 3 (*James Joyce*, p. 219).[6]

Joyce's well-known ordeal over the publication of *Dubliners* began in February 1906, after Richards had accepted the volume, when he sent after it "Two Gallants," which Richards dispatched to the printer unread.[7] During the spring, writer and publisher exchanged respectively indignant and insistent letters—and Joyce wrote the last new story he would write for more than a year, "A Little Cloud"; he mentioned it to Richards on February 28 and March 13, and completed it April 22. On June 23, he informed Richards that he had received the manuscript for changes; and on July 9, he wrote, "I return you today the manuscript of *Dubliners* which you suggested in your letter of 19 June that I should alter.... I have rewritten the first story in the book *The Sisters* and included the last [i.e., fourteenth] story *A Little Cloud*." He also had deleted six instances of "bloody" and altered "Counterparts" to mollify Richards; but Richards objected to nothing in "The Sisters." Joyce's recasting and expanding the story had been not compromise but creation. He never before mentioned working on it to Richards; and the wording of the letter suggests that his creative act occurred after June 19. At any rate, "The Sisters" was the young James Joyce's first short story and his last, before "The Dead"—many times longer than most of the stories and strikingly mature—was written more than a year later.

While finishing "The Dead," he told Stanislaus he would rewrite *Stephen Hero* in five long chapters; his short novel or long story was completed on September 20, 1907, and two months later he had drafted and revised the first version of the first long chapter. What I propose was the initial stage of his fiction writing had been superseded, although the *Portrait* ("entirely reconceived, reorganized and newly styled as *A Portrait of . . .*," Gabler, "Introduction," p. 10) was not yet fully in progress.[8]

The manuscript fragment of *Stephen Hero* bears notations for adapting portions of it to the *Portrait*.[9] But an index of Joyce's growth during the first stage of his fiction writing is his dissatisfaction with his "marvellous novel"—even if ironic, his epithet of June 1904 is significant—by the spring of 1905. That dissatisfaction is the negative beginning of his development of a poetics of autobiography. As early as November 19, 1904, he wrote to Stanislaus from Pola, "I am afraid I cannot finish my novel for a long time. I am discontented with a great deal of it and yet how is Stephen's nature to be expressed otherwise. Eh?" (*Letters* II, p. 71). It would be almost a decade before he himself answered his question, with brilliant success.

By April 4, 1905, he could write to Stanislaus from Trieste, "I have now finished another chapter and am at Chapter XX. This is a terrible opus: I wonder how I have the patience to write it. Do you think other people will have the patience to read it?" (p. 87). And in the postcard of May 27 announcing that Stanislaus would receive the mostly extant eleven University College chapters "in a fortnight," he wrote, "I intend to rewrite some of the beginning which, I think[,] is not well written." Presumably, he then returned to his more general misgiving; and time did not elevate his estimation of *Stephen Hero:* Spencer quotes a letter from Paul Léon written "at the end of 1938," declaring that Joyce "calls [it] a schoolboy production written when he was 19 or 20 [*sic*]" (p. 8).

The surviving "University College episode" has some effective portrayal of Stephen Daedalus's world, and its satire often is done with deft irony. Ellmann justly calls Joyce "justly proud of" (*James Joyce*, p. 207) the "incident in Chap. XXIII" he boasted of to Stanislaus, in which Stephen Daedalus impulsively proposes to Emma Clery that she sneak him into her house and bed for one night, after which they will never speak: it builds nicely on previous elements in the chapter, such as the location of their earlier walk together and the passage beginning "A certain extravagance began to tinge his life." But this rich fictionality is the exception: the too-frequent detailed monologic account of the "hero's" conversations, observations, reflections, and movements explains Joyce's lack of "patience" with his novel (half yet to do).

The young writer James Joyce's first major project was a *Künstlerroman* whose protagonist was a facsimile of himself, and whose subject was his own life experience; and he had abandoned it despite the approval of his brother and the others who read it. He had grown to expect more of himself as a writer of fiction than they did.

The young writer had done so when almost half the stories in the original *Dubliners* were unwritten, including two of the "stories of my childhood." A developing Joyce would write them and revise their companion, his first short story; then, a year later, as his last work on *Dubliners* before he wrote "The Dead" (and began the *Portrait* proper), he would metamorphose "The Sisters" in a second, extensive, revision. The three stories span the period of his growing maturity as a writer.

# 3

# James Joyce and "I"

Of the five stories young Joyce wrote about denizens of Dublin during the four months after he abandoned his novel about himself, two were "stories of my childhood." Despite Stanislaus's admonition to Colum in my epigraph to the previous chapter, a witness has attested that one of them, "Araby," is not "purely imaginary" beyond "the house in North Richmond Street" (and encounters with "urchins")—that in fact it depicts an incident in the young writer's life experience. Such a proposal about a story like "Araby," even were it by a writer less autobiographical, would scarcely surprise. Joyce's declaration to Stanislaus was unlikely to have been a claim—in despite of his brother's certain knowledge—that he himself was the Dubliner (the implicit subject) of the first three stories of *Dubliners;* yet the testimony exists.

It invokes the most immediate question young Joyce's "stories of my childhood" poses about the relation of his life and his art, antecedent to whether his phrase only signifies he is using his life experience as material, or asserts he indeed is writing about himself. And the question is complex: What is the actual extent of veridical autobiography—Joyce's fidelity to (his own "childhood") history—in those three narratives either by an adult about himself when a boy, or by three different adults about themselves when boys?

The second alternative might seem to obviate the question for (at least) two of the boys and their older narrator-selves. I believe it would not, but would raise instead the secondary question, Whether one or all three (or none), and if any the tertiary question Which, of the three boys-and-narrators is or are autobiographical.

Both the mentioned departures from veridical autobiography Joyce made in the *Portrait*—appropriating a friend's experience for, and incorporating his brother's temperament in, his facsimile Stephen—bear on the question of how the young Joyce related "my childhood" to his art in the three stories. Although the mature writer transmuted J. F. Byrne's ephemeral encounter with Father Joseph Darlington, Joyce actually helped himself to it when not yet twenty-three: on January 13, 1905, about the time he was writing as "Stephen Daedalus" his fourth story intended for the *Irish Homestead*, he informed Stanislaus "I have finished Chap. XV" of *Stephen Hero* (*Letters* II, p. 76). And his second departure in the *Portrait* is anticipated in "A Painful Case," written that July or early August (Gabler, *Dubliners*, p. 5), little more than a year after "The Sisters." As Stephen is to do, its protagonist James Duffy recalls young Joyce intellectually: he shares his interest in Nietzsche, when young had his interest in socialism, has translated Hauptmann's *Michael Kramer,* and has named his occasional observations on life "Bile Beans." However: that was the title "Jim suggested for" his brother's observations, which like Duffy's were on pinned loose sheets; two of them are appropriated for Duffy; and Duffy has Stanislaus's mandarin contempt for socialism, his "intolerance of drunkenness," generally his solemn, austere temperament: "I served as model" (*My Brother's Keeper,* pp. 165–66, 73).

In other words, both departures from veridical autobiography Joyce made when creating Stephen that were not invention but derived from his experience, he made very early. Moreover, while "An Encounter," written in September, does not give its unnamed protagonist Stanislaus's temperament, this story largely based on a historical experience of the Joyce brothers abandons the pattern in *Stephen Hero* of autobiographical protagonist and brother-companion, substituting for Stanislaus the less congenial (apparent) invention Mahony.

But departures from autobiography are precisely that. And the most significant light that examining the range of ways the mature Joyce used and did autobiography casts on the young writer's "stories of my childhood" illuminates the radical contrast with his early practice when not writing his abortive *Künstlerroman:* like Lawrence and other writers, the young Joyce used himself and his experience in those stories; but he did so pragmatically, for he was not being autobiographical—the child James Joyce was not their subject.

The extent and ways he both drew on his experience and eschewed fidelity to his own history in them can be illustrated by referring yet again to Stanislaus's testimony about "the house in North Richmond Street described in 'Araby.'" His next sentence quotes the first paragraph of "Araby" on the neighboring "uninhabited house," and respecting what his brother's narrator calls its "square ground," interjects "—a garden with apple-trees" (p. 79). In his story about the advent of erotic urges in a boy, the young writer enlisted that real garden, significantly modified: the narrator's account of "our house" in its second paragraph includes "The wild garden . . . contained a central apple tree and a few straggling bushes."[1] In making his art when mature, Joyce gave radical priority to his experience. His creation of the boy's primal garden out of the real—but neighboring—garden "with apple trees" does just that; yet it is a creation.

His departures from veridical autobiography relative to "the house in North Richmond Street" are more extensive. It is a dead-end (British *blind* suits the story) street running north from the North Circular Road almost to the Royal Canal. The Joyce family lived at no. 17 according to Richard Ellmann, no. 13 according to Peter Costello ("By an odd coincidence there was another John Joyce living at 17 . . ."), and no. 12, to judge from Stephen Dedalus's address and from "12 Norse Richmound" in a partial and non-chronological list in *Finnegans Wake* of the family's many addresses to Joyce's twentieth year; their tenure began in either "late" 1894 or 1895 (Ellmann), or in "early" 1896 (Costello), and extended through 1895 (Ellmann), "only a few months" to "autumn" 1896 (Costello), or three years to late 1897 or some time in 1898.[2] The conflicting house numbers are important only as they reflect on Joyce biography; but the uncertainty about when the boy James Joyce lived at 17 or 13 or 12 North Richmond Street impedes ascertaining historical verisimilitude in any or all of the "stories of my childhood."

*My Brother's Keeper* specifies the months following the Intermediate Examinations in which Joyce won his second "exhibition" as "the summer holidays that were to furnish either the idea or the emotional environment for the few [three] stories of childhood" (p. 82). Joyce was thirteen, the year 1895 (*James Joyce*, p. 47, and *Years of Growth*, pp. 130–31); and in "The Sisters," after originally withholding the year, then giving it as 1890, in the final version he dated Father Flynn's death July 1, 1895. This apparent eventual victory for veridical autobiography also seems to confirm Stanislaus's generalization about "the summer holidays." However, both the other stories explicitly take place during the school year. More important, the Araby Bazaar occurred more than a year before the summer of 1895.[3] This fact not only reflects on Stanislaus's generalization, but also signifies another violation of historical verisimilitude: Araby preceded the earliest date (late 1894) for the Joyces' residence on the street actually mentioned only in "Araby."

Though it is not named in either of the other stories, internal evidence locates the boy's home close to North Richmond Street—so that it could be his street—in both. The Joyces moved there from Millbourne Avenue in

Drumcondra, about a half mile northwest, a more rustic location—and more rustic than that to be inferred from either story—north of the Tolka River (which flows roughly parallel to the Royal Canal); and their next four addresses all were in Fairview, also north of the Tolka, and northeast of North Richmond Street (see *Letters* II, p. lv). From about his twelfth to nineteenth years, Joyce lived in the northeast quadrant of Dublin above the North Circular Road. (Eccles Street is in that quadrant, west of North Richmond and just below the North Circular.)

Of his addresses during this period, only North Richmond Street is consonant with that of Joyce's boy in "The Sisters" and "An Encounter." The narrator of "The Sisters" reports, "after breakfast I went down to look at the little house in Great Britain Street" (p. 11): for a young boy, the Flynns' "little house" on what is now Parnell Street is within easy walking distance of none of Joyce's Drumcondra or Fairview addresses. And none of those addresses could enable the boy in "An Encounter" to hide his school books "at the end of the garden where nobody ever came and hurr[y] along the canal bank," and to live "nearest" to the three boys' place of rendezvous, "the Canal [Newcomen] Bridge" (p. 21). The real "uninhabited house" described at the beginning of "Araby," which "stood at the blind end" of North Richmond Street "in a square ground," also backed on the Royal Canal, so that "the garden where nobody ever came" in "An Encounter" sounds like its garden.

But is it? To mention the proximity of the canal to the house at the dead end of North Richmond Street is not an instance of biographers' bad habit, because that real Dublin street where Joyce really lived is named. However, it is named in "Araby": the boy's street is not identified in "An Encounter." The fact his address and that of the boy in "The Sisters" is consonant with North Richmond Street could signify that while Joyce violated verisimilitude in "Araby," since he did not live there at the time of the Araby Bazaar, in the three stories he kept close to his own experience when situating the home of each boy. Or it could signify that all three boys have the same address.

The latter would be the case if they are a single boy; but whether they (and their older narrator-selves) are one or three has been a much debated question. The coherence of the stories, which derives from similarities, sequencing, and intertextual elements, encourages the assumption that all have the same protagonist-and-narrator. Even a single address for him when a boy can be hypostatized, as having been disclosed with increasing specificity through the three stories in sequence; but there is more persuasive evidence that they constitute a sequence.

Of their similarities, plainly the most blatant is that those three stories grouped together at its beginning all have, and uniquely in *Dubliners,* a first-person narrator, and that in all three the narrator is an adult telling about himself when a boy. In none of the three does the boy appear to have any sisters or brothers. Parent figures, who appear in only two, in both are an uncle, named Jack (John Joyce's familiar name) in "The Sisters," changed from John in the first revision (Gabler, *Dubliners,* p. 126), and an aunt, unnamed: Cotter in that story speaks of the boy as their child (p. 10). (In *Ulysses,* Mulligan refers to his mother [1.195/p. 7] as "the aunt" [1.139/p. 6].) In "The Sisters" the boy is fascinated by language; in the other stories he is bookish. All three begin with a depiction of his domestic circumstances, but essentially portray an experience he has in the outside world; and in all three, that experience is disturbing. Finally, in all three— explicitly in the others and deducible in "The Sisters"—the boy has learned from the disturbing experience. In sum, they are overtly a group of very similar stories about—at the least—very similar boys.

The fact that one is the first story Joyce wrote, and the other two "of my childhood" are among the last four written for the original volume, suggests his intention to create a coherent group. That they are in the order of their composition might seem haphazard, were it not for the elements that make them a sequence.

In the extensive criticism published over the years on "An Encounter," "Araby," and above all "The Sisters," a number of sequencing elements have been suggested. Some of these are like the putative gradual revelation of the boy's address: accepting them does young Joyce's artistry little credit. For example (in sequence): Father Flynn intended but failed to take his sisters on an excursion to the birthplace of the three in Irishtown, which is south of the Liffey; the two boys of "An Encounter" travel toward, but do not reach, their destination, the Pigeon House, which is south of the Liffey; and the boy travels to Westland Row (now Pearse) station, which is south of the Liffey, and from there on a special train to fulfill his quest at Araby (the historical Araby was at the Royal Dublin Society in Ballsbridge)—but is disappointed when he does so. However, those sequences in the three stories that concern the true subject of each— the nature and experience of its protagonist—more rewardingly assert their coherence. For example: in "The Sisters," the boy's disturbing experience imparts to him knowledge solely about the world; in "An Encounter," the knowledge is mostly about the world and partly about himself; and in "Araby," it is still partly about the world but mostly about himself.

Of the sequences concerning the boy, the most significant is that of his age. The young Joyce achieved it both simply and definitively: by portraying the onset of puberty. In "The Sisters" as originally written and first revised, the boy's age is vaguely indicated, once: the narrator reports "I said nothing" during the closing conversation between his aunt and Eliza Flynn, "being too young" (Gabler, *Dubliners,* p. 144). In contrast, the final version of the story begins with the boy's naive response to the words *paralysis, gnomon,* and *simony;* that is followed by the conversation between Cotter and his aunt and uncle about "children" like him; immediately thereafter, to supplant "the heavy grey face of the paralytic" in his imagination when in bed, he "tried to think of Christmas"; when he walks to the Flynn house alone, "I wished to go in and look at him but I had not the courage to knock"; on the visit with his aunt, he "hesitated to enter" the room containing the body, then "went in on tiptoe"; during the final conversation, now offered crackers, "I declined because I thought I would make too much noise eating them"; finally, he has left his sherry on the table, goes to taste it "under cover of" a pause in the conversation, "and then returned quietly to my chair in the corner" (pp. 9, 10–11, 12, 14, 15, 17). Joyce's final revision carefully portrays a distinctly young boy, so that the absence from the protagonist's consciousness of any thought of girls through all versions has become a significant negative part of the portrayal.

The advance in age of the boy in "An Encounter" is signaled in its third paragraph: although "doors of escape"—his central motive in the story—are "opened" by "the literature of the Wild West," he "liked better some American detective stories which were traversed from time to time by unkempt fierce and beautiful girls" (p. 20). To the sadistic pedophile's question in the "encounter" itself, the boy replies that he has no "sweetheart"; but his classmate Mahony has "three" (p. 25), so it is not an incongruous question for boys their age.

"Araby" dramatically portrays—it is the lever of the story—the advent of erotic longing in a boy, and its consequences. He still is young enough both: to believe the deceased priest who preceded his family in the house "*very* charitable" for leaving "*all* his money to institutions" (my emphasis) though he had a living sister; and, of the priest's books he found, preferring to Walter Scott's *The Abbot,* whose protagonist is a boy and young man devoted to a queen, the lurid *Memoirs of Vidocq*—to do so for the juvenile reason that "its leaves were yellow" (p. 29). But the extent of his young devotion to the unnamed adolescent girl who shares the family name of the poet of "Dark Rosaleen" is elaborately expounded in three successive paragraphs. He watches furtively until "Mangan's sister" leaves for school in the morning, and follows her; "Her image accompanied me" everywhere; "My eyes were often full of tears"; and so on until, at the end of the third paragraph, in a swoon, "I pressed the palms of my hands together until they trembled, murmuring: O *love*! O *love*! many times." The paragraph following this climactic expression of erotic rapture by one who "did not know whether I would ever speak to her or not" about his "confused adoration" begins, "At last she spoke to me." Unlike their earlier "few casual words" she brings up Araby, and he becomes now totally "confused" (pp. 30–31). He is still a boy; but he is older than the boy in each previous story, in a distinct sequence.

The coherence achieved by their similarities, and by Joyce's manifest sequencing of them, is reinforced by the recurrent details and motifs in the three stories. The cohesive effect of these details and motifs is limited, not least because none seem to recur in all three; but they cannot be gainsaid. Among the most often cited are that in "An Encounter" and "Araby" the boy is a quester who experiences dis-illusion, and that "The Sisters" and "Araby" share an orientalist element. More important than these familiar common elements are the religion-related ones in the latter two stories. The dead Father Flynn was discovered laughing in his confession box in the dark chapel, and in "Araby" the boy reveals his state of mind in the darkened room in which that other priest had died. Father Flynn's decline began when he dropped, and in the final version of the story his corpse is holding "loosely," a chalice; and in a famous metaphor the boy calls "her image," which "accompanied me even in places the most hostile to romance" (p. 31), a chalice. (The young Joyce's use of *image* for an obsessive and emotionally profligate mental icon anticipates Yeats's in "Among School Children.")

The narrator's word "romance" in the context of "chalice," in combination with other words grouped around it, some also metaphors—"litanies," "chanting," "prayers," "praises," "adoration"—and with the boy's prayerful attitude ("I pressed the palms of my hands together") as he repeatedly "murmur[s] O *love*!" in the room associated with the death of the "Araby" priest, signals the function for "Araby" of its religious intertextuality with "The Sisters": to help portray the boy's erotic fervor as perverted religiosity, and so both deleterious and futile. Those consequences of his perversion are conveyed by his extravagant association of the "chalice" he "bore . . . safely through a throng of foes" ("her image") with the Holy Grail. The *title* of the third book he found, *The Devout*

*Communicant* (a "diffuse and redundant" collection of *Pious Meditations* [*Joyce Annotated*, p. 43]), functions ironically in this context. (Joyce here anticipates his portraying, and identifying, the etiology in Catholic Ireland of a slightly older Stephen Dedalus's confusion of the erotic and the religious.) And when near the end of the story the boy "recognised" in the darkened Araby hall "a silence like that which pervades a church after a service" (p. 34), the potential reciprocal comment on religious "adoration" is made, and "Araby" repays its debt to "The Sisters."

But although the young Joyce purposely created a coherent sequence of three "stories of my childhood," he withheld from them a single protagonist (and consequently, narrator). Strictly speaking, the boy in "Araby" has not been given different neighbors from the boy in "An Encounter," as some critics have suggested. The boy in "An Encounter" is one of a large group: "We banded ourselves together, some . . . almost in fear: and of the number of these latter . . . I was one" (p. 20). And the point has been made that the two classmates with whom he plans his truancy live elsewhere. In other words, his playmates are not identified as (different) neighbors.

Nevertheless, the neighbor and principal companion of the boy in "Araby," Mangan, is not mentioned as one of the many playmates of "An Encounter." That he is not a close friend (yet) could signify a different age in the same boy-protagonist; but if so, a brief mention of the neighboring future friend as one of the group would have been apposite. A more striking absence, if the stories are about a single boy, is his name. "The Sisters" was first revised, and "Araby" if not both other stories written, after Joyce described the three as "of my childhood"; so he could have made his protagonists explicitly one boy, even by so simple a device as giving the boy in all three stories a (single) name, disclosed in dialogue. He declined to do so at that stage; and in his final revision of "The Sisters" almost a year later, he abandoned a reticence which (in contrast to his elaborate refusal in *Ulysses* to specify whether or not Bloom is Jewish) had no purpose—by making the protagonists explicitly three. For in finally placing Father Flynn's death in 1895, he specified the time of that first "story of my childhood" as more than a year after the only other datable event in the stories, the Araby Bazaar.

By that new detail, the young Joyce reversed what would have been the chronology if the sequence of progressively older protagonists in the three stories were a single boy—he pointedly differentiated the boys. And when during that final revision he added to "The Sisters" the youngest boy's reflections on the three "strangely" sounding words, giving him alone of the three (like young Stephen Dedalus) a fascination with language, Joyce augmented the differentiation.

The very extent of the similarities he gave boys whom he also kept distinct affirms his functional treatment of history, including his personal history. The point was made that if they are different boys, it might seem only one at most can be his autobiographical embodiment. That would be true—as logical—if he were being strictly veracious historically. But when he represented "my childhood" by three distinct boys who also are similar, young James Joyce denied exclusive historical authenticity to any single one of them: if one is like him, all are, so none is his historically authentic single autobiographical embodiment. In the sequence of three distinct boys he created, his practice was to subvert potential historical verisimilitude in order to eschew autobiography.

His practice comprised not only the protagonists of the stories, but also the circumstances and the incidents. It is generally agreed that he subverted little history in "An Encounter": much of the boy's experience in his "adventure," if not his companion or the consequent nature of his final realization about himself and the "stupid . . . Mahony" (p. 25), is veridical autobiography—"of my childhood." Stanislaus's comment in a letter to him after reading the manuscript of the story, quoted above, attests that it was "based upon his actual personal experience," as Stanislaus put it in *My Brother's Keeper:* "In 'An Encounter' my brother describes a day's miching which he and I planned and carried out while we were living in North Richmond Street" (p. 79).

The companion replacing Stanislaus who is the subject of the boy's final realization subverts history; but he also is a more suitable foil for the protagonist than a Stanislaus/"Maurice" character would have been, exemplifies young Joyce's objectifying his experience as material for art. And regarding the central element of the story, the boy's "encounter" itself: is it solely a report of the one Joyce experienced? Does it owe anything to an encounter related in the epiphany he numbered "(22)," written at Mullingar, where he stayed when eighteen and nineteen, which is between "Two Children" and a violent beggar? The epiphany ends with "The Lame Beggar" saying, "I'll cut ye open. I'll cut the livers and the lights out o' ye" (*Workshop of Daedalus,* p. 25). How can it be determined that the incident Joyce apparently witnessed is unrelated to "An Encounter"?

In the case of "Araby," at least its final circumstances were "based upon his actual personal experience," according to the testimony of the witness mentioned in the first paragraph, a contemporary of Joyce's at Belvedere College, William G. Fallon. It has been cited by critics to make that point, and is mentioned with the story in both recent biographies (*Literary Life*, p. 35; *Years of Growth*, p. 129); in my judgment, it shows that even simple testimony can promote the "bad habit":

> *Araby* is one of the most poignant stories in *Dubliners*. . . . Strangely enough, I remember meeting Joyce on the very evening that he went to this bazaar. It *was* called *Araby*. I had just got off the train at Lansdowne Road when I spied him. . . . It was a Saturday night. When we reached the bazaar it was just clearing up. It was very late. I lost Joyce in the crowd, but I could see he was disheartened over something. I recall, too, that Joyce had had some difficulty for a week or so previously in extracting the money for the bazaar from his parent. (*The Joyce We Knew*, pp. 47–48)

Fallon reports he too was in the English class taught by Joyce's early mentor, George Dempsey (p. 42); he is named in two consecutive epiphanies as at the Sheehys' house along with a less young Joyce (*Workshop of Daedalus*, pp. 23, 24); and the *Portrait* mentions "a boy named Fallon in Belvedere" who had "a silly laugh" (p. 145). So there is no doubt he could have come upon his classmate Joyce and accompanied him to the Araby Bazaar on Saturday, the night in May 1894 the boy in "Araby" attended it. (In the *Portrait*, Heron chides the disdainful boy Stephen who "doesn't go to bazaars" [p. 76].) But Fallon's testimony is taken as evidence for the autobiographical basis not just of trivial details in the story like the night it takes place, but also of its climax and conclusion. Even were the memory of a memoirist about an event more than seventy years before (see *The Joyce We Knew*, p. 49) to be reliable, how reliable would be the perception by a thirteen-year-old boy that a twelve-year-old boy "was disheartened"? And how significant of autobiography in "Araby" is the boy or octogenarian Fallon's "over something"?

Moreover, in "recall[ing]" Joyce's "difficulty for a week . . . extracting the money," the aged Fallon recalls strange knowledge for a mere acquaintance. His supposed recollection of that knowledge may derive from his familiarity, when he wrote, with "one of the most poignant stories in *Dubliners*," whose conclusion turns on the boy's too-late receipt of the needed money. And while Fallon does not claim to know the cause of the twelve-year-old Joyce's perceived state of mind that Saturday night, his distinctly remembered thirteen-year-old perception of it may be attributable to the same "poignant" fictional source.

More important for the question of veridical autobiography in "Araby" than Fallon's testimony about Joyce himself is his "I lost Joyce in the crowd." Delayed until late the Saturday night of Araby, Joyce's boy travels "alone in the bare carriage" to arrive "ten minutes to ten" (p. 34) at a carnival that is empty and closing. The historical Araby was neither. It had been scheduled to end Saturday night (May 19), as does Araby in the story, but because of its popularity was extended through the next Tuesday. Moreover, according to reports in the *Freeman's Journal,* "nearly one-third of the population of Dublin, visited the fete" during its eight days, and the "crowd" in which the boys were separated numbered, for all of Saturday night, eighteen thousand people. Congested rather than deserted at "ten minutes to ten," the real Araby also was bustling rather than closing: at the chief performed attraction, "Café Chantant," which in the story is closed, the last show did not begin until ten-thirty; and the last train left the Araby siding at Lansdowne Road at eleven-thirty.[4]

Like anyone else, when twelve as at any other time, James Joyce could well have been "disheartened over something" that night; and it is possible he had difficulty getting money to attend Araby. But the first point is a boy's perception, the second one trivial even if true: if Fallon's "very late" was later than the time in the story, the bazaar may have been "clearing up" but, by his own testimony, was crowded—so Joyce would not have had his character's experience because of a delay in arriving; and both points are the testimony after more than seven decades of a man who had read "Araby." What is important for the question of veridical autobiography is not this dubious testimony, but the state of the Araby the boy visits in "Araby," which is instrumental to his realization at the end of Joyce's story. And in creating the empty and closing carnival, Joyce departed radically from the Araby he had experienced.

Of the three "stories of my childhood," "The Sisters" is least about Joyce's childhood historically: Stanislaus was right that the boy's relationship with a priest and experience of his death have no biographical basis. Flynn is the maiden name of Joyce's maternal (Murray) grandmother, Margaret Theresa, who had at least four sisters and a brother. The historical chronology suits the three generations in the story, but little else in history bears on Father James Flynn and his sisters of the story.

Two widowed sisters of Margaret Theresa Flynn Murray, Julia Clare Lyons and Ellen Callanan, kept the "Misses Flynn" music school with Mrs. Callanan's daughter Mary Ellen, at their home, 15 Usher's Island (*James Joyce,* p. 245, and *Years of Growth,* pp. 25–26). Joyce portrays the spinster "Misses Morkan" (Julia and Kate), Mary Jane, daughter of their dead "brother Pat," and the house on Usher's Island in which they keep their school, in "The Dead" (p. 176); and in *Ulysses,* "Miss Kate

Morkan" is given as Stephen's godmother, and as living "in the house of her dying sister Miss Julia Morkan at 15 Usher's Island" (16.139–41/p. 547). Moreover, as Gabriel Conroy presides at the annual Christmas dinner party of his aunts the Misses Morkan, so John Joyce (the husband of their niece, not their nephew) "carved the goose and made the speech" (*James Joyce*, p. 245) at the annual party of May Joyce's aunts Julia and Ellen; and the older Joyce children attended as well.

Joyce's striking verisimilitude respecting the historical "Misses Flynn" in "The Dead" (and *Ulysses*) simultaneously denies any Joyce family connection to the fictional priest and two sisters to whom he gave that (common Irish) name in "The Sisters." Moreover, their social class, clearly delineated in their origin in the slum, Irishtown, and in Eliza Flynn's speech solecisms, distinguishes them from Joyce's mother's Flynn relatives.

Costello's *Years of Growth* identifies, and associates the Flynn sisters in "The Sisters" with, two spinster sisters named Monahan whom Mary Jane Joyce "must have come to know" ("had apparently come to know") when her oldest son was eleven or twelve; those sisters ran a drapery shop in Great Britain Street and had a brother (not a priest) named James (pp. 119, 129). The Monahan sisters' first names are not given, but if Costello's inference is correct and Joyce knew them, he was not doing autobiography in portraying the Flynn sisters of "The Sisters" but, like every writer, exploiting his experience.

The chief importance of the Flynn name for attributions of autobiography in "The Sisters" is to support the belief that the story is "based on the death of the old, paralyzed, and demented priest to whom [Joyce] was related on his mother's side" (*James Joyce*, p. 163). However, there is no evidence he had any such relation, on either side. Apparently he was related to a priest out of favor with the Church: a maternal uncle not of his mother but of his father. Stephen's Great-uncle Charles in the *Portrait* is based on William O'Connell; and William's brother Charles (godfather of Joyce's brother Charles) apparently "was silenced" by his superiors because he "declined to accept offerings from his parishioners."[5] Both real and fictional priests were unconventional; but there is no similarity between the circumstances of Father Charles O'Connell's real suspension from priestly duties and the fictional suspension of Father James Flynn— or between the men themselves, to judge from the scant historical evidence.

Although "The Sisters" is invention, a confirmed boyhood experience of its author more suggests autobiography in it than his possible acquaintance with the sisters Monahan. According to *The Years of Growth,* "on 3rd March 1894 old John Murray," Joyce's mother's father, widower of Margaret Theresa, the Flynn sister who was her mother, died "in a coma induced by a paralytic stroke" (p. 125) at his son John Murray's house, which Joyce frequented when a boy. However, the suggestion of biographical significance in the boy's response to Father Flynn's death in "The Sisters" is not warranted. John Murray was Joyce's grandfather, and he may have been drawing on an affecting boyhood experience; on the other hand, the available evidence indicates that once again Joyce was using his experience, not doing autobiography. His attitude toward John Murray, and hence the extent of personal loss he experienced over the last illness and death, though unknown, can be inferred. Costello makes the point that the old man "is strikingly absent in Joyce's fiction" (p. 128). And while he was growing up, his father expressed toward his grandfather "an unrelenting hatred and unremitting virulent abuse that amounted to an obsession," for example calling him "the old fornicator," because he had married again after Margaret Theresa's death (*My Brother's Keeper*, p. 51; Stanislaus mentions their grandfather's death without comment). Costello's conclusion that "this was a significant death for Joyce, for it eventually provided the impetus for the first story of *Dubliners*" (p. 128) seems to be biographers' habit.

It seems to be so not only because positive evidence is lacking, but also because a very different kind of "impetus" exists: George Russell's undated letter beginning, "Dear Joyce Look at the story in this paper The Irish Homestead. Could you write anything simple, rural?, livemaking?, pathos? . . . so as not to shock the readers" (*Letters* II, p. 43). And "The Sisters" itself seems to owe more to the story ("Our Weekly Story") Russell sent Joyce, "The Old Watchman," by one Berkeley Campbell, than to anything in his own life.[6] It does not owe a great deal, and the young writer fully if obliquely acknowledged his debt by a number of details. The date of the issue Russell sent, July 2, is the date of Father Flynn's death in the *Irish Homestead* version of "The Sisters." The narrator of "The Old Watchman" is an adult who "was a small boy of about twelve" when he met the ailing old watchman, who "was apparently about sixty-five," the age of Father Flynn. The watchman was a Protestant, but the son of the dean of St. Patrick's Cathedral, and he had ruined his life. The only name in the story, that of "the other workman," is Father Flynn's, James. Finally, the narrator reports, "I used to go and see him very often" during his final illness, and "I was awfully sorry when he died." The sentimental story young Joyce almost playfully drew on, the pound

Russell's letter offered ("It is easily earned money"), the opportunity for publication (even if in "the pigs' paper"), all are more substantial etiology for "The Sisters" than his own boyhood.

The veridical autobiography in that first of Joyce's "stories of my childhood" does not extend beyond his experience—the personal import of which is unknown—of an aged man's last illness and death following a paralytic stroke. The more substantial autobiography in "An Encounter" includes a day's truancy for the adventure of walking abroad in the city, and the consequent frightening meeting with a sadistic pederast. Finally, the boy Joyce would have been like countless other boys if he had undergone something like the inchoate erotic attachment and disillusion portrayed in "Araby";[7] but historical evidence exists only for contacts with poorer children, North Richmond Street—where he did not yet live—and his having attended the Araby Bazaar on the Saturday night of its Dublin visit, along with thousands of other people.

Young Joyce signed the three stories printed in the *Irish Homestead*, the next two (possibly three: see Gabler, "Introduction," p. 5) he wrote, and some contemporaneous letters to friends, "Stephen Daedalus"; moreover, he was writing *Stephen Hero* and would write the *Portrait* and *Ulysses*. Under the circumstances, that he named Stephen Daedalus as the author of "The Sisters"—with its first-person narrative of a protagonist whose personal and social circumstances are very like what his own were when a boy—certainly encouraged autobiographical inferences about it and the two similar stories that begin *Dubliners*. Nevertheless, the small extent of veridical autobiography in the three stories demonstrably confutes such inferences: in none of them is the writer the subject in disguise. This precludes the apparent meaning when he characterized them to his own younger brother as "of my childhood." The meaning of his assertion must be sought not in the facts of his life, but in the stories themselves: the experiences told of three distinct but similar middle-class Catholic (their social class and religion are dwelt on in each story) Dublin boys.

The first of the two related reasons I gave for inquiring what his assertion meant is that it embodied his understanding then of the relationship of his life and his art; the second is that the three stories record the very young writer's evolving the beginning of his mastery in making art out of life. My first reason demands attention to the boys' experiences; my second, to the tellers about those experiences the boys become.

# 4

# "Stories of My Childhood"

On May 5, 1906, Joyce declared: "My intention was to write a chapter of the moral history of my country and I chose Dublin for the scene because that city seemed to me the centre of paralysis. I have tried to present it to the indifferent public under four of its aspects: childhood, adolescence, maturity and public life. The stories are arranged in this order. I have written it for the most part in a style of scrupulous meanness and with the conviction that he is a very bold man who dares to alter in the presentment, still more to deform, whatever he has seen and heard" (*Letters* II, p. 134). He or she also is bold who dares to quote these four sentences, the second one already mentioned in my opening pages: they probably are Joyce's most familiar statement about his own work. The passage occurs midway in the eloquent first and longest of the letters he wrote to Grant Richards during their exchange about *Dubliners,* which follows the young and unknown writer's noble letter (April 26) inviting return of the manuscript, with its ringing conclusion: "It would be almost a disaster to me but I am afraid the service which you ask me to do for your printer's conscience is not in my power" (*Letters* I, p. 61).

He was being slightly disingenuous in the passage: although his point about Ireland's chief city is sensible, he probably "chose" Dublin for more obvious reasons. But "scrupulous meanness" is qualified by "for the most part"; and on the whole what he wrote gives little reason to doubt he was sincerely describing his conception of his twelve-story manuscript. I quote it because it provides a context heuristic for understanding his assertion to Stanislaus just over seven months before, concerning the three stories which essentially are not about "my childhood." In addition to its specifying an impersonal (a general) "childhood," the context the passage provides is Joyce's declared "intention to write . . . moral history," and his specified source for his book: what he "has seen and heard."

Set into this context, the knowledge that however "intensely, intimately autobiographical" the work of the mature writer, young Joyce's practice in the three "stories of my childhood" was not so, clarifies his phrase. For the context sanctions a deconstruction of its genetic preposition—one not beyond the farthest horizon of *différance* (*en abyme*), but less "playful" and more pertinent. It sanctions excluding from young Joyce's "of"— sanctions designating "bad habit"—the word's reflexive signification *about*, in favor of the other relevant (and the principal) one among its significations, the derivative *from:* the stories, his letter informed Stanislaus, originate in his own experience when a child.

In the range of ways he implicated his life in his fiction, the three stories are at the extreme of using it strictly as material. They draw upon the middle-class Catholic Dublin boy Joyce's experience, and represent the young writer's understanding of it, using fictional (invented) characters and mostly fictional circumstances; he himself was strictly source, as distinct from subject.

Fundamental as it is, the distinction sometimes is difficult to apply. In "The Dead," Gretta Conroy's deceased young Galway admirer even has the same first name as Nora Joyce's similar admirer; and Joyce may well have portrayed his own in Gabriel's complicated response, which consummates the story, when each was told by his wife about the dead youth. To declare that "The Dead" is an autobiographical story for these reasons, or is not—the author partly subject or strictly source—is possible only if *autobiographical fiction* is suitably defined, which is to say defined by tautology.

But until the triangle crucial to "The Dead," Joyce practiced an impersonal conception of fiction throughout *Dubliners:* that is the significant point for understanding his relationship to the three non-autobiographical boys. Even when he is a close source for his characters (as for the boys, and for James Duffy in "A Painful Case"), the characters never exist to represent James Joyce—he is never the tacit subject. In "The Dead" itself he (apparently accurately) portrayed the Flynn sisters' Christmas dinners he attended—but no children are among the guests.

This impersonal fiction was anticipated as early—if his brother's report of its title piece and general account of it are accurate—as "Silhouettes," the lost series of "short stories" (or "sketches") he wrote while in secondary school, "in the style of *Dubliners*," recording "life as he knew it," "the life that passed before his steel-blue eyes" (*My Brother's Keeper,* pp. 74, 104–5, 106). Moreover, most of the extant "epiphanies," which he began while at the university, in 1900 (*James Joyce,* p. 83), record either incidents or psychological experiences (called "dream-epiphanies" by Stanislaus) in which he does not figure, or incidents in which he designated himself—even when a child—"Joyce." His loss of "patience" with *Stephen Hero* while he was writing *Dubliners* may have been because that novel, in which he is subject and not strictly source, was failing to "impersonalise" (make "dramatic") "the personality of the artist," in the words he later gave Stephen Dedalus (*Portrait*, p. 187)—was not solving the problem of creating effective autobiographical fiction that he intentionally avoided in the "stories of my childhood."

When with the *Portrait* he resumed his endeavor to solve that fundamental artistic problem, he devoted two paragraphs to an account of the boy Stephen's first experience of Dublin, to which he made the Dedalus family move "from the comfort and revery of Blackrock" (p. 67) at about the age he himself had been taken there from the same southern suburb (*James Joyce*, p. 35).

The first begins "Dublin was a new and complex sensation," describes the boy's wanderings about the city, records "The vastness and strangeness of the life suggested to him by" goods being unloaded from ships, and recalls his earlier "wandering . . . in search of Mercedes." It ends with Stephen's "wander[ing] up and down day after day as if he really sought someone that [!] eluded him"; and he is said to have "A vague dissatisfaction."

The other paragraph dwells on this "embitterment," and on its causes in himself and his family's adversity. Its central passage is a familiar one: "He was angry with himself for being young and the prey of restless foolish impulses, angry also with the change of fortune which was reshaping the world about him into a vision of squalor and insincerity." But the remaining two sentences in the paragraph are more pertinent here: "Yet his anger lent nothing to the vision. He chronicled with patience what he saw, detaching himself from it and tasting its mortifying flavour in secret" (pp. 67–68).

The boy Stephen's "chronicl[ing] with patience what he saw, detaching himself from it," recalls Stanislaus's "the life that passed before his steel blue eyes and [the passage continues] unblinking gaze at home and in the streets of Dublin," about his brother when a boy.

Much in the two paragraphs about Stephen recalls the boy of "An Encounter" or the boy of "Araby"; both can be said to be "the prey of restless foolish impulses." But that is because they and the boy of "The Sisters" are, as Stephen's tacit original who is their creator became, Dublin boys, subject to the outer and inner consequences of that fact. Joyce gave to none of them, only to the boy Stephen, his own practice of witnessing those consequences with detachment. I shall endeavor to show how carefully he delineated each of the three characters of the "stories of my childhood," and the three narrators they have grown into. My point here is that he individualized them because James Joyce, Stephen's subject, is for them strictly a source. They are, like the older protagonists of the other stories, Dubliners.

Their stories readily fit his conception of his manuscript—his program in *Dubliners*—young Joyce articulated to Richards: the effect on the sensitive child James Joyce of what "he ha[d] seen and heard," along with the young writer's diagnosis of causes, both external and internal, provided the "childhood" component of "a chapter of the moral history of my country." Youthful work, his "chapter" treats politics explicitly only in "Ivy Day in the Committee Room."[1] But the social concern the young writer declared to Richards, which is suggested in his brother's testimony and which he ascribed to Stephen in the *Portrait* passage, cannot be gainsaid.

He "inten[ded]" his book to be an account of the condition of his contemporaries in Catholic Dublin, Ireland ("a chapter of the moral history of my country"). In the twelve-story *Dubliners* he had submitted and was describing to Richards, then, each of the three stories out "of my childhood" is a sub-"chapter": each contributes to his program by portraying "the centre of" Ireland being experienced by and affecting a different one of its children. Their function in his "chapter" may be the best explanation why not one of the three boys has a conventional family: parents, sisters, brothers.

The first of the three is sketchy—in the full sense of the word. A man narrates an account of his experiencing when a Dublin boy the shabby dependency in later life, and ignominious death from unspecified causes, of a failed priest once highly enough regarded in the Church to have been sent to study at "the [Irish] college in Rome," but always mentally flawed. The man says he believes Father Flynn talked to the boy because neither of his sisters was intelligent, but also declares "He had an egoistic contempt for all women-folk and suffered all their services to him in polite silence."

The relationship between priest and boy is not divulged beyond "he taught me to pronounce Latin in the Italian way" and "He often put me through the responses of the Mass." That it was slight is indicated by the first part of the story, which focuses on the boy's chagrin that he has failed to be the one to discover Flynn has died, and that he has been mistaken in believing the death would occur at night. The second part takes the boy to Father Flynn's house door, where he reads the death notice, is surprised the priest is not older, and recollects for the narrator to describe the moribund man and his situation. The third narrates the visit of the boy in his aunt's company to "the dead-room," and presents his surprise that the corpse is not smiling. The last and longest part makes the boy silent witness to the platitudinous exchange between his aunt and the dominant sister Eliza, including Eliza's postmortem self-justification, complaints about the burdens imposed by her brother's death, and denigration of him: he "was always a little queer"; "his scrupulousness . . . affected his mind. The duties of the priesthood were [sic] too much for him"; "—It was that chalice he broke"; and finally, the laughing in his confession-box that ended Flynn's ministry and made him an aging (and misogynist) burden. The other character indicated in the title, Nannie, is physically afflicted and subjugated.

Like Father Flynn, the Church is misogynist and sustained by women; but Flynn does not (effectively) represent the Irish Church. Any similitude is vitiated by its having explicitly discarded him as an incompetent agent; the boy's "uncle" and "old Cotter" agree "they" will not "bring him to the chapel." The boy's specific experience in young Joyce's first "childhood" sub-"chapter" has been of a priest's feeble dependency and death, and of piety, love, and charity in that impecunious Dublin family.

In the autograph (holograph) twelve-story manuscript Joyce sent Richards on December 3, 1905, "The Sisters" is revised in a few details from the story published more than a year before (August 13, 1904) in the *Irish Homestead*. (Some revisions may have been out of the newspaper's house styling; the original manuscript is not extant.) The corpse's vestment was changed following Stanislaus's letter of October 10 (1905) answering Joyce's questions; it holds a cross in place of "his rosary"; and wording was altered or added here and there. But "The Sisters" in the original *Dubliners* is essentially as written at the beginning of July 1904, when Joyce was twenty-two.

Almost exactly two years later (I have proposed it was between June 19 and July 9, 1906), he subjected his story to a revision and expansion that transformed it; and on July 9 he sent Richards "The Sisters" in its final form in the fourteen-story manuscript. His last work of fiction before he wrote "The Dead" and began the *Portrait* more than a year later, the transformed story demonstrates his artistic development to the threshold of maturity, as I hope to show in the next chapter.

But it was the story as substantially written in July 1904, and the two other stories of boys as written one month apart in September and October 1905 (see Gabler, "Introduction," pp. 5, 6) Joyce had in mind in his assertion about them that autumn to Stanislaus, and in his description the following spring to Richards of the volume containing them.

The fact he radically changed "The Sisters" necessitates establishing that the extant texts of the two 1905 stories render them essentially as he originally wrote them, not only for considering his conception of them at the time, but also for tracing his early development. A brief review of the textual history of *Dubliners* establishes for "An Encounter," and probably for "Araby" as well, that he never made significant changes.

First of all, the two stories differ only slightly in the text of *Dubliners* finally published June 15, 1914, from the fair copies in his holograph used as printers' copy; and the great majority of the differences were the familiar undesired departures in printings of James Joyce's texts (such as added commas, hyphenated compound words, and in dialogue the substitution of quotation marks for his Gallic dashes). This is certain about "An Encounter," for which his fair holograph copy is extant; and it is probable about "Araby," for two reasons: "there are no major variations among the three texts available" (*In Search of James Joyce,* p. 38); and it is short, less than three-fourths the almost identical length of "An Encounter" and the revised "The Sisters."

The complementary indication he never made significant changes to either story is that the extant holograph of "An Encounter" so close to the text eventually published in 1914 is Joyce's original 1905 one, made for the twelve-story manuscript he sent Richards shortly after he wrote the story. This is averred by Gabler in a historical exposition of "The Document Relationships" (Gabler, "Introduction," pp. 18–21). When Richards rejected the (revised) fourteen-story *Dubliners* on September 24, 1906, Joyce sent his manuscript with minor new revisions to John Long, who rejected it on February 21, 1907. He did not again submit it to a publisher until after "The Dead" was written, to complete the volume, on September 20, 1907. After almost two years of rejections, Maunsel and Company signed a contract to publish *Dubliners* on August 19, 1909. Galleys and early page proofs were set in June 1910 from that holograph manuscript. After Maunsel (George Roberts) refused to publish (on September 11, 1912), Joyce somehow ("by a ruse") obtained a complete set of proofs; these apparently were used by Richards to set up the book published in 1914 (see Gabler, "Introduction," pp. 9–16).

The textual history is much more complex than is suggested by this account.[2] Not only the holograph of "Araby," but those of six other of the twelve stories in the manuscript Joyce sent Richards in 1905, and two more of the eventual fifteen stories in manuscript, have been lost. (Two of the nine lost story manuscripts, and one for which the Richards holograph survives, exist in earlier holographs, presumably the ones Joyce sent Stanislaus.) Of the seven extant manuscript stories behind the Maunsel proofs, which in turn are behind the first edition, internal evidence shows that "Grace" is in a state written later than the "Grace" (last of the twelve completed in 1905) included in the fourteen-story manuscript returned to Richards—with some stories altered to placate him, and a new holograph of "The Sisters," transformed—in July 1906; and "The Dead" (an incomplete text) dates from 1907. Therefore, aside from the superseded "Sisters," only four story holographs in the volume sent Richards on December 3, 1905, are extant: "An Encounter"; "A Painful Case"; "Ivy Day in the Committee Room"; and "A Mother." (All four were written during August and September.)

Unless external evidence (such as an account in dated correspondence) exists, the loss of the other seven prevents drawing, from significant revisions he may have made later to those seven stories, conclusions about Joyce's development as a writer by the end of 1905. An illustrative case occurs in "The Boarding House," of which Stanislaus's slightly earlier copy, but not that Joyce made for the twelve-story manuscript, survives. The published story contains ninety-five crucial words not in Stanislaus's copy. They are the six sentences beginning "Then late one night"; and they are crucial because they alone in the story establish that Bob Doran has been seduced. Joyce is not indicting Polly Mooney, but providing another sub-"chapter" of "moral history."[3]

In the six added sentences, Doran recalls Polly knocking at his door perfumed and "glow[ing] warmly" after her bath, to relight her candle (p. 67). The incident is markedly like the woman's appeal to *"mon ami Pierrot"* in the familiar French folk song: "*Ma chandelle est mor-te / Je n'ai plus de feu / Ouvre-moi ta por-te / (Pour l'amour de Dieu).*" Joyce may have made his (witty?) deft and crucial addition to the version of "The Boarding House" preserved in Stanislaus's copy: a bit later in 1905 when he wrote out the (lost) Richards manuscript of the story; to that manuscript in 1906 before he returned the (augmented) volume to Richards; to it after 1906 but before the volume was temporarily accepted in 1909; or only in early proofs.

However, this problem does not arise with the two "childhood" stories. The point has been made that, in addition to the holograph of "The Sisters," which was transformed in 1906, that of "Grace," made after Richards rejected *Dubliners,* and that of "The Dead," created in 1907, four stories in the manuscript volume temporarily accepted by Maunsel in 1909 exist—and that all are from the fair copy of twelve Joyce sent Richards on December 3, 1905. None of these four manuscripts of stories written in the late summer of 1905 bear significant revisions made between then and the extant partly late and partly final page proofs pulled by Maunsel in the summer of 1910, and used to set the published *Dubliners* in 1914.

The manuscript of "An Encounter" has two canceled words restored in 1910; and Joyce changed half a dozen other words in proof, the most significant of which is "sage-green" to the more appropriate "bottle-green" for the man's eyes; for the reasons given, "Araby" too apparently is essentially the story Joyce wrote in 1905. If he saw fit to change only details in either one subsequently, not only are they exemplary of his development at twenty-three, but they attest to his abiding satisfaction with them for representing a decade later the "childhood" part of his program in *Dubliners:* his "intention" as he described it to Richards in those four sentences the following spring.

In the first sub-"chapter" of the two, a man narrates an account of his experiencing when a Dublin boy the working of social class, sexuality, and violence. Class bias is portrayed initially in "An Encounter" when the Latin teacher, Father Butler, discovers the boys' magazine and expresses surprise at "boys like you, educated": "I could understand it if you were ... [*sic*] National School boys"; the priest's pause is as expressive as what he says. The narrator of "The Sisters" portrays class difference without bias, calling the sisters' meager shop "unassuming." (In the reworked story the three "women of the people" become two "poor women," Eliza's discourse contains solecisms, and the boy notices the worn heels of Nannie's shoes; but bias remains absent.) In contrast, the boy in "An Encounter" has been exposed to class bias—and has assimilated it: the children his companion Mahony harasses he thinks of as not just poor but "ragged" (attendees of a "ragged school," where children were given clothing); on first sight, he observes that the old sadistic pedophile is "shabbily dressed"; as the man speaks, "I noticed that his accent was good"; though as avid a reader of the boys' magazines as his classmates, he pretends to have read the novels the man mentions—covets the social status of superior culture implicit in his teacher's attack on those magazines;[4] finally, when the man asks "did [Mahony] get whipped often at school," he becomes indignant, and—using his teacher's invidious class marker at the beginning of the story—asserts (privately) "we were not National School boys to be *whipped,* as he called it."

Sexuality, introduced by the boy's inchoate preferring to "the literature of the Wild West," the "detective stories . . . traversed . . . by unkempt fierce and beautiful girls," then is combined with the climactic expression of violence in the story, his "encounter" with the sadistic pedophile.

The man's talk goes quickly from the weather, to literature, to a lurid reference to Bulwer-Lytton, to his question "which of us had the most sweethearts." His refusal to believe the boy has none seems inconsequential as he speaks admiringly of girls' "soft" hair and hands, although "all girls were not so good as they seemed to be." When he leaves "for a minute or so, a few minutes," the boy refuses to see what the "queer old josser!" is "doing!" (so the narrator cannot say); but whether or not he is masturbating, Mahony's reaction makes clear it is opprobrious. Although "considering whether I would go away or not," the boy intends to remain in the company of this cultured man who has favorably contrasted him to Mahony, for he proposes to Mahony that they use pseudonyms. He leaves "in agitation" only after the man describes how he "would whip him and whip him," "if ever he found a boy talking to girls or having a girl for a sweetheart," especially (pointedly) "if a boy had a girl for a sweetheart and told lies about it"—and after, as well, the man's "voice, as he led me monotonously through the mystery, grew almost affectionate and seemed to plead with me that I should understand him." If the boy's "agitation" is a response to threatened violence, it also responds to harsh disapproval of normal sexual impulses, and seems precipitated by an attempted seduction to a frightening sexual alternative. Addressing objections to sexual references in "Counterparts" in his second letter of their exchange (May 13), Joyce asked Richards "Why do you not object to the theme of *An Encounter,* to the passage 'he stood up slowly saying that he had to leave us for a few moments & c . . .'?" (*Letters* II, p. 137); his apparent bewilderment is understandable.

It is violence, including the climactic threatened violence inseparable from sexuality in his "encounter," that is the predominant element in the portrayed environment of this Dublin Catholic boy. The opening paragraph describes the daily (capitalized) "Wild West" battles the boys' older playmate Joe Dillon arranged and always won. The words "But he played too fiercely for us" are not solely explanation, for they are juxtaposed against the previous sentence, which declares "His parents went to eight-o'clock mass every morning" and speaks of his mother's "peaceful odour." The next paragraph reiterates the apparent incongruity of violence and Catholicism in Dublin, announcing initially "Everyone was incredulous when it was reported that [Dillon] had a vocation for the priesthood";

but its second and last sentence puts incongruity in question with the information that Dillon since became a priest. And the paragraph after that begins the scene in which Dillon's younger brother is threatened by the teacher, a priest, with corporal punishment, a scene that affirms the connection between Dillon's violence and his religious "vocation."

Bridging the violence and threatened violence at its beginning, and the petition to the boy to accept violence at the climax of the story, are violent inclinations and acts, mostly by his companion. Mahony's contrast to the timid younger brother with whom Joyce himself had the one substantial historical experience portrayed in the three stories, illustrates both the distinction between the writer's life as source and as subject, and Joyce's programmatic agenda in the three stories.

Mahony has brought a slingshot with which to kill seabirds and pigeons at the Pigeon House. Recalling Joe Dillon's "play," he harasses the younger poor children until dissuaded by the boy. And he chases the cat, presumably to use the slingshot on it. However, Mahony is not exceptional: the poor boys "fling stones at" them; and although the boy declines Mahony's "propos[al] that we should charge them," he joins Mahony in "arrang[ing] a siege," and in enjoying the prospect of the younger Dillon's corporal punishment. Mahony's again chasing the cat, and throwing stones at "the wall she had escaladed," coincides with the proposed violence of the sadist. That occurs in two paragraphs. In the first, the man further distinguishes Mahony from the boy as "rough"; and "His mind ... seemed to circle slowly round and round its new centre" (prior to his brief leave-taking it had been "circling round and round" girls) of whipping "rough and unruly" boys. In the second, the "new centre" is shown to embrace the protagonist. Variants of *whip* occur nine times in the two paragraphs.

This sub-"chapter" of young Joyce's "moral history" portrays one of Dublin's middle-class children being inculcated with class bias, and subjected to an environment in which violence and the threat of violence pervade almost all aspects of his life: school, play, sexuality, and religion.

How the last of these affects the next-to-last in a Dublin child's experience of what should be a normal stage of growth, is portrayed in "Araby," by a man's account of his confusing them when a boy. Two points made in the last chapter are that the lever of the story is the advent of erotic longing in the boy, and that he expresses his fervor as perverted religiosity.

While the boy of "An Encounter" is less precocious sexually than his companion Mahony, this boy becomes more so than his playmates. The change in him during the story occurs in two sequent phases; and Joyce specifies, in the narrator's dramatic presentation of its initial phase, the religious cast of the boy's inchoate sexuality.

After the two paragraphs introducing "North Richmond Street" and "our house," the second of which depicts the boy's childish innocence (and contains the proleptic title *The Devout Communicant*), a paragraph describes his play with neighboring boys following their (separate) "dinners." But that third paragraph of the story concludes with his "looking at" his chief playmate's older sister when she calls Mangan in from their doorway: "Her dress swung as she moved her body and the soft rope of her hair tossed from side to side." The three paragraphs that immediately follow describe the boy's new and obsessive infatuation with his neighbor in a pattern of religious images and tropes, concluding with the vivid "I pressed the palms of my hands together until they trembled, murmuring: *O love! O love!* many times." The girl's name, "like a summons to all my foolish blood," is never given: she is the chance catalyst for the advent of erotic longing in the boy—the onset of his puberty ("everyman's puberty rite," in Beck's phrase).

Immediately after the three paragraphs beginning "Her image" and ending in the repeated "*O love!*" that describe the first phase of the boy's developing sexuality, the second phase occurs. "At last she spoke to me," the next (seventh) paragraph begins. "While she spoke ["was I going to *Araby*"?] she turned a silver bracelet round and round her wrist"; he looks at her neck, her hand, and "the white border of a petticoat, just visible" in the light of the street lamp. "—If I go, I said, I will bring you something"; and the following paragraph describes the second phase of his erotic infatuation. Having presented the promise he had made her, the narrator declares, "What innumerable follies laid waste my waking and sleeping thoughts after that evening! .... At night ... and by day ... her image came between me and ... the serious work of my life which ... seemed to me ... ugly monotonous child's play" (32).

Significantly, both phases of the portrayed development of the boy's longing for Mangan's sister are precipitated by his experience of her physical presence. The nature of "her image," which has now totally disrupted his normal life and state of mind, is specified a third time the night of his "journey." During his tortured wait for his uncle's return with money, when his alienation from the life of his former playmates is dramatized by his looking down on them from "the upper part of the house" and hearing their cries "weakened and indistinct," he also looks at her house, and "I may have stood there for an hour, seeing nothing but the brown-clad figure [lit by the street lamp at, specifically, "neck," "hand" and "border below the dress"] cast by my imagination" (33).

Unlike the "images," the "presences" in "Among School Children" that "all heavenly glory symbolise," what the boy calls "her image" after each phase of his developing ardor begins, is totally physical. Hence, "Her image" that "accompanied me" among the Dublin crowds—the familiar "my chalice" that "I bore . . . through a throng of foes"—in the three paragraphs depicting the onset of his erotic fervor, is his experience of her very physical "presence" that initiated this first phase: his "looking at her" moving body and hair. Joyce gives him his extravagant metaphor invoking the Holy Grail to epitomize deftly the perverse religiosity of what should be normal developing sexual desire—a boy's or girl's undergoing "puppy love."

The narrator does not recall what he answered when Mangan's sister began their conversation by asking if he planned to go to Araby; but his promise to "bring [her] something," "If I go," promptly becomes an obsessive "purpose" ("my desire") to proffer what is in essence a puppy-love gift. The Holy Grail allusion in the first phase of his erotic infatuation helps make his "journey" to secure the gift, grotesquely, a quasi-religious quest. And it is relevant that their Catholic religion is instrumental: she cannot visit Araby herself because of a retreat in the convent where she attends school that coincides with the week of the bazaar (32).

The "pitilessly raw" morning of his "journey," his uncle's presence prevents his habitual spying on her house from beneath the hall blind, which he had "pulled down . . . so that I could not be seen" (30); so he misses the chance to leave for school when she does, "and already my heart misgave me" (33). The morning's portents of failure are reinforced by the long delay he suffers (his suffering described in detail) because of his uncle's absence, by the "intolerable delay" before the train's departure, and by his difficulty recalling his mission, twice (34, 35); and the portents are fulfilled when he concludes his "journey." He spends half the florin given him—generous in a Dublin in which Eveline earns seven shillings a week as a store clerk (38)—to gain admission to the bazaar, because he has arrived late. His carfare costs four pence each way (he has a sixpence and two pennies left); and holding in his hand only the two pennies (35), he goes to a stall in the closing bazaar that sells "porcelain vases and flowered tea sets."

He witnesses the flirtation between the three English clerks, which the young woman interrupts to ask "me did I wish to buy anything. The tone of her voice was not encouraging." Politely he "lingered," though "my stay was useless"; but he does not then seek at another stall a love-gift costing two—or all his available four—pence:

> I turned away slowly and walked down the middle of the bazaar.
> . . .
> Gazing up into the darkness I saw myself as a creature driven and derided by vanity; and my eyes burned with anguish and anger.

The syntax ("I saw myself as . . . ; and . . .) of the story's final sentence, set off as a paragraph, suggests that the narrator is strictly reporting a judgment he passed on himself at that moment, and the feelings it induced. As a boy he had been "driven [throughout, until] derided" by the "vanity" of his mission/quest; and his frustration caused "anguish," his self-importance/overconfidence, "anger." But the sentence is as carefully worded as any in *Dubliners*.

The word "creature" alone, whether it or just its signification originates with the boy, extends the reference beyond himself. It invokes the lever of the story, wholly ignored in his judgment on himself. The boy knows the "*O love!*" he feels for his neighbor came to him involuntarily and naturally: he was created to develop such feelings. Moreover, if the "vanity" is strictly his own ("driv[ing]") self-importance/overconfidence, how can the narrator say he "saw himself" as "derided" *by* it? "Vanity" here means futility as well. And the futility of his mission that derides him, like his natural development, is beyond his control, and so not his fault. It is largely the product of circumstances: the timing of the girl's retreat; his uncle's delay returning home; his expenditure for admission to the bazaar as a consequence; above all, the circumstance of his sudden new erotic feelings, so unlike his happy state when a boy playing. Hence, like "derided," the second of the other pair of epithets, "anger," is directed (at least partly) beyond himself as well.

No more can be inferred with confidence about the boy's awareness at the end of the story. Although he definitely ceases attempting to buy the love-gift, that may be because of timidity and discouragement; or there may be insufficient time ("The upper part of the hall was now completely dark"); or it may be because he recognizes the similarity between the flirtation of the young woman and men and his own relation to the Mangan girl, who when the first phase of his ardor was precipitated "moved her body" so "[h]er dress swung" and "hair tossed from side to side" (30), and who "turned a silver bracelet round and round her wrist" (32) when the second phase was precipitated. Whichever his reason, the final sentence-paragraph affirms disturbing new knowledge about both himself and the world he lives in.

More to the point here, whichever the boy's reason, the narrator he becomes, who first presents him at child's play, then traces with clinical abruptness the etiology of his erotic infatuation, is aware of the similarity between the Mangan girl and the young woman: he provides that specific information about the girl's conduct. And of course the narrator portrays in rich detail the ultimate source of his predicament when a boy, his having perverted the natural development of erotic feeling in himself into a species of religiosity. This last of young Joyce's three "childhood" sub-"chapter[s] of the moral history of my country" depicts the baleful effect of Dublin's dominant religion on what should be a healthy occurrence, the beginning of development *out of* childhood.

The place in his program in *Dubliners,* of the two 1905 stories "of [from] my childhood [experience]," explains both why and in what way young Joyce implicated his own life in them. But to focus on how he related his life to his art, the first of my two complementary subjects, is to neglect many aspects of those stories. Two are touched on in the previous paragraph: the characters of the two boys, and the relationship to their stories of their older, narrator, selves. Both aspects of the stories—especially young Joyce's narrators—are relevant to my second subject, his development as a writer of fiction from the first "The Sisters" of 1904, through the 1905 "childhood" stories (two of the eight he wrote that summer and autumn), to the 1906 "The Sisters."

Although their boy protagonists are the principal focus of most criticism of the two stories, the boys are less existential actors than naturalist subjects. Joyce's primarily psychological portraits of them anticipate his procedure with the boy Stephen Dedalus: he carefully grounds the developing consciousnesses of both characters in the conditions "my country" imposes on them. Indeed, while the boy of "Araby" is deftly individuated in its few pages—by his childish preference in books at the beginning, the obsessive intensity and the stratagems of his infatuation, his capacity for reflection at the end—he is essentially the subject (victim) of his conditions: to the extent his final judgment is of himself, it is mistaken.

The boy of "An Encounter" is much less likable; and the reasons why make him a more autonomous and richer character. His timidity is revealed in the opening account of the "Indian battles," in his reaction to the teacher's "rebuke" to readers of boys' magazines (20), and twice with the pervert: when the man "did not believe" the truth that he had no "sweethearts," he "was silent"; and "I was going to reply indignantly" when the man speaks as though he and Mahony are "National School boys to be *whipped* . . . ; but I remained silent." His craving for "real adventures" (the phrase is repeated) in spite of extreme timidity, and his initiating one by organizing the truancy and excursion, are sympathetic traits. So too is his perceptiveness, displayed in his observations about the man. In addition to the class marker of his accent: the man is "strangely liberal in a man of his age" regarding "sweethearts"; nevertheless, "I disliked the words in his mouth and I wondered why he shivered once or twice"; when the man begins "to speak to us about girls," he suspects either insincerity or obsession (26); and he decides on the latter when the man becomes "as if magnetised again by his speech"—this time about "chastising boys," especially "if a boy had a girl for a sweetheart and told lies about it" (27); finally, as the man speaks of the pleasure that would give him, the boy notices "his voice . . . grew almost affectionate and seemed to plead with me that I should understand him."

The boy's earlier devising pseudonyms for himself and Mahony signifies that he expects Mahony to stay when the man returns; and his also "considering whether I would go away or not" can only be because he is disturbed by the man. The man's words directly threatening him, and his perception about the man's voice saying them, eventually frighten him away. But when Mahony leaves, his willingness to remain alone with the man until that point makes sense only if the "encounter" is a "real adventure," although one alarmingly different from his romanticizing; and so the willingness does him credit.

Set against his authentic adventuresomeness in despite of timidity, and his perceptiveness, are two negative traits. His class snobbery has been discussed. It joins with his deviousness when "Mahony asked why couldn't boys read" some of Bulwer-Lytton and he, who knows why no more than does Mahony, "was afraid the man would think I was as stupid as Mahony." This is one instance of Mahony's function in the story as the boy's foil, a function most overt when the man refuses to believe he has no "sweetheart" and "I was silent": "—Tell us, said Mahony pertly to the man, how many have you yourself?" Throughout their "encounter" Mahony is forthright and he not. (Mahony even leaves because he has spotted the cat—although he is prudent enough not to return, and may even have been looking for the cat.) Similarly conditioned, Mahony shares the boy's class bias—but not his pretentious mendacity: although the boy's reading matter is the same as that of his schoolfellows, including Mahony, snobbishly "I pretended that I had read every [!] book [the man] mentioned." His refusal to respond or look at the man when Mahony exclaims

"—I say! Look what he's doing!" and his proposing the pseudonyms are other instances of his deviousness. The story ends, to his credit, with his judgment on both negative traits. The dissembling pseudonyms are a "paltry stratagem," and toward Mahony running to his aid "I was penitent; for in my heart I had always despised him a little."

These final words seem to paraphrase II Samuel (Kings in Joyce's Vulgate) 6:16, in which Saul's daughter Michal "despised him [King David] in her heart" for conduct she considers undignified, and is punished. Being always tacit, an allusion cannot be proven; this intertextuality could instead be chance, or young Joyce's unconscious echo. But the biblical passage is directly relevant, functions allusively by reinforcing the boy's judgment on his snobbish pretension. Given the boy's limited reading, the apparent allusion presumably is not his; but while an explicit reference the narrator were to make to the Second Book of Samuel (or of Kings) would be his reference, the allusion cannot be simply attributed to him. It is tacit, not explicit, and he has not shown familiarity with the Bible. A good starting-point for discussing the narrators of the two stories is the fact of radical uncertainty whether the allusion is the narrator's or his twenty-three-year-old creator's.

More instrumental uncertainties concern the narrator and himself as boy-subject. When the former occupant of the boy's house in "Araby" who "had left *all* his money to institutions and the furniture of his house to his sister" is called "a *very* charitable *priest*," the three words here italicized, especially the intensive, suggest irony—prohibit simply reading the judgment as characterizing the boy's naïveté. And when later the narrator says "I imagined that I bore my chalice safely through a throng of foes," the prominent reference to a chalice common to that story and "The Sisters" is the author's work, and "throng of foes" the narrator's phrase. But is the extravagant metaphor in the sentence, "bore my chalice," how the boy "imagined" his devoir to the girl's "image"? It seems to be, and to be revealing about the boy; but it could be the narrator's trope for his state of mind when the boy. The case is unlike the narrator's words describing the boy's thoughts and then reporting his feelings, in the sentence-paragraph that ends the story; for the source of the metaphor is uncertain, and affects, again, characterization.

But such uncertainties are exceptional. Usually both narrators clearly differentiate themselves from the boys they were. They assume four distinguishable stances, two reflexive, two identified with the boys; and they move from one to another sometimes in a single sentence. As the mature Joyce's various ways of embodying his life in his fiction provided a useful context for considering the young Joyce's practice, so a review—which will be largely elementary, but brief—distinguishing the six forms or modes of disclosure ("telling") he practiced in his mature fiction is a useful context here.

The mode he originated (in *Ulysses*), the "non-human voice" David Hayman named *The Arranger* and describes as "a significant, felt absence in the text," is so because it is a clamorous presence calling attention to itself with typography, interpolations, and innumerable other abrupt extravagances. As "something new in fiction" (Hugh Kenner), this mode of disclosure relates to the two narrators only as signifying young Joyce's potential.[5] Of the five modes he shared with most writers, one tends to be overlooked, but strictly speaking is no more "the author" than the other four: an implicit (a self-effacing or "transparent") arranger. That implicit arranger disposes the printed words of the narrative—into separate paragraphs presenting different segments of dialogue, for example, or (in this century) into a sequence representing as words the largely non- or preverbal phenomenon, thought, either in interpolations of inner (*intérieur*) "monologue" or in an uninterrupted "stream." Dialogue, the graphic forms of actual words of the language representing them as being spoken, is a third mode.

The primary concern here is with the other three modes of disclosure. All are narrators: two kinds of narrator are nominally external (to their narratives) and so both anonymous and capable of omniscience; one of those and the third are literally narrators because objective, palpable.

The word *narrator* can be not literal but a metaphor, akin to the metaphor *speaker* for a hypostatized source of printed assertions that have no reflexive reference, even implicitly, and so no identifiable source *as speech* (have no literal speak-er): for example, Shakespeare's "The expense of spirit" sonnet. *Narrator* is a metaphor when used to signify the hypostatized source, lacking reflexive reference, of a printed narrative. The source not only is external to the narrative and so capable of omniscience about it, but is impalpable, objectively nonexistent, and so necessarily metaphorical: the hypostatized source of "autonomous" or "dramatic" narrative that aspires to an idiolectic state, as in most fiction of this century, including the *Portrait* and the early chapters of *Ulysses*.

Also external to the narrative and so capable of omniscience, but palpable, objectively present as speaking to an acknowledged and sometimes even addressed reader the printed words of the narrative—possessing identity though not identified, opaque where the other is transparent—is the anonymous self-referential quasi-authorial narrator usually avoided in fiction of the twentieth century. As though playfully invoking his Victorian predecessors, in *Ulysses* Joyce has the narrator advert to his (her, its) words introducing Bloom to the novel ("Mr Leopold Bloom ate with relish the inner organs") almost two hundred pages later: "As said before he ate with relish" (11.519–20/p. 221), and two pages after that, "Bloom ate liv[er] as said before" (569/p. 223); a sayer is saying the sayer "said before."

The third kind of narrator is her- or himself a character within the narrative, and so both palpable and not capable of omniscience. Moreover, like the other overtly narrating literal narrator, the character perforce acknowledges the reader. After the three "childhood" stories, Joyce did not use this narrator again until the egregious bill-collector in Barney Kiernan's pub in the twelfth chapter of *Ulysses*.

Joyce also evolved there a hybrid of the character-narrator and the literal (palpable) external narrator. He used intermittently in that chapter and began to use systematically in the next, a narrative voice or style that is not a character yet is identifiable rather than anonymous—because (parodically) imitative. And being ventriloquy, each of these voices from other writers Joyce employs to narrate, like the character-narrator and the palpable external narrator, perforce acknowledges the reader.

The voice that narrates the major (Gerty MacDowell) part of the thirteenth chapter of *Ulysses* is a parody of a significant cultural artifact published exactly fifty years before the year of the novel, the immensely popular sentimental novel by Maria S. Cummins, *The Lamplighter*.[6] The fourteenth chapter is narrated in the chronological series of parodied English prose styles. Following the Nighttown chapter, Joyce made an increasing rapprochement to the character-narrator. The narrative voice of the sixteenth chapter approaches an (identifiable) internal narrator because it parodies Bloom trying to impress, and so establish rapport with, the young intellectual and poet Stephen Dedalus; Joyce actually specifies this Bloomian voice and its function in a proleptic paragraph that interrupts the series of prose styles two chapters before (14.1174–97/p. 340). The encyclopedic catachetical respondent in the seventeenth chapter, being a comically pedantic and typically error-prone know-it-all (*Monsieur-je-sais-tout*)—like Bloom—is so conspicuous as to approach a character-narrator even more. If Molly also seems a character-narrator (of "Molly's soliloquy") in the last chapter of the novel, that is a tribute to Joyce's achievement in the mode he employed for disclosure there—in his implicit arranger of words arranged to simulate an uninterrupted segment of her thoughts.

*Dubliners* has nothing like the resplendent narrativity the mature Joyce evolved while writing *Ulysses,* of course; but its young early modernist author shows developing skill with the character-narrators of its first three stories and the narratives of its others. The latter stories usually are "dramatic," with an external narrator having to be hypostatized; but occasionally a palpable narrator intervenes. For example, in "A Mother," one of the four stories extant as Joyce wrote them out in 1905, the second paragraph begins, "Miss Devlin had become Mrs Kearney out of spite" (136).

His character-narrators of "An Encounter" and "Araby" are equally unconstrained, and their situation is inherently more complicated. An index of the young Joyce's development toward maturity as a writer is their difference both from the character-narrator of the original 1904 "The Sisters," and from that of Joyce's revision of the story the year after he created them.

The point was made that both character-narrators assume four distinguishable stances, and move from one to another sometimes in a single sentence. Two stances are reflexive, two identified with the boys they were, and whose stories they are narrating. In both the first two stances, the character-narrators are akin to the literal, because objectively present, narrator external to the narrative; in the other two, their kinship is with the impalpable source of "dramatic" narrative. The distinction between the first two stances of the character-narrators is the degree in each of self-referentiality. In one, they blatantly obtrude their presence as narrators on their narratives; in the other, they are inconspicuously but tangibly present. The distinction between their two self-effacing narrative stances is the treatment in each of the experience of the boys they were. In one, it is reported; in the other, the boy's experiencing consciousness is rendered. In other words, from the most self-assertive of his four stances to his most self-effacing, the character-narrator of each story: (1) blatantly asserts himself; (2) is inconspicuous but tangible; (3) reports his experience when a boy; and (4) presents the boy's experiencing consciousness.

From familiarity with Joyce's later and so much other modernist fiction, the fourth stance or direct rendering of the boy's consciousness has been assumed to be more frequent than it is in the two stories. In both, the narrator himself tends to be tangible at and near the beginning, then largely retires behind the experiencing boy. The "Victorian" first stance of the two narrators as well as their characteristically modernist fourth one is relatively rare.

Exemplifying their four stances by rhetorical analysis of their narration may seem pedantic, but displays an important aspect of Joyce's fiction-making in 1905. The stances can be distinguished readily in the initial two paragraphs of each story, and illustrated further primarily with passages already mentioned in other contexts.

Exemplary sentences at the beginning of "An Encounter" include:

> It was Joe Dillon who introduced the Wild West to us. . . . His parents went to eight-o'clock mass every morning in Gardiner Street and the peaceful odour of Mrs Dillon was prevalent in the hall of the house. But he played too fiercely for us who were younger and more timid. He looked like some kind of an Indian when he capered round the garden. . . .
>
> Everyone was incredulous when it was reported that he had a vocation for the priesthood. Nevertheless it was true. (19)

The first sentence of each paragraph exemplifies the second stance of the character-narrator: he is tangible but not obtrusive. The brief statement that at some date after the story Joe Dillon became a priest asserts the later existence, and so the blatant presence, of the narrator.[7] The third stance, reporting the child's experience, dominates the rest of the excerpt from the first paragraph. However, the phrase "was prevalent," and the "But" connecting the parents' religiosity and Mrs. Dillon's "odour" with Joe's violence, render the boy's experiencing consciousness. (The conjunctions *but, for,* and *and* frequently mark his movement from one stance to another.)

The only other instance I find in the story of the blatant first stance occurs when the narrator explains why the boy "examined the foreign sailors to see had any of them green eyes": "for I had some confused notion. . . ." (23). The narrator is intruding himself with both "confused" and the dots; the conjunction marks the movement.

An instance of the second and third stances juxtaposed in two sequent sentences illustrates their difference neatly: "The mimic warfare of the evening became at last as wearisome to me as the routine of school in the morning because I wanted real adventures to happen to myself. But real adventures, I reflected, do not happen to people who remain at home: they must be sought abroad" (21). An exemplary instance of the second stance is the report that "of . . . the reluctant Indians who were afraid to seem studious or lacking in robustness, I was one" (20). The next sentence shifts from the second: "The adventures related in the literature of the Wild West were remote from my nature," to the third: "but, at least, they opened doors of escape." In the next sentence, about the "American detective stories traversed from time to time by unkempt fierce and beautiful girls," "traversed" and "unkempt," and the fact that he is speaking about the boy's general experience rather than disclosing a particular one, affirm the discreet presence of the narrator.

As in the first paragraph, the rare fourth stance always occurs as a development out of the third: a report of an experience moves into a rendering of the boy's experiencing consciousness. An instance occurs in his initial "encounter": "He seemed to be fairly old for his moustache was ashen-grey" (24). Sometimes the narrative moves from report to rendering and back. When the boy is waiting at the rendezvous:

> I sat on the coping of the bridge admiring my frail canvas shoes . . . and watching the docile horses. . . . All the branches of the tall trees which lined the mall were gay with little light green leaves and the sunlight slanted through them on to the water. The granite stone of the bridge was beginning to be warm and [the movement back] I began to pat it with my hands in time to an air in my head. I was very happy. (21–22)

Like the second and third stances, the third and fourth are juxtaposed in sequent sentences, at the end of the story: "How my heart beat as he came running across the field to me! He ran as if to bring me aid" (28). Its next and last sentence, with the unattributable allusion, returns to the third stance using a conjunction, then moves by way of another from the third, reporting an experience, back to the second (with which the story began), narrating a general situation: "And I was penitent; for in my heart I had always despised him a little."

As the boy in "An Encounter" is more fully developed and less attractive than the boy in "Araby," so the narrator of "Araby" is more fully developed and less attractive than the narrator of "An Encounter." The achieved differentiation of a less and a more attractive boy, and a more and a less attractive narrator, bespeaks not only artistic invention, but the author's distance from his characters.

The reason why the narrator of "Araby" is less attractive than the narrator of "An Encounter" is not moral but aesthetic. Exemplary sentences in his first two paragraphs include:

> North Richmond Street, being blind, was a quiet street except at the hour when the Christian Brothers' School set the boys free. An uninhabited house . . . stood at the blind end. . . . The other houses of the street, conscious of decent lives within them, gazed at one another with brown imperturbable faces.

> The former tenant of our house, a priest, had died in the back drawing-room ["drawingroom" in Gabler]. Air, musty from having been long enclosed, hung in all the rooms. . . . I liked the last [of the three books] best because its leaves were yellow. . . . He had been a very charitable priest; in his will he had left all his money to institutions and the furniture of his house to his sister. (29)

The problematic last sentence, which could be either rendering the boy's consciousness or blatantly obtrusive irony, has been discussed. That blatant first stance is definite in the arch personification and pathetic fallacy of the third sentence; and at the beginning of the next paragraph of the story, "the houses had grown sombre" and "the lamps of the street lifted their feeble lanterns" (30). The initial sentence combines the second stance and, with the words "set the boys free," rendering those boys' experience, a modification of the fourth to which I shall return. In the remainder of the passage, as in most of both stories, the narrator either is tangibly but unobtrusively present ("An uninhabited house . . . stood," "The former tenant . . . had died"), or is reporting the boy's experience ("Air, . . . long enclosed, hung," "I liked the last best because"); however, "musty" renders that experience.

One subsequent instance of the narrator's first stance is a declaration of failed memory. After reporting the boy's experience ("I did not know what to answer") when the girl whose name he withholds "asked me was I going to *Araby*," he declares "I forget whether I answered yes or no" (31). His later reports of the memory lapses the boy had, "The sight of the streets . . . recalled to me the purpose of my journey" (34), and "Remembering with difficulty why I had come" (35), illustrate nicely the difference between the first and third stances. Drawing less attention to himself is a confession he makes of ignorance: he says that when looking at the girl's house from "the upper part of the house," "I may have stood there for an hour" (33). More obtrusive than either of these instances of the first stance, as much so as his unfortunate fine writing at the beginning of the story, is his exclamatory judgment, after "her name was like a summons to all my *foolish* blood" (30), which is almost as clinical as the other narrator's "for I had some *confused* notion": "What innumerable follies laid waste my waking and sleeping thoughts after that evening!" (32).

Although he draws attention to himself more than the narrator of "An Encounter," the narrator of "Araby" (as he must do, given the nature of the story) both reports fully the boy's experience of growing erotic obsession and renders the boy's experiencing consciousness. The descriptions of the girl's physical presence, and of the details of it "cast by my imagination" when he is looking at her house, are as the boy is experiencing it. And the three paragraphs recording the growth of his obsession are more in the third stance than the second, and end partly in the fourth. The second of the paragraphs is almost all a report of his experience, from "Her image accompanied me," through "These noises converged . . . for me," "I imagined that," "I myself did not understand," "I could not tell why," "I thought little of," "I did not know whether . . . or if," to its end: "my body was like a harp and her words and gestures were like fingers running upon the wires" (31). The third paragraph in the sequence moves from the second stance, which reports experience but in an adult's diction ("impinge," "incessant," "sodden"), to alternate sentences in the fourth and third, to the alternation repeated in the climactic sentence of the whole sequence:

> One evening I went into the back drawing-room. . . . Through one of the broken panes I heard the rain impinge upon the earth, the fine incessant needles of water playing in the sodden beds. Some distant lamp or lighted window gleamed below me. I was thankful that I could see so little. All my senses seemed to desire to veil themselves and, feeling that I was about to slip from them, I pressed the palms of my hands together until they trembled, murmuring. . . . (31)

Apparently, the only strict instance of the narrator's fourth stance in the remainder of the story is "After an intolerable delay" ("the train moved") (34). But reports of the boy's experience approach rendering his experiencing consciousness when he enters Araby ("I *recognised* a silence like that which pervades a church after a service. I walked into the centre of the bazaar *timidly*"), and in the final clause ("and my *eyes burned* with *anguish and anger*").

This more fully developed of the two character-narrators Joyce created at twenty-three also employs a particular modernist strategy to portray a character not himself when a boy, though only once or twice, and tentatively. During his wait for his uncle the night of the bazaar, his aunt's visitor "stood up to go," and the rest of the sentence gives Mrs. Mercer's words as though they are the narrator's own—he employs free indirect discourse (33); the colon after "go" signifies his tentativeness. The phrase for the end of the school day in the first paragraph, "set the boys free," may not be a second instance, for "set . . . free" could be not the boys' but the narrator's own words; and free indirect discourse requires language identifiable as that of a character or a cultural group. Normally, the strategy is used with an impalpable (metaphorical) narrator; its use increases modernist idiolexis by transmuting that ghostly entity's normal discourse into an idiom whose source is the very subject of the narrative.

Free indirect discourse as a strategy of Joyce's fiction has been examined by prominent critics in recent years. Their studies tend to treat the fiction as a whole, more or less synchronically, focusing on *Ulysses*. An exception to that focus is a chapter of *In Search of James Joyce*. In "Semiotic Approaches to Joyce's 'Eveline,'" Robert Scholes describes Joyce's incorporating into the second story he wrote, at a necessarily indeterminable time after its appearance in the *Irish Homestead* on September 10, 1904, "Joyce's kind of ventriloquial effect, in which he narrates in the voice of a character while seeing the character as a third person" (p. 155).

However, when providing examples from "Eveline" earlier in the book, Scholes declares that such revision of *Dubliners*, "a system whereby the events and characters . . . determine the diction and syntax of the narrative prose . . . paves the way for the experiments of Joyce's later fiction" (p. 40). "The Uncle Charles Principle," Hugh Kenner's familiar name for the strategy ("method"), comes from the first of the recent studies, a chapter with that title in his *Joyce's Voices:* when the self-deluding Uncle Charles is exiled to "the reeking outhouse" at the beginning of chapter II of the *Portrait,* the narrator says he "repaired to his outhouse"; about "Joyce's method" (p. 16) Kenner observes succinctly, "'repaired' wears invisible quotation marks" (p. 17). But he traces the strategy no farther back than the solecism-and-cliché in the first sentence of "The Dead," "Lily . . . was literally run off her feet"; and his central subject is the Bloomian narrator of the sixteenth chapter of *Ulysses,* called in the final sentence of "The Uncle Charles Principle," "Joyce's return to the tonic of his method: . . . a stylistic homage in Bloom's style to Bloom" (p. 38). Denis Donoghue also focuses on that chapter in "Is There a Case against *Ulysses?*" a spirited rebuttal of the quasi-Marxist charge that the novel embodies "Joyce's subjectivity and the conservative ideology of the self."[8] Donoghue approaches the linked charges of subjectivity and solipsism by way of a grammatical analysis of free indirect discourse (it is in the "middle voice" between active and passive), and an exploration of its general linguistic significance.[9] In my final example, "The Benstock Principle," Shari and the late Bernard Benstock argue that the emphasis in "The Uncle Charles Principle" on "Joyce's method" of free indirect discourse offers too limiting an account of "what narrationally occurs in *Ulysses*"; and they propose "extending narrative influences" to all aspects of "the contextual setting of action in the text."[10]

Even my cursory accounts suggest the intrinsic value of these critical studies. But three points must be made respecting their pertinence to free indirect discourse and the young author of "Araby." The first is that what the strategy/system/method does—why a writer would use it—is the central (albeit a relatively simple) question; and the answer is not grammatical or otherwise linguistic, or even philosophical or sociopolitical, but formal and rhetorical. The second point is that while Joyce created narrative strategies in *Ulysses* that can be related to it, it was used by others both during and before his time, as its approximate synonyms in French (*style indirect libre*) and German (*erlebte Rede*) suggest.[11] The last point is that the synchronic approach which emphasizes *Ulysses* obscures a fact significant for his development: he adopted the strategy when a young writer.

The first point can be expounded most briefly. I call free indirect discourse a *strategy* because it is a writer's calculated action toward a desired end. The end may be to diminish the external source of the narrative or, expressed positively, to increase idiolexis. The end may be also, or instead, to render character: by presenting directly a character's particular idiom, free indirect discourse renders her or his consciousness as it perceives and thinks. Too often, that it characterizes deftly is ignored in discussions of it, and would seem to be the principal or even the sole reason for its use in fiction not concerned to eliminate the narrator.

Such fiction was the rule before modernism. "The Benstock Principle" makes the second point, declaring the "discovery" that a character's "voice is inserted in impersonal, third-person narration. . . . [It] belong[s] to a tradition of narrative analysis defined at the turn of the century in Europe" (p. 11), and citing studies of the history of the strategy (nn. 2 and 3). However, tracing uses of it before Joyce requires precision. The most famous novel by a writer he admired, *Madame Bovary*, often mistakenly is said to use *style indirect libre*. Flaubert's cool portrayal of his exemplary romantic, Emma Bovary, provided a model for Joyce and other modernists of the objective representation of a character's consciousness; but consistently he refuses to relinquish the narrative to her *style*.[12]

Nevertheless, free indirect discourse antedates James Joyce considerably. Austen's assertive anonymous narrator, that adornment of her fiction (absent from the rash of movies) who/which judges both explicitly and ironically, uses it to portray (and judge) the protagonist of *Emma,* for example, when she begins to "lament and exclaim" in chapter XXX. Since Emma's diction is not distinct from the narrator's, the free indirect discourse of the narrative is in its syntax and exclamatory punctuation: "The loss of the ball, the loss of . . . and all . . . ! It was too wretched! Such a delightful evening as it would have been! Everybody so happy, and she and her partner the happiest!" And, as almost random examples at the other end of the nineteenth century, two stories published the same year (1897), one with an assertive Victorian narrator, the other with an impalpable modernist one, both use the strategy to characterize. In H. G. Wells's "A Perfect Gentleman on Wheels" (*Woman at Home*, April), a privileged young snob is attempting to repair a young woman's bicycle: "And curiously enough the wheel would not go on right, and there was a difficulty about the chain. One or two of the little nut things may have lost themselves in the grass, and—trivial though they were—this complicated the business." Nothing readily substitutes—as deft characterization of his pomposity, smugness, and ignorance—for ("trivial") "little nut things may have lost themselves." The other story is Conrad's first or second, "The Lagoon" (*The Cornhill*, January). A white man is being taken to a Southeast Asian friend, and a single paragraph is given over to the boat's polers: "The polers . . . would have preferred to spend the night somewhere else than on this lagoon of weird aspect and ghostly reputation. . . . White men care not for such things, being unbelievers. . . . To the warnings of the righteous they oppose an offensive pretense of disbelief. What is there to be done?"[13] Here the strategy also promotes the modernist effacement of an external narrative source; but that is not its purpose, for the polers are incidental to the story, and could have been ignored.

My third point, that Joyce used free indirect discourse when a young writer, is not supported by Scholes's demonstration of its absence from the original *Irish Homestead* "Eveline," and the impossibility of dating Joyce's revisions to "Eveline" incorporating it. Moreover, the holographs of other stories in which he conspicuously used the strategy, such as "Clay" and the two he added to the original twelve in early 1906, "Two Gallants" and "A Little Cloud," are not extant. And one that is, the manuscript of "The Boarding House" presumed to be Stanislaus's, which "is dated 1 July 1905" (Gabler, "Introduction," p. 5), proves that Joyce later added an instance of it to his description of Jack Mooney (see p. 220, l. 40), and incorporated it at the end of the paragraph showing Mrs. Mooney's thoughts as she is about to confront Bob Doran (p. 223, ll. 136–38; Gabler records accidentals only in his "Historical Collation," but p. 418 of that reveals the slang word for salary in the passage, "screw," lost quotation marks: Joyce made them, as Kenner put it, "invisible"). Again, when he did the revisions (and the paragraphing) cannot be determined.

However, a possible use of the strategy does occur in the 1905 manuscript when, after three more sentences, "she thought of some women she knew who could not get their daughters off their hands." And he definitely used it less than three months later in 1905 (p. 5), in "A Mother." "Mrs Kearney," he wrote: "bought some beautiful white ribbon in Brown Thomas's to let into the front of Kathleen's dress. It cost a good penny; but there are occasions when a little expense is justifiable" (p. 300, ll. 82–85). He revised both key phrases, to increase the characterization and more firmly establish the source of the final platitude: "a good penny" became "a pretty penny"; and "beautiful white ribbon" became "lovely blush-pink charmeuse." Still, his use of the strategy is in the original fair copy he sent Richards on December 3, 1905; and he did not improve on his youthful work for nine years: the changes first appear after the 1914 proofs, in the published book (see p. 300, notes for ll. 83, 84).

Finally, there is the story young Joyce wrote after "Eveline," and submitted to the *Irish Homestead* a few days before he left Dublin in 1904. In "After the Race," when only twenty-two, he used the strategy for both the protagonist and his father. Jimmy is having difficulty hearing "light" and "quick" remarks in the open car, and "Besides, Villona's humming would confuse anybody: the noise of the car, too." Two paragraphs later: "it had been his father who had suggested the investment; money to be made in the motoring business, pots of it." The only alterations to what he wrote then, done at some indeterminable point and appearing in the 1910 (Maunsel) proofs, were his change of "motoring (business)" to "motor," and of the final word in the second passage, "it," to "money" (p. 202, l. 91).

Although Joyce would rely increasingly on free indirect discourse as a narrative strategy in his fiction, and in *Ulysses* would evolve from it in unprecedented ways, the young writer occasionally used it, beginning with his third published story. That is a mark of his development from his second; moreover, the strategy figures prominently in the extensive revisions he made to precisely the *Irish Homestead* "Eveline."

That second *Irish Homestead* story, in turn, was more finished than his first, which was slight and badly flawed. The transformation of "The Sisters" he achieved after an interval of two years is a historical datum of his evolution as a writer to the threshold of maturity.

# 5

# Transforming "The Sisters"

As most teachers (and coaches) know, development and achievement are reciprocals. To adapt James's famous declaration in "The Art of Fiction" about "character" and "incident": What is development but the determination of achievement? What is achievement but the illustration of development? By a fortunate historical circumstance, young Joyce's development from his first published story to the threshold of maturity has a documentary record: his progressive achievement through three datable states of that story.

Written in July 1904, when he was twenty-two, "The Sisters" was revised slightly fifteen months later and made the first story of *Dubliners*. Then by early July 1906 he had wholly transformed into an accomplished work of art what in essence he wrote almost exactly two years earlier, altering and augmenting, but retaining the elements of, that indifferent story with the same title. The Gabler edition of *Dubliners* provides a synopsis of the three states of "The Sisters" (pp. 124–57), printing on facing pages the manuscript volume's initial and successor holographs, and keying to the earlier (1905) holograph variants from (its few revisions of) the text that had been published in the *Irish Homestead* in 1904.

Young Joyce's achievement in transforming "The Sisters," a concrete "illustration of" development more than a year before he wrote "The Dead" and began the *Portrait*, betokens his evolving mastery, and poetics, of the making of art out of life.

\* \* \*

Of course he was an impressive young writer when he had completed his original *Dubliners* in late 1905. The surviving drafts of four of the other eleven stories, so little different from their proof states, reveal that. But although he revised "The Sisters" when he placed it at the head of the volume, his slight alterations after more than a year did not improve it much.

To the story's original approximately seventeen hundred words, fewer than twenty words were added, half of them incorporating the Flynn sisters' new offer of sherry to the boy and his aunt. Other alterations of substance, mentioned earlier, are of the corpse's vestment (from "his brown habit" to "as for the altar") and rosary (which became a cross), and disclosure of the year on the card announcing Father Flynn's death. Of altered wording, some is insignificant: words and word order were transcribed from the *Irish Homestead* text (or the lost original manuscript), then canceled and replaced (ms. pp. 1.16, 2.14, 5.25); in the same paragraph, a hyphen is removed from between two words and one inserted between two others (3.3 and 3.12). But most is purposeful. For example, "I think" becomes positive ("you see"), when Eliza declares her brother's "scrupulousness . . . affected his mind"; and in the "dead room," "the candles seemed like" becomes objective ("looked like"). Perhaps the most significant revision accomplished by altered wording is a slightly changed narrator—including his relationship to the boy he had been—through the young author's increased development for him of what I have called a narrative stance.

The changed narrator was touched on in the third chapter of Magalaner's *Time of Apprenticeship:* the first part of "The Evolution of *Dubliners*" (pp. 73–86) is a redaction of "'The Sisters' of James Joyce" (*University of Kansas City Review* 18 [1952]: 255–61), "[a] careful look at the three versions of 'The Sisters'" (261). Magalaner's is the longer of the two earliest comparative discussions of the versions, now more than four decades old; the other is three pages in Hugh Kenner's *Dublin's Joyce* (London: Chatto, 1955). Both discussions focus on possible symbolic meanings of changed and added details in the final story; and both tend to conflate the two earlier versions because they are so similar.[1] But Magalaner's does draw attention to a difference: the altered phrasing in two of the three short sentences after "Old Cotter and my uncle were talking" that describe Cotter in both earlier versions. In both, the passage introducing Cotter directly follows—to begin the scene in the boy's home—the opening account of his lone vigil under Flynn's window. The three sentences, with the altered phrasing in parentheses after the original, read:

> Old Cotter is the old (was a retired) distiller who owns the (owned a) batch of prize setters. He used to be very interesting. . . . Now I find him (Afterwards he became) tedious.[2]

Magalaner observes reasonably that young Joyce's alterations "give distance to [the] narrative" ("the distant tone"), but also that in the original version "it is as though the boy narrator were speaking to 'Mangan's sister' [in "Araby"] down the block on the evening of the priest's death" (pp. 82–83). The inference that in the story as first written the boy himself could be narrating shortly after the event (it cannot be that evening), is contradicted by "adult cadences" (Kenner, p. 50) of the character-narrator such as (even before the Cotter passage) in the second paragraph, "the ceremonious candles in whose light the Christian must take his last sleep."

But as first written, the story allows no specific alternative inference about the narrator's relationship to himself as experiencer. Although he both uses adult diction, and did not join the conversation in the Flynn parlor, "being too young," these facts fail to distinguish an adult narrator from a child experiencer. The most egregious reason why they fail is because, while most of "The Sisters" is told in the past tense, not the historical present, Cotter exceptionally "is" and "owns" in the original sentences. He is contemporaneous ("Now I find him") both with the boy and with the narrator; so is Nannie, who not just did so then—when in "the dead-room"—but now "prays noisily." And both Cotter and his setters are familiar to an otherwise absent auditor.

The few words altered in the three sentences in 1905 eliminated the narrative anomaly. The "distant tone" Magalaner observed, when the character-narrator put Cotter in the past (Nannie also "prayed" in 1905) and removed a specific auditor, is young Joyce's having caused the passage to contribute to a stance for the narrator distinct from him when the boy; it is what I have called the second stance, in which as narrator he is inconspicuous but tangible ("Afterwards he became"). In the fall of 1905 "The Sisters" gained a usually discrete character-narrator, one more like those of the two "childhood" stories written at the time. And Joyce augmented the more distinct identity he gave this narrator by altering the "ceremonious candles" passage to a more pompous "in *the light of which* the Christian . . ."

Slight as they were, the young writer's alterations to the sentences about Cotter, and to "prays" and "whose (light)," constitute the most significant revision he made to the story in 1905, at least in the present context, because they modestly "illustrate" his development at, as James put it, the art of fiction.

Unfortunately, this revision did not make the relatively more distinct (more realized) narrator integral to "The Sisters," because the boy he more distinctly once was, and whose experience he is reporting, is no more integral to the story than when Joyce wrote it the year before. Both earlier comparative studies found fault with "the boy narrator"—as Magalaner repeatedly called "I"—in the 1904 and 1905 versions. Kenner observed, "the boy-persona is an excuse for working in a grown-up commentary" (p. 50). Magalaner wrote more precisely of "This one-leveled and not very imaginative sketch": "Though it is presented from the point of view of the boy, the telling does not reveal the boy to us except in the most mechanical and pedestrian way. . . . In other words . . . the story might have been narrated just as effectively by the aunt of the boy or by Cotter or even by one of the sisters" (p. 74). And both studies emphasize that in his final revision into a fitting initial story for *Dubliners,* Joyce made "The Sisters" the boy's story, by portraying "the consciousness of a young boy" (Kenner, p. 51).

However, in the first two versions the boy had not been merely a fortuitous—but happily perfunctory—witness, and an "excuse for . . . a grown-up commentary." Young Joyce had been more positively at fault in those versions. For the irrelevant witness-become-narrator also was disrupting his own story of Flynn's death, by persistently and gratuitously calling attention to his younger self throughout most of its first part.

In the last chapter, the brief discussion of the original story and the slight 1905 revision disposed "The Sisters" in four parts, for convenience: the boy's vigil and then discovery at home that Father Flynn has died; his visit to the Flynns' house door and recollections of Flynn; his subsequent visit in his aunt's company to "the dead-room"; and the conversation of his aunt and Flynn's sister Eliza in the Flynn parlor. In that brief discussion the first part of the story was described as focusing on the boy's chagrin that he both failed to discover Flynn's death and wrongly believed it would occur at night. That focus is the disruptive element, a deep fault in "The Sisters" before young Joyce's transformation of it in 1906.

In the two earlier versions, the story begins "Three nights in succession I had found myself" on the Flynns' street "as if by providence," and presents the boy's experiences and thoughts into the following night, on which the action proper begins (G124). The narrator that night calls "whimsical" what "may have been the same providence that led me there" the three previous nights—because that night it led him as boy elsewhere, "to take me at a disadvantage." Following his arch fourth mention of "providence," the narrator announces that at supper he "found myself a prophet" (G126) for anticipating Flynn's death, which was reported by Cotter before his arrival home. Cotter is introduced; the dead priest is discussed briefly; and in a paragraph concluding the first part of the story, the boy according to its initial word (he is not distinct from the narrator in the remainder) declares, "So old Cotter had got the better of me for all my vigilance of three nights," expresses his "annoy[ance]" at the turn of events, and finally his chagrin at being a flawed prophet: "I was sure he would die at night" (G128). (This certainty is inconsistent with "I seemed to understand that it would occur at night" in the opening paragraph in both earlier versions, an uncertainty that also subverts narrative authority.)

This boy, apparently less interested in the dead priest he had come to know than in learning of and being able to announce his death, is not just a fortuitous witness to Flynn's story or an "excuse for . . . commentary"; he is a second subject of "The Sisters" in his own right. Moreover, the (unattractive) subject is not developed: the boy's petty actions and attitudes are fully presented in the first part of the story, and then just dropped. For its first part alone, "The Sisters" must be judged markedly inferior to the eleven other stories in the 1905 volume.

It was this "sketch" of the late life and death of a failed priest witnessed by the narrator as an irrelevantly self-important boy, only slightly altered from its initial state of 1904 when Joyce composed his volume in 1905, that became in 1906 his story—so rich as to have prompted more criticism than almost any other in *Dubliners*—of an attractive boy's experience of the priest's late life and death.

He kept much of the original, although some of it he used differently. The result of his excisions from it and additions to it is a text more than three-fourths (about 1,400 words) longer. The first part he about doubled in length. The opening scene of the boy's lone vigil has cuts that balance his additions. But the brief exchange at home, in which Cotter declares Father Flynn's "upper storey . . . was gone," the aunt asks "Do you think they will bring him to the chapel?" and both men answer in the negative (G128), he replaced with the story's long discussion of Flynn dominated by Cotter ("I have my own theory"); and the short final paragraph registering the boy's chagrin, he replaced with the new boy's bedtime revery-become-dream about Cotter on Flynn and Flynn himself. In the second part, he removed the short negative description of Flynn, and altered and expanded his presentation of a consequently more attractive Flynn's relationship with the more attractive boy. In the third ("dead-room") part he added a few sentences to the boy's perceptions and thoughts. And he extensively revised and expanded Eliza Flynn's speeches in the last part, the scene in the Flynns' parlor.

The two longest additions Joyce made to "The Sisters" are accounts of Flynn by other characters (Cotter and Eliza, respectively) in the boy's presence, that are filled with suspended meaning and innuendo; *Joyce, Bakhtin, and Popular Literature* exaggerates only slightly in proposing that the adult conversations Cotter and Eliza dominate comprise "Far more than half of the text" in the final story (p. 25). The other major additions depict the boy in bed following the Cotter episode, and Flynn and their relationship as recalled by the boy in the second part. Two of the four major added passages portray the attitudes of adult Dubliners to Flynn and one Flynn himself, but always as the boy's experience; the fourth portrays the boy on Flynn directly. These and other additions Joyce made can be shown to function for "The Sisters" in a way similar to the six sentences he added to "The Boarding House," of Polly Mooney's perfumed late-night visit to Bob Doran's room: the additions are instrumental in his realizing, and so they guide our understanding, a story that is much more difficult than "The Boarding House."

\* \* \*

The nature of young Joyce's achievement (development) in his transformation of "The Sisters" can be illustrated succinctly by way of the new boy (as narrated) on Cotter. The anomalous witness of the 1904 "Now I find him tedious," become a distinct narrator's (no less gratuitous) report, "Afterwards he became tedious," finally functions in Cotter's transformed and elaborated role in the story.

In an act of modernist parsimony, Joyce removed the "prize setters" from the sentences introducing Cotter. Also, he deftly replaced "Cotter is [then "was"] a retired distiller" with the comment that Cotter's "talking of faints and worms" was part of "endless stories about the distillery," and Cotter's "tedious" effect with a skillful return to the subjectivity of the 1904 version, by way of a distinct (the third) narrative stance: "but I soon grew tired of him and his endless stories . . ." Moreover, this statement— employing the epithet that replaced "tedious"—is repeating the key epithet of the expletive sentence which, complete with exclamation mark, has just rendered the boy's consciousness in the fourth stance: "Tiresome old fool!" And the boy's silent exclamatory outburst is motivated by Cotter's fragmentary aspersions against an unnamed person he astutely identifies as Father Flynn (9–10). (The aspersions resume after his silent exclamation and remarks about Cotter.)

The boy's outburst itself, his own idiom and so authentic free indirect discourse in a character's narration, is development beyond the character-narrator's tentative rendering of Mrs. Mercer's words in "Araby" the year before; it approaches Joyce's mature narrative virtuosity. But the silent outburst affirms Joyce's development equally by its function in the plot. The reason for the boy's vehemence is provided in the opening account of his vigil under Flynn's window, in which Joyce has given him a distinct relationship with the old priest.

Joyce's transformation in the opening passage of both the boy's character and the plot of the story—and as well the artistic development attested—can be seen from a comparison between the supplanted and the final manuscript before the words "Old Cotter" begin the scene at the boy's home in both versions. A 27-line paragraph replaced 28 lines in two paragraphs; the slant (/) indicates manuscript lines:

| | |
|---|---|
| Three nights in succession I had found / myself at Great Britain Street at / that hour, as if by Providence. Three / nights I had raised my eyes to that / lighted square of window and speculated. / I seemed to understand that it would / occur at night. But in spite of the / providence which had led my feet / and in spite of the reverent curiosity / of my eyes I had discovered nothing. / Each night the square was lighted / in the same way, faintly and evenly. / It was not the light of candles so / far as I could see. Therefore it had / not occurred yet.<br><br>On the fourth night at that / hour I was in another part of the / city. It may have been the same / providence that led me there—a / whimsical kind of providence—to / take me at a disadvantage. As I / went home I wondered was that / square of window lighted as before / or did it reveal the ceremonious / candles in the light of which the / Christian must take his last sleep. / I was not surprised, then, when at / supper I found myself a prophet. | There was no hope for him this time: it / was the third stroke. Night after night / I had passed the house (it was vacation / time) and studied the lighted square / of window: and night after night / I had found it lighted in the same / way, faintly and evenly. If he was / dead, I thought, I would see the / reflection of candles on the darkened blind / for I knew that two candles / must be set at the head of a / corpse. He had often said to me: / —I am not long for this world— / and I had thought his words / idle. Now I knew they were true. / Every night as I gazed up at the / window I said softly to myself the / word *paralysis*. It had always / sounded strangely in my ears / like the word *gnomon* in the / Euclid and the word *simony* in / the catechism. But now it sounded / to me like the name of some male- / ficent and sinful being. It filled / me with fear and yet I longed / to be nearer to it and to look / upon its deadly work. |

The only active subjectivity in the original version is announced by the word "speculated" at the end of the second sentence, and fulfilled after four more sentences with "Therefore [an unspecified] it had not occurred yet." In the transformed passage, not only is the central information about Flynn's mortal condition no longer coyly withheld by the narrator; in addition, the story's abrupt very first sentence, which discloses it and the cause of death as well by rendering the boy's thoughts, also begins the exposition of the central element of the plot—soon to cause his silent outburst against Cotter—his involvement with Flynn: "There was no hope for him this time: it was the third stroke." Then in two sentences the boy reveals that concern about Flynn has motivated his vigil "Night after night" (for an unspecified number), and expresses his "thought" that if Flynn had already died two candles would be displayed. Fanciful talk about (and the agency of) some anomalous "providence" has been cut out; and the narrator's obtrusive "ceremonious candles" pietism—which also indicates a high degree of religious indoctrination in the boy—has been replaced by the simple "thought" about what "I knew."

Less than half the length of the earlier passage both assimilates what is functional in it and inaugurates the plot. The account of the boy's lone vigil then gains two wholly new elements. The first is that Flynn had "often" (further portraying their relationship) told the boy of—and "Now I knew" he had mistakenly disbelieved—the approach of death. (His mistake in thinking Flynn is not yet dead, formerly emphasized, is ignored as of no importance to this boy.) The second new element concerns the word he "said softly to myself," "Every night as I gazed up at the window," a word he formerly associated with two less common italicized words because all three "had always sounded strangely in my ears." His reflections on *paralysis,* "now" become a word both sinister and fascinating, which characterize him further, also augment the portrayal of his concern about Flynn. The *meaning* of the less common words, *gnomon* and *simony,* is not "strange" like their sound, since he specifies where he read them. *Paralysis* does not denote a concept, as they do, instead is "the name of some maleficent" reality that is particularly strange because he has never "look[ed] upon" it: he does not know what the paralysis "deadly" to Flynn is.

With this new beginning to "The Sisters," Joyce transformed the boy's character by way of a transformed relation to Flynn and (consequently) to Cotter; and he prepared for the more elaborate role he gave to Cotter through the first of his major additions.

It should be mentioned that his greater artistic virtuosity often is expressed as his character-narrator's greater competence. The opening passage first renders then reports the boy's consciousness, never supplanting or combining with it: for example, the adverb in "sounded strangely" is not slovenly English, but describes his auditory experience when the man was the boy—signifies his actual young ears' hearing of the sounding of those three words. Thereafter, the narrator's tangible presence in the story is relatively rare and always unobtrusive: the complex syntax of passages like the description of Flynn taking snuff (12); adult diction like the last phrase of that passage, especially its five-syllable word ("quite inefficacious"); the forms "paralytic" and "simoniac" in his rendering of the boy's consciousness in bed, since the boy knows the root words (11); and writerly touches like "then said shrewdly" and "then she continued" (16, 17) during his presentation of Eliza's much-lengthened speech in the parlor. Also, his discourse is improved; for example, "there used to be a notice hanging" (G132) became "a notice used to hang" (12).

The boy's conflict with "Old [always capitalized in the final story] Cotter" when he returns home, prepared for in his lone vigil, is begun by Cotter's initial fragmentary aspersions against—he realizes—Flynn ("something queer ... uncanny ... one of those ... [sic] peculiar cases"), which occasion his silent exclamatory outburst and "staring" at Cotter. The conflict continues with his ironic thought that Cotter was not "giving us his theory" about Flynn's peccability, and his uncle's announcing the death of "your old friend" in response not to his questions (in this final version of "The Sisters" the boy volunteers no words and speaks only four), but to his staring at Cotter. He resumes "eating as if the news had not interested me" because "under observation," his uncle "explain[s]" to Cotter his close relationship with Flynn, his aunt asks (as she will do in the Flynns' parlor) "mercy on his soul," and Cotter resumes his attack on Flynn—after looking at the boy and so clarifying whose "observation" has caused his dissembling: "I felt that his little beady black eyes were examining me but I would not satisfy him by looking up from my plate" (10). The aunt's repeated inquiry why associating with Flynn was "bad for children" elicits from Cotter only more vagueness, and the scene ends with an elaboration by the boy of his first silent exclamatory outburst: "Tiresome old red-nosed imbecile!" (11).

In the supplanted version of this scene, when the men agree Flynn will not be admitted to the chapel, it is after Cotter has called him *non compos mentis*. In the supplanted version of the fourth part and final scene of the story, Eliza denies that very charge to the boy's aunt, but ambiguously: "—Not that he was anyway mad, as you know yourself: but he was always a little queer. Even when we were all growing up together he was queer" (G146). Joyce removed from "The Sisters" this definitive characterization of the priest's lifelong mental state, and replaced it with characters' inferences—about a recent development.[3]

His new representation of Flynn has two elements. One comprises the two longest additions he made: Cotter's vague censure, accompanied by the boy's rejection of it; and the corresponding imputation by Eliza in the final scene about Flynn's recent mental state. The other new element occurs between this added brace of aspersions by Cotter and Eliza; with the boy's revery-become-dream, it completes his four major additions to "The Sisters": he created an expanded (and altered) narrative portraying Flynn's actual recent behavior.

Cotter's new vague charges in the family scene in the revised story, which combine with the new responsive silent secret hostility of the boy on Flynn's behalf to provide its central conflict, are not accepted but not rejected by his aunt and uncle. Flynn is never called a priest: even when the uncle praises him, it is "the old chap [who] taught him a great deal" (10). However, unlike the other priests in *Dubliners*—the bullying snob Father Butler in "An Encounter," the seedy spoiled priest Father Keon in "Ivy Day in the Committee Room," the sophistical Father Purdon in "Grace"—whose faults are presented concretely, the physically debilitated Flynn only has faults imputed by others. Joyce's excising Cotter's assertion of and Eliza's confirming testimony to Flynn's (lifelong) mental "queer[ness]" in the original version, and his substituting vague aspersions by Cotter and imputations about Flynn's mental state when an old man by Eliza, created an open question out of a fact.[4] Excisions he made can, like additions, be heuristic.

The second major addition to the story follows immediately the boy's second silent outburst, and elaborates its portrayal of Flynn and their relationship. He is in bed, trying "to extract meaning from [Cotter's] unfinished sentences," and—presumably partly because of them—confronting the "grey face" of "the paralytic": although Flynn has died, "it desired to confess something." He falls asleep and dreams of Flynn's disembodied face: "I felt my soul *receding into some* pleasant and vicious *region;* and there *again* I found it *waiting for* me [my emphasis]." In a familiar passage, the face "smiled continually" as "it" confesses "murmuring"; and (in his dream) the boy "too was smiling feebly as if to absolve the simoniac of his sin" (11).[5]

This second major addition, which concludes the first part of the story, seems to have two striking elements: the continually smiling, insistently disembodied face of Flynn; and the dream-confession to, and dream-absolution by, the boy of a sin far more available to priests than to lay people. The source of the specific judgment of the "simoniac" is ambiguous. The word (like "paralytic") is the narrator's; but did he make the judgment itself when the boy, because the boy considers Flynn to have used spiritual things if not his priesthood for worldly gain, and so in his dream has caused Flynn's face to confess that? Or is the judgment retrospective, made by himself as narrating adult? In other words, does the boy understand sufficiently the theological concept *simony* for the meaning of "simoniac" to have originated with him? However, the ambiguity is not very important. The form of "The Sisters" indicates that Flynn's conduct is only one element, and not the defining one, in the experience that constitutes the boy's story. And respecting Flynn's conduct itself, whether the specific charge of simony originates with the boy or not is less pertinent than his awareness that Flynn has done something—that is specified by the adult narrator's word—warranting contrition.

The boy's relationship with Flynn is announced in the first words of the transformed story, dramatized in his silent conflict with Cotter, and elaborated by his revery and dream. In the second part of the story, Joyce altered and expanded both the original portrayal of Flynn, and the original account, by himself-become-narrator, of the boy with Flynn; one result is that both the confession the new boy dreams, and the smiling disembodied face that makes it, are explained.

Joyce's first significant alteration in the second part is the date given on the card the boy finds announcing Flynn's death when he goes "The next [changed from "following"] morning to look at" the Flynns' house (11–12). The change of year (withheld in 1904) from 1890 to 1895 has been discussed: his dating this story of a manifestly younger boy the year after the bazaar of "Araby" helps him individuate the protagonists of the three "stories of my childhood." By changing the day from July 2 to July 1, Joyce made Flynn's death coincide with the Feast of the Most Precious Blood, and so linked it to both the chalice he notoriously dropped and the one (defiantly?) placed in his corpse's hands—if not by, then in accord with the wishes of, Eliza or both sisters.

In both versions of "The Sisters," the second part of the story is organized around the boy's confronting Flynn's death notice. In both: his initial reaction to the card is given; Flynn himself is described; the narrative returns to (his standing before the card in) the present time of the story; then the narrative describes his boyhood relationship with Flynn. The revised second part has a second return to the present time of the story for a new final paragraph.

The changes Joyce made to the original two passages of the boy in the present time are less extensive than those involving Flynn, but are significant. In the original story, the boy's initial reaction to the card is only that Flynn "looked much older" than the age given on it, before as narrator he begins his description of Flynn (and his sisters: "neither . . . was very intelligent"), by saying that he "often" visited the priest in the company of his aunt, who always brought a gift of snuff (G134). And in the other present-time passage in the original story, that following his description of Flynn, the narrator portrays his young self as reflecting coolly on his difficulty believing Flynn has died, because "his life was so methodical and uneventful." This introduces the second descriptive passage, portraying a limited relationship between them during visits made with his aunt, and attributing ("Perhaps") it to the combination of Flynn's refusal to speak to "women-folk" and lack of "friends or visitors" (G136, 138). Flynn and he are not even clearly alone together.

In the revised story, the boy's initial reaction is "The reading of the card persuaded me that he was dead and I was disturbed to find myself at check" (12). And Joyce's portrayal of the new boy as having a new close relationship with Flynn continues with his words introducing his description of the priest: "Had he not been dead I would have gone into the little dark room . . . to find him sitting. . . . Perhaps my aunt would have given me" snuff to take with him: his visits have been frequent, to Flynn himself, and not occasioned by visits to the house by his aunt. Following his description of the priest himself, which is briefer than in the original story, and devoted to Flynn's palsied snuff-taking, the new boy still standing before the card reflects that he "wished to go in and look at him." However, he lacks "the courage to knock"; and he walks away slowly, in the sun, reading in shop windows: "I found it strange that neither I nor the day seemed in a mourning mood and I felt even annoyed at discovering in myself a sensation of freedom as if I had been freed from something by his death" (12).

Between the narrator's altered and diminished description of Flynn himself, and his altered and considerably expanded account of his boyhood relationship with Flynn, Joyce placed this altered and expanded second passage in the present time of the story. It emphasizes the conflict in the new boy between his concern for and loyalty to Flynn through most of the first part, and his revery and dream (with accusation) at its end. His concern and loyalty make him not only wish to see Flynn's body, but also "annoyed" that in place of mourning he feels, significantly, "a sensation of freedom . . . from something."

The actual nature of their relationship, which has caused the negative bedtime experience of Flynn Joyce added for him, causes this extremely negative added feeling consonant with it. And Joyce replaced the narrative of the original boy's limited relationship with the priest in the original story, and the misogyny and lack of society he as narrator infers for it, with the detailed description the revised story presents, of the relationship of boy and priest, introduced by the boy's "wonder[ing]" at his "annoy[ing] . . . sensation of freedom"—"for . . . he had taught me a great deal" (12–13).

To motivate the boy's wholly new and complicated involvement with Flynn, Joyce made changes in 1906 to Flynn's character. And, commensurate with his no longer being simply "always . . . queer," the changes largely dignify him. Three are excisions from the original boy's description of him. Originally: his sisters "used to look after him, feed him and clothe him"; he required "almost stone deaf" Nannie to read the newspaper to him daily until he "tired" of it, when he "rattle[d] his snuff-box . . . to avoid shouting at her"; and he "suffered all their services to him [those of "women-folk," including the many gifts of snuff brought him by the boy's aunt] in polite silence" because of his "egoistic contempt" for women (G134, 136).

In addition to eliminating his original portrayal of a testy, imperious, and dependent bigot, Joyce altered his portrayal of Flynn's infirmity. Originally, Flynn takes snuff with a "large trembling hand" (G134), and "When he smiled he used to uncover his big discoloured teeth and let his tongue lie on his lower lip" (G138). The vivid depiction of Flynn's smile along with the boy's initial "feel[ing] uneasy" about it, he retained in his new briefer description, with the difference that the boy's changed attitude is the result not of becoming "used to it," but of getting to "kn[o]w him well" (13). And Joyce portrayed more graphically Flynn's physical debility. Now the boy is obliged to empty into Flynn's "black snuff-box" his aunt's present of snuff he now himself brings; and Flynn's palsied snuff-taking is fully described. But with its first sentence Joyce caused his altered story to disclose that Flynn has suffered two strokes; as a result, both the priest's more graphically portrayed debility and his retained grotesque smile become simply (familiar) consequences of a natural misfortune. Joyce's changes made the no longer "always . . . queer" character also no longer unsympathetic.[6]

The explanation of the new boy's new ambiguous attitude toward the afflicted and criticized priest is provided by his new account as narrator of their sessions together. In the original story, after proposing the "queer" priest's reason for their limited association, the narrator gives—briefly and in consecutive sentences—only two details of it: "He had studied at the college in Rome and he taught me to pronounce [in 1904, "speak"] Latin in the Italian way. He often put me through the responses of the Mass, smiling often and pushing . . . snuff . . . " (G138). The second part of the original story then ends (with the narrator's description of Flynn's smile and of his initial and subsequent boyhood responses to it). Joyce kept both details of their association in the revised story. And between them he placed his addition of more than two hundred words describing their sessions.

The first of the two retained details of the priest's instruction to the boy he only modified to elevate Flynn: "He had studied in the Irish college in Rome and he had taught me to pronounce Latin properly" (13). The other became: "Sometimes he used to put me through the responses of the Mass which he had made me learn by heart; and as I pattered he used to smile pensively and nod his head, now and then pushing . . . snuff . . ." (13). In the first part of the sentence, "often" became (only) "Sometimes," and Flynn "had made" the boy memorize the responses. Hence: his visits were more frequent than in the original story; Flynn (in his uncle's words to Cotter that he quotes) "taught him a great deal"; and what Flynn taught him included training to be an altar-boy. In the second part of the sentence: Flynn took snuff only "now and then"; the narrator uses the dismissive "pattered" (from *Paternoster:* in the words of the OED, prayer or talk "without much regard to sense or matter") to describe the boy's responses; and Flynn's smiling not only was accompanied by nods as though certifying the boy's accuracy, but was "pensive."

Flynn's "pensive"—both thoughtful and sad—smiles as the boy "pattered" are mentioned after smiles and nods that occur just before the quoted sentence begins; those earlier smiles conclude the hundreds of words Joyce added to the story between the brief clause about "the Irish College" and that about "the responses of the Mass." The added passage illuminates the epithet *pensive* and a good deal more.

Introduced by "as my uncle had said . . . he had taught me a great deal" (12–13) and the detail about Latin pronunciation, it portrays the circumstances of Flynn's religious instruction to the distinctly young boy. The priest's "great wish for" the boy the uncle also spoke of to Cotter normally alludes to a vocation for the priesthood; and the added passage, like the two retained and modified details between which Joyce inserted it, describes sessions formally consonant with a priest's directing a boy toward that eventual vocation.

However, they seem to be only formally so. The passage has five sentences, the last of which complements the second after the intervening two provide a context for them. The description of their sessions Joyce added begins by specifying "stories" Flynn told the boy "about the catacombs and about Napoleon Bonaparte," and his explaining "the meaning of" priests' vestments and "the ceremonies of the Mass." This first sentence describes appropriate religious instruction for a very young Catholic; Napoleon's supposed statement—either fictional or cynical—that the day of his first communion was the happiest of his life, was "a staple of First Communion (or pre-Confirmation) classes in Ireland" (*Joyce Annotated*, p. 152).

With the second sentence, the passage changes direction. It begins, "Sometimes he had *amused himself by* putting difficult questions to me" (my emphasis) about fine moral distinctions. In the third sentence, the narrator declares that the questions "showed me how complex and mysterious" were "certain institutions of the Church"; and the fourth sentence makes clear the boy has in mind the administering of communion and absolution. (Significantly, his explicit reference is to "the Eucharist" and "the confessional": the first invokes the role in the story of chalices, the other both Flynn's "confession-box" and his own revery and dream of the night before.) The narrator says the boy felt awed by "the duties of the priest towards" the two sacraments. Then the sentence describes the boy as "not surprised" to be told by Flynn that the Church fathers had "elucidat[ed] all these intricate questions" in "books as thick as the Post Office directory and as closely printed as the law notices in the newspaper."

Only after this account of the effect of Flynn's questions on the boy, and of Flynn's description to him of the moral writings of the Church fathers on such questions, does the last sentence of the added passage reveal how he responded to the "difficult" ("intricate") questions about "sins" the second sentence says Flynn posed. "Often when I thought of" the voluminous "elucidating" by the Church fathers, the narrator begins, "I could make no answer or only a very foolish and halting one . . ." And the latter part of the last sentence in the added passage gives Flynn's response to the boy's frequent helplessness before the "difficult questions" he "amused himself by putting": "upon which he used to smile and nod his head twice or thrice."

Flynn's conduct here is very different from his pensive smile with nod "as I pattered," altered from a simple smile in the original story, which is mentioned in the next sentence, that depicts him training the boy to assist in the celebration of the Mass.

Relevant to what Joyce wrought in the passage he added to the original two brief details of the boy's sessions with Flynn, is the added third occasion on which the boy is acting in the present time of the story, the short paragraph that follows his description of the priest's grotesque smile and his own "uneasy" feeling "before I knew him well," to end the second part of "The Sisters" (13–14). Walking "along in the sun," the boy "remembered Old Cotter's words and tried to remember what had happened afterwards in the dream." The "pleasant and vicious region" (11) of his dream—in this paragraph it is "some land where the customs were strange," and "Persia [a non-Christian country], I thought"—comes back to him; but not the latter (and important) part of it. I hope to show below that his account of his sessions with Flynn that precedes this paragraph also explains his lapse of memory.

In transforming "The Sisters," Joyce deftly plotted it so that the innuendos he gave Cotter motivate the boy to express in response both contrary elements of his attitude toward Flynn: his affectionate loyalty, and his unconscious disapproval. Joyce accomplishes this with Cotter's vagueness. The innuendos do not signify that he concurs with Eliza—as the original Cotter does—that Flynn is mentally unbalanced. Had they signified Cotter's agreement with her, they might have motivated the boy's silent vehemence—but not his dream of Flynn's confessing "to me," or in the morning his first having "a sensation of freedom," then as he walks away from the Flynns' house his recalling "Old Cotter's words," and attempting to recall his subsequent dream. Cotter calls Flynn "queer," "uncanny," "peculiar," warranting a "theory"; and he decries exposing children to "things like that" because "their minds are so impressionable" (10–11). He may share the general adult view of Flynn, and so believe Flynn's potential egregious influence on a child is the product or even mere spectacle of a priest's mental unbalance. But the boy understandably does not construe his vague aspersions so; the boy promptly considers Flynn guilty of something he must confess, and relates Cotter's aspersions to Flynn's guilt: he considers Flynn responsible for his acts.

Moreover, nothing in the actual portrayal of Flynn suggests that he is other than completely sane; that is why Joyce took pains to change a datum of the original story into characters' opinions. And Flynn is no ordinary parish priest, but learned, for his intellectual ability caused his superiors to send a lower-class (Irishtown) young man to the Irish College at the Vatican. It is this sane and learned old priest who asked the boy disturbingly finical moral questions, and characterized to him as Flynn did the library of Catholic scholasticism that addresses such questions. If the attitude toward their prodigious volume, of the former student of those writings by the Church fathers, in fact was simply respectful, why did he smile and nod at the boy's dismayed response to his description of them? And why did he decline to provide answers—the "elucidating[s]" contained in the so "thick" and "closely printed" books—to the questions he had put?

Flynn's nodding smile seems to have involved (antithetical) religious instruction. If he was exploiting the boy's puerility for his own pleasure, he would have "amused himself" more by revealing the answers to his "intricate" questions. But he was not acting reprehensibly as a teacher, for he responded to the boy's bewilderment as though it is sound—sensible: a nodding smile as response suggests mild mirth and affirmation.

Yet the passage does not specify what he was affirming. The sequence of relevant sentences is:

> he had explained to me the meaning of the different ceremonies of the Mass and of the different vestments worn by the priest. Sometimes he had amused himself by putting difficult questions to me, asking me what one should do in certain circumstances or whether such and such sins were mortal or venial or only imperfections. His questions showed me how complex and mysterious were certain institutions of the Church which I had always regarded as the simplest acts. The duties of the priest towards the Eucharist and towards the secrecy of the confessional seemed so grave to me that I wondered how anybody had ever found in himself the courage to undertake them; and I was not surprised when he told me that the fathers of the Church had written books as thick as the *Post Office Directory* and as closely printed as the law notices in the newspaper, elucidating all these intricate questions. Often when I thought of this I could make no answer or only a very foolish and halting one upon which he used to smile and nod his head twice or thrice. Sometimes he used to put me through the responses of the Mass which he had made me learn by heart; and, as I pattered, he used to smile pensively and nod his head. (13)

Flynn's questions "showed" the boy how "complex and mysterious" were officiating at the Mass and taking Confession; the boy "wondered" how any priest had "the courage to undertake" those "institutions." He mentions Flynn's characterization of the patristic writings in this context. And Flynn, instead of providing answers to his questions from those writings, "used to smile and nod his head twice or thrice" in response to the boy's bewilderment.

What Joyce may have wrought in the five-sentence passage he added at this place when he revised "The Sisters," is a depiction of a priest both giving religious instruction and "amus[ing] himself"—indulging (expressing) himself—by subtly ridiculing the religion. If that is so, Father James Flynn, in the idiom, has lost his faith: Joyce portrays him as expressing publicly—although *faute de mieux* to a child—his religious skepticism or even secret apostasy. And the sin the boy attributes to the—in the narrator's word—simoniac, then is explained by Flynn's attitude, which means that the boy apprehended it. He had seen the old priest of whom he was fond ridiculing, and so no longer fully believing in, their religion. And Flynn's nodding smile was his endorsing the boy's response to the otiose volume of the patristic writings about "circumstances" and "sins."

Since I share Joyce's hostility to institutional religion, it would be gratifying to be able to persuade myself that he has indeed expressed it through his old priest—made Flynn not only sane, but a skeptic or even an apostate as well. However, the state of mind the priest reveals in the long paragraph Joyce composed to portray the new boy's relationship with the new Father Flynn may have been pathetic rather than combative.

That would be consonant with the general mode of his portrayal of the adult denizens of Dublin in the volume. Moreover, to infer criticism of the Church fathers may be, in the words of one of them, "*praeter necessitam*" ("Occam's razor"). Flynn's attendant nodding could have signified simply that his smile was not mockery of their casuistry but rueful. He too (nodding smile) was unable to derive secure guidance from them: he shared the boy's bewilderment. And so he did not provide the answers to the questions he had put because he could not. He was unable to construe what a priest should do in those circumstances.

With this interpretation of Joyce's portrayal of Flynn in the new long description by the boy of their sessions, the retained Irish College detail preceding it functions in the story by signifying that Flynn knows Church teachings thoroughly enough to have been incapacitated as a priest by his knowledge. The samples of that knowledge he gives the boy reveal the extreme "grav[ity]" of his office, the "courage" it requires—has required of him, a man of moral imagination and fastidiousness who also possesses his knowledge. And his newly "pensive" smile in the retained detail following the passage concerns "the Mass," "The duties of the priest towards the Eucharist." With this interpretation, Joyce's criticism of the Church is more rich and subtle than the creation of a partisan: his priest is a victim, not a rebel.

One favors this interpretation over the other partly because, with the added "pensive," the two retained details around the new passage support it. One favors it even more because of the prominence in Flynn's history before the boy's sessions with him of a dropped chalice ("the Eucharist") and "his confession box" ("the confessional"). However, this knowledge of Flynn's history anyone familiar with "The Sisters" has, is not shared by the boy experiencing the sessions: it is revealed to him only in the Flynns' parlor in the long last part of the story. And the possibility that Flynn is a skeptic or apostate cannot be ruled out at this point by a first reader.

The fact is not trivial. Young Joyce's impressive achievement in his revision of the second part of the story can be appreciated only by reading phenomenologically, not in the literary-critical but in the root philosophical sense of Husserl: the reader's knowledge of Flynn must unfold as the developing "object" presented by the story, for he or she to understand Joyce's portrayal of this stage in the boy's chronologically increasing enlightenment that constitutes "The Sisters" transformed.

That the significance of Flynn's conduct with the boy is (temporarily) ambiguous is one aspect of the account of their sessions in the first story of *Dubliners* that has not been generally noted; another, linked to the ambiguity, is that the enlightening passage Joyce added to this part of his original story actually portrays a stage in the boy's own enlightenment.

It derives from the boy's *experience of* his recollection of his sessions with Flynn. Ultimately, the account given must be the narrator's report, like the two segments that precede it, the description of Flynn (shortened from the original), and the second passage in the present time of the story, which has the boy "walking away slowly" in the sun, feeling "annoyed" by his "sensation of freedom," and "wonder[ing] at this for . . . he had taught me a great deal." The account of their sessions follows these reported reflections directly. And it is followed by the new last paragraph of the section, in the present time of the story: the placement of the boy's account indicates that he has been thinking about the sessions *while* he walks "in the sun." In other words, the narrator reports not his memory of the sessions, but the boy's having actively recollected them: he depicts his boyhood experience, like "sounded strangely" for the three italicized words. This fact is signified promptly by the consequence of the boy's experience: the boy is certain no longer of what he has characterized at the beginning of his recollection as Flynn's having "amused himself by putting difficult questions." For the final paragraph begins, "As I walked along in the sun I remembered old Cotter's words and tried to remember what had happened afterwards in the dream"; and the last words of the paragraph are "But I could not remember the end of the dream" (13–14).

What the boy is unable to remember is Flynn's continually smiling and confessing face and his own responsive "smiling feebly as if to absolve the simoniac of his sin": he recalls Cotter's aspersions, but cannot bring to mind the expression in his dream of his own corollary disapproval. His experience recollecting the sessions seems to have blocked out his sense of Flynn's sinfulness, expressed just before the recollection in his "sensation of freedom," and shortly after it begins by his believing Flynn "had amused himself" with the questions.

In a fine touch of characterization, young Joyce presents a boy learning negatively, realizing inchoately from his recollection of their sessions that Flynn may deserve not reproach but sympathy, and that he himself does not know what the truth is. For he is yet to learn that this priest's "courage" failed him with respect to "the Eucharist" on one notorious occasion. Whether the sin he charged Flynn with unconsciously the night before is general improper deportment as a priest in their sessions, or he is familiar enough with the concept of simony to have agreed with his specification as adult narrator that Flynn used religion for personal gain, is unclear. (The gain could be companionship, or snuff, or both; or he could simply be clinging to his priestly status for its material advantages when he cannot fulfill the office.) But the boy is unable to recall his charge; and the narrator's "simoniac" loses force to the extent that Flynn is an object of sympathy.

Confused about Flynn's state of mind as he may be, the boy knows Flynn is fully competent mentally, and so knows him better than do the adults in the story, who attribute his recent conduct to mental as well as physical debility. (Cotter is vague about both its cause and its effect—but not Eliza.) However, it is important for the story that the boy not only does not share, but shows no awareness of, the general adult misconception about Flynn—until the adults' conversation in the last scene (fourth part) of the story.

Moreover, the boy's (and narrator's) moral judgment of Flynn is only incidental to the central business of "The Sisters": Flynn's situation itself is the significant element, the remainder of the story shows. A key to Joyce's own moral position here—with relevance for his general project in *Dubliners*—is the implicit question: What does a priest, discarded by the Church as "queer" because his knowledge and temperament made him incapable of performing his office, and grown sick and nearly destitute, do in Dublin in the 1890s?

The very short next episode of "The Sisters," the visit by the boy and his aunt to "the dead-[*sic*]room" I have designated the third part, Joyce expanded by more than half from barely two hundred words in the original version of the story. He replaced a brief statement that Nannie conducted the visitors to and into the room with a passage that increased the length of the part by a third; the sentence about Nannie's noisy praying he replaced with two about the boy while she prayed. In addition to these two new passages, he changed two words and added one, in two consecutive sentences. And to the first paragraph of the next and final part of "The Sisters," the scene in the Flynns' parlor, he added a brief transition sentence. Though the changes are not extensive, some are vital elements of the transformed story.

The first and longest added passage characterizes the feeble Nannie, and then describes the boy's entry to the room. Although "beckoned ... encouragingly" by "the old woman," he "hesitated to" follow his aunt in, whereupon Nannie "began to beckon to me again repeatedly" and he enters "on tiptoe" (14). The narrator says he "had not the courage to knock" in the morning; his trepidation seems to extend to confronting Flynn's corpse.

The shorter added passage of two sentences replaces the narrator on Nannie's praying. In the first, the boy "pretended to pray" although unable to "gather my thoughts" because of "the old woman's mutterings." In the second, he remarks Nannie's misfastened skirt and down-at-heels shoes, confirming his inability to pray.

At this point in both versions of "The Sisters": "The fancy came to me that the old priest was smiling as he lay there in his coffin," and a new paragraph begins, "But no. When we rose and went up to the head of the bed I saw that he was not smiling." The two consecutive slightly altered sentences follow.

In the first, the description of Flynn lying "solemn and copious in his brown habit," his "hand loosely" holding "his rosary," which Joyce had changed in 1905 to "copious, vested as for the altar" and "a cross" (G144), in 1906 was unchanged except for "a [*not* "his"] chalice." Joyce transcribed the first two letters of "cross," then erased them (G171) and made his substitution. Through the sudden inspiration of "chalice" (the 1905 change of dress seems almost generative), Joyce enlisted Flynn's vestments in an invocation of the priestly office; and that invocation achieved by the laying out that had been given her brother's corpse augments Eliza's elaborate new account of him to the boy's aunt in the final scene of the story.[7]

In the second slightly altered sentence, the neutral adult word "distended (nostrils)" Joyce changed, as part of his systematic transformation of "The Sisters" into a story both about and through the experience of the boy, to "black cavernous." To the clause before that, "His face was very grey and massive," he added a single word, perhaps the most important new word in "The Sisters": "His face was very truculent, grey and massive" (14). The new word that alters the original "solemn" expression the boy finds in both versions (instead of the smile he expects in both), is the final element of an important addition Joyce made in transforming his story: he created a pattern inaugurated by the boy's dreamed pair of smiles. The very truculent face of the corpse also is the final element of the pattern chronologically; but significantly, it is not the last in the story (in the boy's experience). At this point, Flynn's surprising fierce expression in death is an increment in the knowledge about him the boy takes to the Flynns' "little" parlor, the scene of the fourth part of the story.

With Cotter's expanded role and the episode of the boy in bed, the length of its first part in the revised story is about double that in the original story. The length of its final scene and longest part Joyce somewhat more than doubled; one consequence is that a third of the original became almost half the story. Its revisions and expansion indicate that he intended the scene in the parlor to culminate the prior experience the boy brings to it, and so to complete the story of the boy's experience into which he was transforming "The Sisters." In it, the boy learns about Flynn's performance of the "grave" (requiring "courage") "duties of the priest towards the Eucharist and towards the secrecy of the confessional." He then learns about the living adult Dubliners.

In both the original and the revised story, the scene begins as the boy and his aunt enter the parlor. In both, the prompt talk about the deceased has two general subjects. The first comprises the fact of his death, the difficulties attendant on it, and the sisters' ministering to the old man previously. The other concerns his mental state: its etiology, and his former colleagues' reports on and judgments about it. For the sake of clarity, the extensive changes Joyce made to this final part of his story will be described consecutively, in eight distinguishable corresponding segments of its original and revised versions.

In both versions, the first segment is a paragraph of exposition prior to the first dialogue. Originally, that describes three of the four people present with, in 1905, the "visitors . . . given a glass of sherry each" (G144). Eliza, mentioned twice previously (during the negative description of Flynn), is ignored. Of the others, Nannie and "I . . . being too young" both "said nothing," though Nannie's "lips moved . . . with a painfully intelligent movement"; "but my aunt said a great deal for she was a gossip, a harmless one" (G144). And the boy's loquacious aunt shares with Eliza the ensuing dialogue to the end of the original story.

In the revised paragraph, the narrator's brief explanation of the boy's silence is replaced by him portrayed refusing crackers because eating them "would make too much noise"; this occurs after "I groped my way towards my usual chair" indicates his emotional state fresh from "the deadroom." The aunt is not described at all; and she is much less prominent in the expanded scene as a whole than in the original one, for almost all the hundreds of new words are spoken by Eliza.

The revised story retains the original final detail in "the dead-room" of the "heavy odour" of flowers, then breaks to the revised paragraph of exposition which begins with the brief new transition sentence, "We crossed ourselves and came away." It is the next sentence in the paragraph that begins the fourth and final part of "The Sisters," the scene in the Flynns' parlor. Also new, the sentence is devoted to the character completely ignored in the original initial paragraph of exposition; and it is richly informative: "In the little room downstairs we found Eliza seated in his arm-[sic]chair in state" (14). Although her presence is implied in its retained title, before this sentence initiating its final scene Eliza is not mentioned in the revised story. And from this first sentence she dominates it, her speeches interrupted only by the aunt's brief responses and by occasional exposition. When he transformed "The Sisters," Joyce made Eliza very prominent in it, much more an instrumental actor than the augmented Cotter or (through the boy's augmented experience and memory), Flynn.

For the purposes of his story, Joyce not only greatly expanded the role of the originally "[not] very intelligent" Eliza, he also metamorphosed her into a complex and strong character. The transformation of the two sisters from ciphers into individuated characters that he began with Nannie in the previous scene, he completed with skillful economy in this one. Introduced to the story as assertive, Eliza later is shown to be—the word is the narrator's—shrewd. And she is characterized further by way of class markers: solecisms like Nannie's "*Freeman's General*" in the original version (G138) and "rheumatic wheels"; and nonstandard English like "she and me." In two important retained phrases: "the duties of the priesthood was too much for him," Joyce changed from "were" (G146); and "we done all we could for him," he changed from "did" (G148) and had her say in response to the aunt's new "you did all you could for him" (15).

The characterization of Eliza in the expository initial paragraph is implicated in the account of her sister that follows its sentence presenting Eliza "in state." Described without ridicule in the previous scene as old, deaf, and feeble, Nannie is portrayed: proffering sherry and cream crackers; "at her sister's bidding" pouring the wine; and disappointed at the boy's "refusal" of the crackers. Nannie's then sitting silent and inactive "behind her sister" for the rest of the story is emblematic.

The second distinguishable segment of the original parlor scene, between the expository paragraph and the aunt's asking "Did he [dots for ellipsis] peacefully?" Joyce reduced to one-third its length. Originally, Eliza says "—Ah, well, he's gone!—" and the aunt asserts "—To enjoy his eternal reward" as "a good and holy man." But Eliza demurs: "—He was a good man but . . . you see," he was "disappointed," his "life . . . crossed—." The aunt's polite response to this is treated as an interruption by Eliza, who begins her detailed account of her brother's lifelong mental state: not "mad," but always "queer," "Even when we were all growing up together"; "One time he didn't speak hardly for a month. You know, he was that kind always—." The aunt suggests that Flynn read too much; Eliza responds it was not reading but "his scrupulousness . . . that affected his mind," and "The duties of the priesthood were too much for him—" (G145–46).

As has been pointed out, Joyce removed from "The Sisters" Eliza's explicit declaration that Flynn always was mentally unstable, in order to turn a permanent character-trait into a late development imputed by other characters. He retained and used later in the scene not just Eliza's final sentence (with the class marker inserted), but her whole final assertion, as well as her initial ones that Flynn was "disappointed" and "his life . . . crossed." In the short corresponding segment of the revised story, the aunt says in a single sentence both the "—Ah, well, he's gone" and her own former pious response ("to a better world"); and Eliza only sighs, before and after.

In the original story, the third short segment of the scene comprises only the aunt's question, did Flynn (avoiding the word) die "peacefully," and Eliza's reassurances: "He had a beautiful death"; he received the final rites; "He was quite resigned—" (G146–47).

The original text Joyce retained, slightly altered, in the revised third segment. But he added to it:

—He looks quite resigned, said my aunt.
—That's what the woman we had in, you know, [revised before publication to "in to wash him"] said. She said he just looked as if he was asleep, he looked that peaceful and resigned. No one would think he'd make such a beautiful corpse.
—Yes indeed, said my aunt. (15, G147, G172)

After seeing, on the variously smiling face he had known, Flynn's "truculent" final expression, the boy whose story "The Sisters" has become "grop[es]" to his "usual chair in the corner"—to witness the gross misrepresentation of Flynn's true final state committed by the adults, including "the woman we had in," who have shared what he has seen. And this experience of his takes its place in the plot of Joyce's transformed story.

The fourth distinguishable segment of the scene is devoted to the difficulties attendant on Flynn's death. The original version (G148), Joyce quadrupled in length in the revised story. The aunt has three new short speeches. In the first, she takes over Eliza's former "we did all we could." Her praise is followed by a seven-word paragraph of exposition: "Eliza smoothed her dress over her knees" (15). Then Eliza responds with an exclamation (she makes it in the next segment, in the original story): "—Ah, poor James!" followed by the short original segment, slightly revised, including—now echoing the aunt—"done all we could." The major part of Joyce's expansion then begins. Eliza describes the extensive help of the priest who administered Flynn's last rites, Father O'Rourke. She does not articulate the manifest contrast between her brother and O'Rourke, the effective (and functioning) priest; but when the aunt responds with her second speech, "—Wasn't that good of him?," a nine-word expository paragraph follows: "Eliza closed her eyes and shook her head slowly." The segment ends with Eliza's praise of "old friends" and the aunt's third, polite, speech. Eliza's account of resourceful Father O'Rourke in the added dialogue seems, in the context of the added second brief paragraph describing her gestures, to begin tacitly the disquisition about Flynn's condition for which she appropriates the rest of the story. Both brief descriptive paragraphs are significant: they initiate a pattern Joyce created in the revised story, of calculated gestures complementing Eliza's words about her brother.

The fifth distinguishable segment in the original story, about as short as the fourth, Joyce expanded even more than he did the fourth. It comprises a single speech by Eliza devoted to no longer ministering to Flynn that she begins and ends with her exclamation about "poor James!," and the aunt's declaring Eliza will miss him more "in a day or two" (G150). The revised segment not only has new material, but also incorporates the passage about Flynn's mental state removed from the original second segment, and a detail about him removed from the negative portrayal of him in the original second part of the story (G136), which now is given to Eliza.

The revised segment begins with the original one, slightly altered in phrasing; but it also has an important difference. The aunt's declaring Eliza will miss Flynn, which originally followed Eliza's brief speech bracketed by her "poor James!" exclamations, Joyce caused to interrupt the speech. The importance of this rearrangement is that it permits the story to focus on Eliza when the retained original part of the segment ends:

> Ah, poor James!
> She stopped, as if she were communing with the past[,] and then said shrewdly:
> —Mind you, I noticed there was something queer coming over him latterly. (16)

Her specific instance is the detail from the original second part of the story: finding Flynn asleep "Whenever I'd bring in his soup ... his breviary fallen on [revised to "to"] the floor."

With this modest beginning, Eliza "shrewdly" introduces to the revised "The Sisters" her proposition that in later life ("latterly") her priest brother became "queer." She then departs from it, speaking of Flynn's wish to take the three of them to visit their childhood home. However, this digressive detail palliating Eliza's revelation of her brother's "queer[ness]" when near death is informative: Flynn's planning a trip back to the site of his poor and ignorant beginnings in Irishtown suggests an unconscious desire to undo all that the Church has done for and to him.

A fourth "poor James!" and a responsive "—The Lord have mercy on his soul!" by the aunt follow Eliza's digression; then the revised fifth segment continues with its subject, Eliza on Flynn—punctuated by two more in the series of paragraphs describing her gestures. The first seems to express her concern that the boy is present: "She laid a finger against her nose and frowned: then she continued" (17). The second follows the aunt's pious interjection, and is another of the studied silent elements of her disquisition: "Eliza took out her handkerchief and wiped her eyes with it. Then she put it back again in her pocket and gazed into the empty grate for some time without speaking." This introduces, together, her three statements taken from the second segment of the original scene, about the etiology of Flynn's mental state. In their new form, "—He was too scrupulous always, she said. The duties of the priesthood was too much for him. And then his life was, you might say, crossed." Concurring, the boy's aunt now is the one who says Flynn was "disappointed," and the fifth segment of the scene ends.

All three of Eliza's statements from earlier in the original scene are enriched into dramatic irony by additions Joyce made in revising it. She seems to intend that the first explain the second in both versions; and in the revision, she has already presented Father O'Rourke as a priest whose discharge of his duties is not hindered by excessive scrupulosity. In their *James Joyce's "Dubliners,"* Jackson and McGinley propose reasonably that her first statement is echoing O'Rourke, and write of "too scrupulous": "Joyce was aware of its theological signification: 'prone to unreasonable doubts about sin'" (p. 8); Flynn had suggested to the boy that his "scrupulous" attention to Church doctrine incapacitated him as a priest. Eliza's using the words "his life was . . . crossed" to call her brother beset, luckless, in her third statement, enables Joyce to create an ironic pun in the revision, and even a gesture to Flynn's truculent face. And the boy, who has seen Flynn's face, is enlightened about it and the old priest by all three of Eliza's statements: "too scrupulous" to discharge "the duties of the priesthood," Flynn was trapped in a "crossed" life in both senses of the word. At this point in the revised story, the boy begins to learn some history about his "old friend."

In both versions of the final scene the sixth distinguishable segment begins with the room become silent, contains Eliza's continuing account of the etiology of Flynn's mental state with the chalice he broke and commentary on the incident, and concludes with her "God be merciful to him!" spliced to the previous sentence with a comma in the revision (17). The original brief segment reads:

> Silence invaded the room until memory reawakened it, Eliza speaking slowly:
> —It was that chalice he broke. Of course, it was all right. I mean it contained nothing. But still . . . . . [sic] They say it was the boy's fault. But poor James was so nervous. God be merciful to him!—(G154)

Joyce doubled the length of the segment; he also made much more important changes to it. Having transformed Flynn's insanity from a fact of the story to something (mistakenly) inferred, and as a recent development, by other adult Dubliners, he introduced subsidiary inferences of others—uncertainties—into Eliza's account of the advent of her brother's condition; that account with its new uncertainties extends through this sixth segment and the next one.

After the less extravagant "A silence took possession" Joyce substituted for his narrator's original mixed metaphor of the room "invaded" then "reawakened," the revised segment introduces the newly enlightened boy. "Under cover of" the possessive silence, he tastes his sherry—which has remained on the table—and returns "to my chair in the corner" to be further enlightened; the intrusion seems pointed. Then another of Eliza's histrionic displays replaces her original innocent responding to "memory":

> Eliza seemed to have fallen into a deep revery. We waited respectfully for her to break the silence: and after a long pause she said slowly:
> It was that chalice he broke.... [sic] That was what was ["what was" from G174] the beginning of it. (17)

Her new specifying of a precise "beginning" to her brother's supposed mental condition is followed by the first new uncertainty. Joyce replaced her two positive extenuating sentences with: "Of course, they say it was all right, that it contained nothing, I mean." In the original story, "their" testimony appears only as the (retained) unlikely "They say it was the boy's fault."[8] Beginning with the compound attribution that replaces her original assertion, the revised story has Eliza adopting the reports and judgments of Flynn's former colleagues about the onset of his supposed mental debility, and so setting out—in the boy's presence—the construction of an erroneous inference grounded in uncertainty.

In both versions of the scene the seventh distinguishable segment begins after Eliza's pious invocation of God's mercy, with the aunt's response to her remarks about "that chalice he broke," and ends with the revelation about her brother which is her conclusive evidence of his dementia—and the narrative climax of "The Sisters": that he was discovered "in his confession-box . . . laughing like—softly to himself" (G156). In revising the segment Joyce made certain strategic changes, and filled out Eliza's delineation of the final search that culminated in "their" discovery of Flynn.

His first strategic change is at the beginning. In both versions, the aunt reveals that she had heard about the chalice incident. But in the original she makes the positive assertion, "I heard that about the chalice. He . . . . his mind was a bit affected by that—" to which Eliza responds with a brief account of the climactic discovery, beginning "—He began to mope by himself." In Joyce's revision of the story, the scene has been constituting Eliza's studied disquisition about her brother, and its new focus is preserved:

> —And was that it? said my aunt. I heard something. . . . [*sic*]
> Eliza nodded.
> —That affected his mind, she said. After that he began to mope by himself.

The remainder of the segment is her more elaborate delineation of the discovery of Flynn in his confessional. She repeats "by himself"; the ubiquitous Father O'Rourke is among those who discover Flynn; more detailed, her report also is more idiomatic ("So then the clerk suggested to try. . . . So then they got the keys and"); finally, in place of simply declaring her revelation the new histrionic Eliza poses a question, beginning "And what do you think but there he was . . . ?"

The scene in the Flynn parlor has treated Flynn's death, his mental state, its etiology, and his former colleagues' reports. The eighth segment I distinguish in it, and conclusion of "The Sisters," is the consequence of Eliza's climactic disclosure: Flynn's colleagues' judgment about him. Following "laughing like—softly to himself," the original story concludes tersely with Eliza's statement of it, and the aunt's final piety:

> Then they knew something was wrong—
> —God rest his soul!—

In his revision, Joyce ended the story with Eliza. He interpolated a paragraph of exposition, then had Eliza repeat the climax of her narrative and go on to a significantly altered final statement: the surmise by the colleagues who discovered him. The passage warrants quoting:

> there he was laughing-like softly [*sic*] to himself?
> She stopped suddenly as if to listen. I too listened; but there was no sound in the house: and I knew that the old priest was lying still in his coffin as we had seen him, solemn and truculent in death, an idle chalice on his breast.
> Eliza resumed:

—Wide-awake and laughing-like to himself. . . . [*sic*] So then, of course, when they saw that, that made them think that there was something gone wrong with him. . . . [*sic*] (18)

The richness with which he invests the revised conclusion to "The Sisters" anticipates the mature Joyce. In the paragraph of exposition, "I knew" and "idle" echo the initial paragraph of the story: "I had thought his words idle. Now I knew they were true" (9). As "vanity" in the last sentence of "Araby" means not only self-importance but also futility, so "idle" has two of the word's principal meanings. That it is not in use is almost redundant for a chalice placed in the hands of a corpse; the functional meaning of the word is the evaluative one invoked in the initial paragraph: without worth or significance.[9] The other echo from the initial paragraph reveals a second thing about the boy's state of mind at the end of the story—which otherwise must be inferred from what he has experienced. Eliza's histrionic silence following her revelation, "as if to listen" for Flynn's laughter, prompts the boy really to listen, although futilely, he "knew."

The conclusion of "The Sisters," with the boy's response to Eliza's reiterated climactic revelation, is the appropriate place to consider the pattern involving smiles Joyce added to it, for in the revised story the laughter Eliza discloses at its climax became the final element of that new pattern. The single instance in the original version, Flynn's "smiling often and pushing huge pinches of snuff up each nostril alternately," is almost comically grotesque. In the revised story: Flynn's disembodied face smiles "continually" while it confesses in the boy's dream; he smiles in response; and in the account of their sessions together Flynn (his face) smiles in two successive sentences, first while nodding to the boy's bewilderment, then "pensively" when the boy "pattered" his memorized responses to the Mass. But the smile the new boy at first (in his dream) believes irreverent, and ambivalently both reproves and reciprocates, then in the morning comes to consider ambiguous, the dead Flynn has replaced—to the boy's surprise—with its exact opposite, an expression of fierce anger. The death the boy knows at the beginning of the story is imminent, before its end he knows occurred neither as he had expected it, nor as the adults around him have represented it: Flynn is "solemn and truculent in death"; and they "had seen him" so.

Finally, just before the story ends, the boy learns that Flynn's frequent and different smiles had been preceded chronologically by almost hysterical laughing. Promptly, he judges the appropriateness of a chalice for

Flynn's corpse, and observes that the adults knew ("we had seen him") Flynn's attitude at his death was not as they represented it. And Eliza's concluding speech then augments what he has been learning. After she repeats, for emphasis, her climactic revelation, she ends the story with the confident surmise by Father O'Rourke and the others from their discovery of Flynn laughing in his confession-box: "So then, of course, when they saw that, that made them think that there was something gone wrong with him." The change Joyce made from her original final "Then they knew something was wrong" not only introduces uncertainty ("that made them think"), but reiterates that in the revised story "something" is believed to have "gone wrong" with a formerly normal priest.

Eliza attributes the dementia she claims had befallen her "too scrupulous" brother not only to his breaking the chalice, but also to the "nervous[ness]" that caused the accident. Before he entered the Flynns' parlor the boy was aware of the scruples that might have made one with Flynn's knowledge of Church doctrine nervous when performing the chief office of a Catholic priest. Now he knows beyond doubt that Flynn himself suffered from failure of the requisite courage: what the nodding smile had signified was a sharing of his own perplexity. In the parlor Eliza's calculated disquisition has provided him with the history of the condition, as it developed, of his old and sick smiling and nodding priest: from Flynn's nervousness, to the chalice incident, to his moping, to his sitting "laughing to himself." Flynn's subsequent smiling the boy knew so well before the time of the story—during their relationship—and has dreamed about, occurred between Flynn's almost-hysterical laughing at his predicament and his anger when dying. And Flynn's laughing and anger the boy learns about in reverse sequence, when he accompanies his aunt on her condolence call. In addition, Eliza's account and the conversation of the adults have disclosed to him the misperception—or misrepresentation—of elements of the truth about Flynn by Eliza, the woman who laid Flynn out, the aunt, the churchmen. To Eliza's final words, the long parlor scene in which the story culminates enlightens the boy far more about the adult Dubliners' representation of Flynn than about Flynn himself.

\*   \*   \*

Young Joyce's transformation in 1906 of the indifferent story he had written two years before and revised slightly the year before can be seen as his deriving "The Sisters" from the original bearer of that title the way an accomplished work of fiction is made from its source material. His enabling development was progressive, not sudden, of course: his achievement in "The Sisters" transformed is not to be contrasted with that in the *Dubliners* stories written before it and "The Dead." (For example, "A Painful Case" underwent its extensive revision almost a year before he remade "The Sisters.") But the relevant point about his development is that during the period he was completing "A Painful Case" and the other impressive achievements among the originally twelve stories, that first one proved refractory: the slight revision he was able to make then did little for it.

The sequence and dates of its three texts document that one year later, and after writing all but the many times longer than most, successfully more ambitious than any other, final story of *Dubliners,* he proved able to take "The Sisters" out of its indifferent predecessor. What is signified by his achievement in the few excisions, many alterations, and prodigious expansion reviewed above—the development as an artist he realized in 1906—now can be considered.

The two early critical discussions of his revisions noted that changed details enriched the story symbolically. His sequential changes of rosary to cross to chalice, and of Nannie's proffering nothing to sherry to sherry and crackers, were given as examples. (When he changed the date of Flynn's death, his moving it back one day also served the story symbolically; but his moving it forward five years served *Dubliners* as a whole functionally.) Both Magalaner and Kenner emphasized, however, that the most important change he effected was to make "The Sisters" the boy's story, by portraying his experiencing consciousness.

Sound as their observation is, young Joyce's transformation of "The Sisters" seems not to be fully accounted for by the difference between a story of the events around the death of a priest witnessed by a boy (who, it must be remembered, obtrudes his consciousness extensively), and a story of a boy's consciousness as he experiences those events. What Joyce's revision produced manifestly is far richer than his original story; and the product can be accounted for only by attention to the process.

Stories like "Eveline" (written only a few weeks later in 1904), "Araby," and "A Painful Case" show that he was capable of an impressive story portraying an experiencing consciousness not only when he made his slight revision to "The Sisters," but even the summer he wrote it. And yet his capability did not extend to it, on either occasion. What transpired in 1906 seems to be a dramatic illustration of the profound consequences for the process of fiction-making of a writer's "method . . . governed by . . .

point of view," as Percy Lubbock long ago (in his aptly named *The Craft of Fiction* [1921; New York: Viking, 1957, p. 251]), called the definitive choice the writer always makes, consciously or not.

In the two 1905 "childhood" stories, young Joyce had portrayed the baleful effect of class bias and violence in middle-class Catholic Dublin when experienced by one boy approaching, and of the religion directly by another beginning, normal growth into sexuality; but in 1905 "The Sisters" had remained a story of impecunious Dublin death and piety, with conversations in kitchen and parlor and a corpse, witnessed by an almost silent, responsive boy. When he changed the boy, from a witness with attitudes to the subject, a just-dead priest—when he succeeded in making "The Sisters" about the boy, like the other two "childhood" stories—it was by enlisting for the former witness himself, his aborted then completed visit to that corpse, and the conversations he overheard in kitchen and parlor.

Considered in terms of results, my assertion seems a tautology: he made the story about the boy by making it about the boy. But I am describing what he enacted, which is to say, fiction-making process: he succeeded because he had grown capable of the requisite "method." His transformation of "The Sisters" is not adequately described by pointing out that he made it consist in the boy's subjectivity, because his instrumental method did not constitute a major *alteration* of point of view. Although that more uniformly became what I have called the narrator's third stance, reporting the boy's experience subjectively, his older self still told what the obedient yet observant boy saw, heard, and thought; but the operation of a boy's experiencing consciousness could become itself the subject of this story because Joyce finally had developed the method for dedicating its events—which is to say, what the boy and its three other principal characters do—to *constituting* the (consequently more complex and so different) boy's experience.

In other words, the new method generated new characterizations and circumstances in "The Sisters"; and these are not just complements of, but more radical changes from the original story than, the new (actually, only newly consistent and expanded) subject-consciousness. The catalogue of radical changes: the initial revelation of the boy's emotional involvement with Flynn; his consequent both fierce and silent response to the innuendos of (a consequently also more complex) Cotter; his equivocal thoughts and dream about Flynn, and behavior before Flynn's house; the account that becomes his recollective experience of their sessions, which explains his initial ambivalence and later confusion respecting a consequently altered and more complex Flynn; in sum, everything reified in the many long and short excisions, alterations, and especially additions, through an altered and more developed Eliza's calculated disquisition, more revealing than she intends—though to a young boy; that catalogue of changes derives from Joyce's method of portraying everything else in it as the coherent experience of the subject of his new "The Sisters." In technical terms, all that enrichment devolves, as my repeated "consequently" suggests, out of a new coherent plotting. Young Joyce had gained mastery over material that earlier in his development defeated him. For that reason, his transformation of "The Sisters" marks a kind of accession as an artist. The rich achieved story confirms this.

Awareness of certain of his changes to his indifferent original story becomes special access to its richness, by constraining reading: the agency is not his intention in the alterations and clarifications, but palpable design, shaping. For example, that he took the measures he did to change Flynn from definitely "queer" to mistakenly believed so, indicates the importance of the detail; it combines with the passages he added and changes he made to the narrator's account of his sessions with Flynn, to create a priest who has lost not his sanity but his ability to continue functioning. In the plotted story Joyce created, these two linked innovations also contribute to the boy's culminating experience in the Flynns' parlor.

Nevertheless, knowledge of how Joyce excised from, altered, and added to his original story in transforming it does not give complete understanding of what he wrought, or even intended. Of certain aspects of "The Sisters," reading is not constrained, and critics will continue to interpret them differently. They seem to be of two kinds: undecidable (aporias); and amenable to interpretation.

The boy's responsive smile in his dream of Flynn's smiling disembodied face is "as if to absolve the simoniac of his sin." But the point has been made, there is no way of knowing if the boy has identified, or only the narrator can name, the sin; and there is no way of knowing if even the narrator accuses him: "simoniac" may only serve to articulate the boy's original belief about him. The aporia is not important in the boy's story.

Three others are even less so. Cotter's vague statements make it impossible to know whether he does in fact share the general belief that Flynn has become unbalanced, or suspects something closer to the truth ("I have my own theory about it," 10). Does he want to shield the boy from a spectacle or an influence?—the story never reveals what he is refusing to articulate. And there is no way of knowing why Flynn has not revealed his predicament to anyone but the boy. It could be understandable reticence, motivated by either prudence or fear; or it could be the simple fact that the boy is the only visitor he has. Finally, the possibility that he has either revealed or betrayed himself to his shrewd sister creates a more complex aporia.

Both her having taken the very unusual measure of causing a chalice to be placed in the hands of Flynn's corpse (giving pointed significance to his vestments), and her subtly pejorative disquisition tracing the history of his supposed mental debility, can signify nothing more than an innocent attempt to mitigate the social consequences of her late brother's conduct. Eliza and Nannie can simply correspond to the two imperceptive Dublin women of Stephen's "Parable of the Plums" in *Ulysses: Joyce's "Dubliners"* describes the sisters as representing "pious Ireland's impoverished existence, down-at-heel [Nannie is literally so] and semi-paralyzed in impercipience" (p. 75).

On the other hand, from her introduction to the revised story seated in Flynn's chair, Eliza's appropriation of its long final scene enables the inference that she knows and is misrepresenting the truth. In that case, her initiative with the chalice and her history of Flynn's supposed debility would be a "shrewd" endeavor to mislead. Joyce's emphasis on her histrionic gestures throughout suggests conscious deception. In describing Flynn as "too scrupulous always" and "nervous," perhaps from the time he was "crossed" in the punning sense—that is, became a priest—she has explained (the boy knows) his pathetic condition. But she is tracing dementia; and her specifying what "they saw" and what it "made them think," invoking corroborating authority, contributes to the deception. If deception it is: her histrionics, her treatment of Flynn and his recent history, her invoking the churchmen, all intended to help confirm to her socially superior visitor the general belief that her brother died "queer," not responsible for his conduct, could be to serve a belief she sincerely shares.

Unlike the aporias mentioned, the narrator's inconsistency does affect the boy's story; and unlike the aporias, it is amenable to interpretation. The adult the boy has become presents himself as conventionally pious, even to apparently charging Flynn with a specific serious sin. And he gives innocent reasons why, when a boy, he only "pretended to pray" in the dead-room, and declined the apparent quasi-Communion in the parlor; he also specifies that he eventually "tasted my sherry." On the other hand, he has certain knowledge: what he learned when a boy about the Dublin Catholic adults' misperception and misrepresentation of Flynn in death; and that Flynn's simony was trivial and pathetic—whether for the boy's company and/or the snuff, or merely to avoid being unfrocked. Above all, knowing these things he learned when a boy, he tells his story.

Although the light cast by Joyce's changes to its predecessor story does not fully constrain interpretation respecting the teller of "The Sisters," he is illuminated by it. The same also is true for three other important elements of the story: the quasi-Communion of sherry and cream crackers, the title, and the three added italicized words in its opening paragraph.

The history through the three versions of the symbolic refreshment called by Magalaner "the most important of the additions to the *Dubliners* version" (p. 79), almost confirms that Joyce evolved the generally interpreted analogue to the Eucharist in the final story. But what the sisters' proffered quasi-Communion signifies has no such general consensus. Are they surrogate priests, as some (e.g., Magalaner, p. 80) say? Does the symbolic detail instead invoke the absence of the indispensable priest? Is its irony more general? And what, if anything, is signified by the boy's response beyond, as I point out, emphasizing his presence in the room?

Possibly related to this enrichment of Joyce's transformed story is its retained title, which also has been variously interpreted. And a bibliography of interpretations of the meaning in and for the story not only of *simony*, but of all three italicized words, would be extensive. The special access to "The Sisters" provided by awareness of Joyce's changes indicates how these four important elements may (although not must) be understood.

I have called the aporias unimportant because they do not affect the essential story. It can be described as portraying the boy's experience consequent on his relationship with Flynn; but more precisely, it comprises his experiences of the four specific parts of the story, which are its armature: of Cotter's disparaging and his own ambivalent attitude toward Flynn in the evening; of Flynn's prior dealings with him in the morning; of Flynn's corpse in "the dead-room"; and of the attitude toward Flynn of the adults in the parlor.

The skill of young Joyce's transformation of his original story into one portraying a boy's experiencing consciousness, it should be pointed out, is epitomized in the conjunction he created between the boy's experiences of its armature, and the pattern begun by the first pair of smiles. Those smiles the boy dreams; the second pair he recollects; Flynn's truculent expression he sees; finally, Flynn's laughter that happened first in the series he hears about. Each different particular experience in the four-element pattern—the dreamed, the recollected, the seen, the heard—is the climax of the boy's general experience of one of the four parts of the armature.

The attitude toward Flynn of Cotter and the adults in the parlor occupies about two-thirds of "The Sisters," including its final and much its longest scene. The form of the story indicates, and I propose its retained title signifies, that while Flynn is indispensable to it, all aspects of the boy's experience that implicate Flynn directly actually are secondary in importance to the boy's experience of the attitude toward Flynn of its other adults. Hence, its long final scene: the boy's primary experience in the story occurs principally in that scene.

In that culminating scene of "The Sisters," the boy enters the Flynns' parlor knowing the state of mind of his "old friend" in death. There, he hears the adults around him inaccurately characterize Flynn as having died "resigned"; after that, he learns they believe Flynn to be mentally "queer"; and then he learns of the sequence of events that led to their misapprehension: Flynn dropped the chalice while celebrating a mass; in consequence he "began to mope"; eventually he was discovered laughing in his confessional.

Knowing the priest is sane, and confirming in the parlor that Flynn was revealing his predicament in their sessions, the boy can discern that those events record stages in the breakdown of an Irish priest. Hence, he knows their significance has been misconstrued by the adult Dubliners around him. Finally, in the last sentence of the story, he learns the origin of that misapprehension. It was the respected churchmen making the discovery in Flynn's confessional, types of the principal authorities in his world, who inferred from Flynn's "laughing-like softly to himself" there that he must have become—who originated the belief their fellow-priest was—mentally unstable.

In Flynn's chair, with the boy in his "usual chair in the corner" (14), Eliza is in the place of his late instructor; and conducting the proceedings, she unknowingly informs him. Before entering the parlor he was aware of the smiling then finally truculent Flynn's troubled experience of two of the four Sacraments of the Church relevant to one of its priests, Holy Orders and Extreme Unction. In the parlor, she reveals Flynn's troubled experience of the other two, Communion and Penance (his "nervous[ly]" dropping the chalice and laughing in his confession-box). But she functions for the boy there as *gnomon,* in the broad sense of "that which enables knowledge," less for this reason than for being the instrument of his learning that the adults already know, or learn with him, all he learns from her about her brother, and refuse or are unable to acknowledge its significance.

He knows the adults misperceive or deny Flynn's truculent end, and attribute Flynn's treatment of Communion and Penance to mental debility. The narrator does not reveal how he reacted, when the boy, to his experience of the failures of perception and understanding, or of candor, by Dublin adults, including churchmen and his own surrogate parent, with respect to Flynn's late life and death; but he has directed his story of himself when the boy toward, and ended it with, that experience. And this fact indicates how the most prominent of the three italicized words may function in it.

At the end of the first paragraph of "The Sisters," he reveals that the "being" whose name *paralysis* "sounded to me like" when a boy "filled me with fear, and yet I longed to be nearer to it and to look upon its deadly work" (9); and promptly the boy hears at home that he will not succeed with the literal paralysis of Flynn's final illness. Joyce revised "The Sisters" shortly before sending the fourteen-story manuscript of *Dubliners* to Grant Richards on July 9, 1906; and on May 5, in the first of the four familiar sentences quoted at the beginning of the previous chapter, he described Dublin to Richards as "the centre of paralysis." He had linked the word to his volume from the beginning.[10] (At the end of the newspaper chapter in *Ulysses,* he turned his metaphor into a symbol by having the trams emanating out of central Dublin "becalmed in short circuit" [7.1043–47/p. 122].)

The boy knew before the story that Flynn was confounded—metaphorically paralyzed—by his strict (i.e., orthodox) conception of the duties of the priesthood. More to the point, he learns in the story that the other adults, and Eliza articulates their attitude, consider Flynn, not their Church, to be the cause of his predicament: have been incapacitated for acknowledging the truth about a priest broken by his profound grasp of the demands of his (their) Church. The story portrays a boy learning that Dublin adults are mentally immobilized—metaphorically paralyzed—by their conformity to a hegemony of Roman Catholic piety. For them, the legitimacy of the Irish Church is a categorical given. And although the narrator he has become does not reveal if the boy recognized at the time this etiology for the adults' ideological variant of Dublin's metaphorical paralysis, manifestly the grown man recognizes it, for the story he tells is about his boyhood experience of "be[ing] nearer to it": as a boy he had, at the end of the story he has begun with the word in italics, "look[ed] upon [the] deadly work" of Catholic Dublin's intellectually paralyzing religious hegemony.

If the symbolic Eucharist Joyce created for the story is considered in the context of this metaphorical paralysis of a community, its signification ceases to be problematic. The sherry and crackers symbolize the sacrificial wine and wafer not to invoke Communion directly, but to effect a highly appropriate social trope on the religious rite: the communion the sisters' wine and crackers admit to, and the aunt receiving them participates in, is that of pious Dublin Catholic adults, who misperceive and misinterpret things that are contrary to the religious ideology that has absorbed them, and so has immobilized their intelligence.[11]

This understanding of the word *paralysis* and of the symbolic Eucharist: that both asseverate the realization that is the boy's principal experience in the story, supports my suggestion above that the title "The Sisters" signifies the centrality of that experience of adult misperception and misinterpretation: it evolves in the Flynn sisters' home, and one of them is its agent.

The narrator's report, of his ambiguous response to the proffered social communion when the boy, points to his complicated place in the story he tells. While telling his thoughts and dream in bed the previous night those years ago, the narrator calls Flynn "the paralytic," then in the same passage makes his explicit judgment, "the simoniac." Both his epithets have their limited truth, but both obfuscate: as "The Sisters" creates a significance for *paralysis* different from the one he invokes, so it does for *simony*. After the boy has forgiven him in his dream, he learns of the priest's failed struggle to perform his office, and its pathetic conclusion. The narrator knows that in this context Flynn committed trivial simony: he learned it when the boy. I will try to show that both italicized words the narrator obfuscates the significance of, that "had always sounded strangely in [his] ears" when a boy, Joyce's story applies to him, and *gnomon* as well.

Not only Eliza, but Flynn before her, and even his aunt, are gnomons for the boy in the broad sense of the term. That sense does not enrich the story particularly; and "*gnomon* in the Euclid" (9) invokes explicitly its geometric sense, of the remainder of a parallelogram after a similar one has been taken from one of its corners: the shape of the remainder reveals (provides *gnosis* of) that of the removed corner. For the boy, Cotter's fragmentary aspersions and Flynn's smiles are closer to that sense. But the rich significance of *gnomon* in the revised story is indicated by an early instance of the functional comic wit Joyce used increasingly in *Ulysses* and *Finnegans Wake*.

In the original story, Nannie is seated not "behind her sister" but "in a corner" (G144); and the boy's location in the parlor is not specified. In the revised story, the boy as well as Nannie is situated. And in that culminating scene, he is explicitly where he sat when being tutored by Flynn: "I groped my way toward my usual chair in the corner" (14). It is "in the corner" he previously learned about the baleful effect of the Church on the most admirable kind of priest, the erudite and conscientious Father Flynn; and it is there he learns about the distorted consensus of the adults. Not sharing that consensus, he is the piece taken out of the whole. "Let him learn to box his corner," his uncle specifies at the beginning of the story (11); and by its end he has done so.

The remainder of the parallelogram, not the removed corner, is the gnomon defined by Euclid: here it is the adults around the boy, who reveal their nature (to him) precisely because he is apart from their adult Dublin Catholic "communion." And being him grown up, the narrator also has *gnosis* of that gnomon whose nature the boy apprehended; yet the narrator inconsistently, it has been pointed out, speaks as part of it. The key to the inconsistency is that a gnomon reveals by its own shape the shape of the removed piece. Eventually, Joyce's sub-"chapter of the moral history of my country" turns toward its teller, the Dublin Catholic adult the boy became.

That the silent boy also is guarded, to the point of dissembling, is relevant here. His not expressing his anger at Cotter is merely good behavior for a child; but when his uncle says "your old friend is gone," he, who has just come from his vigil at Flynn's house, responds "Who?" And that is followed by his feigned indifference to the news. His dissemblings in the kitchen follow Cotter's first aspersions against Flynn; but that does not make them any less acts of self-protection in the world of the adults. Later, in the dead-room, he pretends to pray. For his inability to do so, and for his later declining the crackers of the adults' symbolic communion, the narrator provides reasons why both are innocuous actions—preserves his own reputation as then a pious Catholic boy. They sound like lame excuses, but the narrator presents them as the boy's conscious reasons, and specifies that he did sip his wine. All these elements but the boy's silence are new to the revised story.

Also new is a pattern of progressively greater withholding of the boy's reactions to his four crucial experiences as the story progresses; and it is the narrator of a story who reveals or withholds. The boy's silent outrage at Cotter is fully articulated, and his subsequent ambivalence about Flynn that night and the next morning described at length. There is a brief account of his reaction to his memory of the sessions with Flynn. Of his reaction to his discovery that the face on Flynn's corpse is not only not smiling but "truculent," the narrator tells nothing more than that he "groped my way towards" his seat in the corner—provides only this physical symptom of his state of mind. And at the end of the story, after telling that the adults shared what "I knew" about Flynn, and quoting Eliza's reiteration of the almost lurid climax and conclusion of her account of her brother, he withholds totally his reaction when the boy.

Possibly nothing in "The Sisters" before it points as insistently to the narrator as does the conclusion of the story. In both the other "childhood" stories, the boy's reaction to his culminating experience provides closure, even though the narrator knows, and has shown, more about its significance than he was aware of when a boy. The reaction of the boy to Eliza's revelation about the extent of adult misapprehension in his Catholic Dublin world can be inferred easily enough. It is the narrator's action in withholding what he realized about the adults when the boy that calls for scrutiny. That negative action, his declining to articulate what he realized, relates to his conventional piety in the story, and explains his inconsistency: in spite of what he knows about a priest's disablement by his Church and about the intellectual paralysis of Dublin's adult Catholics when confronted with it, as an adult he has joined them. The gnomon reveals the shape of the (once-)removed piece. Hence, at the end of his narrative he refrains from articulating his boyhood reaction to the derogatory truth about them revealed to him. His withholding it recalls the beggar-playwright's changing the ending of his play, also to gain public approval, in Gay's *The Beggar's Opera:* in both cases, his act makes the agent the subject.

This is why all three italicized words in the first paragraph of "The Sisters" ultimately relate to him. The adults in his world when a boy are afflicted with intellectual paralysis; and they are the boy's gnomon of that fact. But they are not guilty of any simony. In contrast, the grown man who tells his story accommodates himself to the hegemony of Catholic Dublin. In doing so, he subverts truth for his convenience as the simoniac does faith. He knowingly conforms to the paralysis afflicting Dublin's adults, and so joins them as gnomon of it. His knowing accommodation to the pious community is prudential, of course; Joyce is signifying by it that a man could not remain in that society otherwise. But it remains self-interested, a metaphorical act of simony against the truth, however understandable. In the context of the power in Dublin of Irish Catholicism, Father James Flynn and the man the boy became are foils.

Each of the two subsequent "childhood" sub-"chapters" in *Dubliners* presents a man telling about how his Dublin Catholic environment influenced his growing self: in "An Encounter" the influence is its snobbery and violence; in "Araby," its sexual repression. Each narrator's understanding of the formative boyhood experience he tells of is part of young

Joyce's story: implicitly, the knowledge has been salutary to the man. But although the narrators are characterized to different degrees, the stories essentially are about the boys' formative experiences.

While this narrator's story also is about his formative experience when a boy, Joyce made "The Sisters" eventually about him, and so turned his narrative into a revelation of how he has coped with that experience. The Dublin man's prudential submission to the environmental pressure on him affirms the force of that pressure. When Joyce transformed the inaugural story of his volume, he made it an eloquent introduction to the baneful power of the Church over the minds and lives of the Dubliners the volume portrays.

Many hundreds of pages have been written to date about a story less than ten pages long, a number of them in this chapter. The fact itself is an index of the artistic richness Joyce achieved when, in the late spring of 1906, a little more than a year before he wrote "The Dead" and began the *Portrait* proper, he metamorphosed the indifferent sketch he had written and published two years earlier, and had retained for his volume almost unchanged a year earlier. His achievement of "The Sisters" simultaneously is his development as an artist, enabling the mature work he would undertake from that point.

# 6

# A Poetics of Autobiography

Near the end of his perceptive chapter on "The Sisters," Beck writes: "This acutely apprehensive child . . . is indeed father to the writer of the *Dubliners* stories. . . . Had he let himself be blunt he could with reason have called the story 'Silence, Exile, and Cunning'" (*Joyce's "Dubliners,"* p. 75). There is Silence aplenty, and the boy has sufficient Cunning to stay silent in certain circumstances; but the narrator's having declined Exile—submitted to Dublin—crucially dissociates both child and man from Joyce (as from his true facsimile Stephen Dedalus).

In the original state of "The Sisters," its protagonist recalls its author less than do either the two boys in the following stories, or James Duffy of "A Painful Case." All three boys are timid, like Stephen when a boy; but like him the latter two also are subject to emerging erotic feelings in a repressive Irish-Catholic society; and Duffy is the adult product of such conditions. In all three cases, autobiographical inference is encouraged by a fact that distinguishes the two boys and Duffy from other *Dubliners* protagonists likened by some to Joyce, such as Chandler of "A Little Cloud": of all the characters in the fourteen stories before he transformed "The Sisters" and wrote "The Dead," only those three gain knowledge about themselves in their situations. It is understandable, given their other similarities to him, that the two boys and Duffy should be mistakenly identified with their creator.

As the historical disparities reviewed in the third chapter belie autobiographical inferences for the boys, so do the different adult Dubliners they become. And so do his age, nature, and way of life in Duffy's case. The second paragraph of that chapter mentions the similarities between young Joyce and Duffy when young (even to their both having translated Hauptmann's *Michael Kramer*); but it mentions also that these personal details are combined with elements of Stanislaus's biography ("I served as model"). Always the parsimonious inventor of character and incident, Joyce was drawing on himself and his brother for a fictional Dubliner who was intellectually active when young. In the three characters he presented two boys subject to, and a mature man conditioned by, the very same middle-class Catholic Dublin circumstances he saw himself as having confronted, and was to depict imposing on young Stephen; but with neither the two boys nor Duffy did he employ a fictional mechanism of displacement to write about himself—as he did with Stephen.

The boy of "An Encounter" exaggerates his interest in literature for snobbish reasons; the literary sensibility of the boy of "Araby" is puerile. The boy of "The Sisters" is less bookish than either, has read only texts imposed on him. Yet when Joyce transformed "The Sisters," he caused its protagonist to share with Stephen as a boy, and himself when a boy, a personal attribute more singular than timidity.

While he withheld his own "Sunny Jim" disposition, perhaps for the good reason that it would seem discordant in the intense and reflective Stephen Dedalus, he reproduced in Stephen personal traits more pertinent to the *Portrait*. One, which was to realize its fullest expression in *Finnegans Wake*, is his apparently congenital sensitivity to sound, language, and the sounds of language. He considered this trait of his own an important enough one in his autobiographical character, when writing the *Portrait*, to make the slightly more than page-long opening portrayal of the very young Stephen conclude with it. When the child's mother says "—O, Stephen will apologise," and Dante replies "—O, if not, the eagles will come and pull out his eyes," Stephen is portrayed as ignoring the threatening situation, distracted from it by words and their sounds. Instead of responding to the adults, he shapes the key words spoken into the two familiar quatrains of four-syllable two-stress rhymed lines, one with the repeated "Pull out his eyes" enclosing the repeated "Apologise," the other reversing the arrangement of rhymed word and phrase.

The closely followed source of this episode, the first of Joyce's "Epiphanies," explicitly situated in the house in Bray where he lived from age five to age ten, has (in fact, Protestant) "Mr Vance—(comes in with a stick)" saying, "he'll have to apologise, Mrs Joyce," her agreeing ("Do you hear that, Jim?"), his threatening (Zeus's?) eagles, and her saying "O, but I'm sure he will apologise"; however, "Joyce—(*under the table, to himself*)" only does what he portrayed Stephen as doing. In the brief autobiographical episode he placed at the beginning of the *Portrait*, he did not just situate the child Stephen in his own specific childhood situation of prohibition and threatened violence; he gave Stephen himself his own specific expression of extreme involvement with sounds, words, and the sounds of words.

And previously, in 1906, he caused the boy of "The Sisters" also to have this important personal trait: the boy's attitude toward the three words put into italics precisely recalls Joyce's own relationship with language. The previous chapter noted briefly that when the narrator says the words "had always sounded strangely in my ears," the adverb is not a solecism, the last phrase not redundant. The boy sounds the words, so that instead of its usual signification of a quality heard (as in "sounded strange"), "sounded" here has its more strict meaning as an active verb: each word (itself) is sounding to him. Hence, the adverb, and the qualifying phrase to signify his experience of the word's sounding.

Not too much should be made of the fact: the three italicized words in the first paragraph function richly in "The Sisters"; and even in the transformed story the narrator remains an adult Dubliner. Joyce himself simply is not the subject of his boy. However, no parsimony of invention required him to give the non-autobiographical boy his own trait: those specific three words important to "The Sisters" could just have "sounded [like] strange [words]," as the rendered experience of a boy more normally responsive to—less especially sensitive to the sounding of—language. The source of that trait in the boy seems to be the motive whose more blatant later manifestations included his naming the Vances in the *Portrait* and giving Stephen his own debts in *Ulysses*.

From his first reported efforts when a schoolboy, young Joyce did two unrelated kinds of writing: "sketches" and other products of observation, and no less self-effacing translations; and alongside this, autobiographical prose as well as the more usual personal lyric verse. This pattern of alternately making himself his subject and turning outward persisted into *Stephen Hero* and *Dubliners*. Young Joyce's first major project was the novel for which he was not a source of material, but the subject; he began that novel "about himself" in Stanislaus's phrase on his (twenty-second) birthday perhaps intentionally, and if so expressed by that his well-known lifelong attitude—itself revealing—to the anniversary date of his own birth.

His abandoning *Stephen Hero* after hundreds of pages, and almost a year and a half, a year of that period while writing stories for *Dubliners*, "chronicled with patience . . . detaching himself," as he later wrote of young Stephen on Dublin, signified his relinquishing—as failed—James Joyce's first major project as a writer, which was autobiographical. And his giving the new boy, when he transformed "The Sisters" in 1906, a personal trait not required by the story, seems to be an inchoative reassertion of the motive for art he had relinquished a year earlier. If so, then gratuitously representing himself, yet functioning in a story not about himself, the boy's Joycean affinity for language merges Joyce's two kinds of writing. It marks the point from which the mature James Joyce would evolve and develop the ability to integrate the reality around him with himself as a single subject of his art: would evolve and develop, that is to say, his poetics of autobiography.

An intriguing possible complement to this autobiographical element in the transformed first story of *Dubliners* occurs in its last story before he wrote and added "The Dead" in 1907. If it exists, it augments the thematic connection Joyce created between the stories that bracket the 1906 volume. "Grace" complements "The Sisters" thematically, not only in its portrayal of the crude religiosity of lay Catholic Dubliners—especially the serene ignorance of their intellectual paragon, Martin Cunningham—but also in its pointed contrast of the successful Father Purdon, the businessmen's self-styled "spiritual accountant," who "won't be too hard on us," to the "too scrupulous always," failed and broken, Father Flynn.

The last story in his volume of twelve in 1905 (and then fourteen in 1906), "Grace" also was the last story he wrote for the original twelve, begun in October after he had written "Araby," and completed in November (Gabler, "Introduction," pp. 6–7). Gabler provides evidence for dating its only extant holograph copy, the fair copy in the *Dubliners* manuscript, a year later (pp. 8, 9). Because no copy of the original 1905 draft exists, there is no way of knowing whether the element which may be autobiographical play dates from seven months before, or was added up to four months after, Joyce's transformation of "The Sisters." If it is autobiographical play, and was in the original draft, it anticipates the positive reassertion of his autobiographical motive for art in the personal attribute he gave the boy in "The Sisters"; if it is, and was added, his play complements that reassertion.

The element of "Grace" which may be playfully autobiographical, bringing a ghost of the author into his volume at its close, is "A young man in a cycling-suit," who suddenly appears at the beginning, briefly is its chief actor, then leaves it, to be mentioned once later by Tom Kernan for his ministration: "—That was a decent young chap, that medical fellow, he said. Only for him—" and "Decent young fellow, he seemed" (160). Reasonably, this evanescent character described only by his clothing has been likened to the man in the macintosh who flits through *Ulysses*.

Other affinities with *Ulysses* include a hated Catholic ("Irish Jew") moneylender, not Reuben J. Dodd, and four of the five principal characters, who recur many times throughout it: Kernan, Cunningham, Jack

Power, and "Charley" M'Coy; even M'Coy's practice of permanently borrowing suitcases ostensibly for his wife's concert tours, of which Bloom is wary in *Ulysses,* is mentioned (160). Of the five principals only the latecomer to Kernan's bedside, Fogarty, his grocer, to whom he owes money, who alone brings a gift ("special whiskey"), and who is least in error during their discussion of Church history and doctrine, is absent from (he is mentioned in) *Ulysses.* In fact, Molly brings up Kernan's mishap and then the other three characters.[1] As the role in the novel of those principal characters of the story suggests, like "The Dead," and more than its thematic complement "The Sisters" or than "Ivy Day in the Committee Room," "Grace" portrays Dublin society.

The put-upon Mrs. Kernan, and the barmen and constable who figure briefly in the opening scene, have their places in that portrayal; but the young man in the cycling suit is an anomaly. He is well-spoken, polite, articulate. And—pointedly unlike the people of that society—resourceful.

The occupants of the pub merely surround the supine Kernan, whose mouth is making "A dark medal of blood" on the floor, trying to identify him. Frightened by his condition, the manager calls a constable; and this comic archetype, complete to "lick[ing] the lead of his pencil," also only tries to ascertain, in order to record in his "small book," the identity of the still bleeding and untouched Kernan. At that point in the story, "A young man in a cycling-suit cleared his way through the ring of bystanders," and "promptly" tends the injured man. (One result is that the constable "knelt down also to help," temporarily suspending his inquiry.) Thereafter, the "young man" helps Power extricate Kernan from the pub and from the constable, deflecting Power's question to Kernan about "this mess" with the urbanely discreet "The gentleman fell down the stairs," and politely twice declines Kernan's offer of a drink; then, Kernan on his way home in his friend's care, he disappears from the story (151–53).

Unlike the ubiquitous man in the macintosh in *Ulysses,* the young man in the cycling-suit advances the action of the story. Strictly speaking, he was not needed. The constable could have been the resourceful minister to Kernan's injury, and Power could still have effected his rescue from the police: the constable and Power could have advanced the action without the young man. But Joyce made this evanescent character indispensable in "Grace."

His appearing to minister to Kernan has been seen as true divine grace, in a story which proceeds to a satirical treatment of the quest for a specious grace by Kernan's group and the other middle-class Dubliners ("gentlemen," 172) at Father Purdon's retreat. He may even himself have been granted what the Maynooth Catechism calls "actual grace": "Sanctifying grace . . . makes the soul holy and pleasing to God. . . . Actual grace . . . helps us to do good works."[2] Moreover, the young man's dress could suggest that he travels because he is a ministering angel.[3]

But he is not presented as a divine traveler, or even a traveling mortal: the story contains no mention of a cycle, not even when he leaves it, on the (Grafton) street outside the pub; after being introduced by age and dress, he is twice called "the young man in the cycling-suit," then three times "the young man," never a cyclist; and above all, no other story in *Dubliners* has any hint of supernatural intervention. An alternative functional explanation of his brief presence in the story would take his simple humane action, so contrasted to the inept or callous behavior of both the "gentlemen" in the Dublin pub and those who serve them, to be part of its satire of the representative Dublin characters' understanding of and aspiration to grace.

This explains the young man's brief presence in the story, and his resourcefulness. But it does not explain his age, or the striking contrast in manners and speech between him and its "gentlemen." Its first words are "Two gentlemen"; Kernan's companions who abandoned him also are "two gentlemen"; Power, who has emerged "from the far end of the bar," is "a tall agile gentleman"; all the men at the retreat are "gentlemen"; even Kernan, although he is dead drunk and "his clothes were smeared with the filth and ooze of the floor on which he had lain, face downwards" (150), is one: the constable and the pub manager "agreed that the gentleman must have missed his footing" (153).

The well-spoken, well-mannered, considerate, and resourceful "young man," whose "The gentleman fell down the stairs" is a tonal key, is insistently distinguished from all the Dublin Catholic "gentlemen" whose class is satirized in the story. And although there is no evidence he is a "medical fellow," he ministers to Kernan knowledgeably. None of the few known (all familiar) photographs before he departed Dublin of James A. Joyce, B.A., and briefly medical student, show him in anything remotely like a cycling suit;[4] but in that young man in the story he began exactly a year after his departure, the author may have been making a ghostly cameo appearance in his volume. It would be a totally gratuitous but inconspicuous, and therefore private and playful, expression of his autobiographical inclination, a kind of fictional signature, in the story that was the last of *Dubliners* until he eventually wrote and added "The Dead." As is the boy's unnecessarily special sensitivity to language and sound in "The Sisters," the evanescent young man in "Grace" could be a functional element of the story with a gratuitous autobiographical dimension.

In 1907, with the final pages of "The Dead," the author implanted his own life experience unequivocally at the end of his volume. That long story or short novel, as long as the first six stories of *Dubliners*, follows "The Sisters" transformed in demonstrating that a major component of James Joyce's evolution to maturity was his increasingly implicating his life in his art, with success: his beginning to develop a poetics of autobiography. The gestation of "The Dead" began about half a year after he transformed "The Sisters," and the writing extended over the latter part of the next half year (*James Joyce,* p. 244; Gabler, "Introduction," pp. 9–10). With it, he moved from implanting a personal trait in a character, and a possible ghost cameo appearance, to making an event in his private life the central element of a long and densely peopled story. The scope, the texture, the nuanced depiction of human frailty and human virtue, even the cumulative narrative rhythm, of "The Dead," affirm its creator's maturity as a writer when he completed it and promptly turned to reattempting his autobiographical novel.

Joyce gave Gabriel Conroy many of his own deeds and experiences, as *James Joyce* points out (pp. 246–47); but until its last pages his story serves to consummate the "chapter" of "moral history" for which he "chose Dublin." Most overtly, it elaborates with qualified benevolence his portrayal in *Dubliners* of middle-class Dublin society, showing, as he wrote to Stanislaus before beginning work on it (and as Gabriel points out more pompously during his dinner-table speech), Dublin's "hospitality, [which] so far as I can see does not exist elsewhere in Europe" (*Letters* II, p. 164). Another dimension of the story, embodied in the exchanges between Gabriel and Miss Ivors, is the nationalism controversy among intellectuals. A third, extending from the maid's resentment of her vulnerability to male exploitation in its opening pages to Gabriel's initial selfishness toward Gretta in its closing ones, is a subtle, but pointed and effective, feminism. Its feminist dimension includes elements like: the fact that all Gabriel's relationships in (and all specified before) the story are (failures) with women; the independent, impressive character of Molly Ivors; and Kate Morkan's complaint about the injustice to her sister Julia done by Pope Leo X's excluding women from Church choirs.

However, these broader, more general dimensions of "The Dead" resolve at its close into Gabriel's climactic confrontation with Gretta's account of herself and "poor Michael Furey." In other words, the story builds through aspects of "moral history" to its protagonist's experience of and response to an experience Joyce himself had had; young Nora's dead young man even had been named Michael (*James Joyce,* p. 243; his surname, Bodkin, is a common Galway one).

In the fourth chapter, the point was made that the origin in Joyce's own life of the triangle crucial to "The Dead" cannot be positively designated either its subject, or strictly its source, material a writer pragmatically uses. The prosperous, conventional, and committed Dubliner Gabriel Conroy clearly no more recalls Joyce himself in circumstances and character than does James Duffy, although he is (eventually) a much more attractive human being than Duffy. The problem arises because Gabriel does not represent Joyce. For that reason, the question whether the origin of Gabriel's triangle in Joyce's own experience of and (presumably) response to his own triangle makes Joyce's strictly the historical source of the otherwise non-autobiographical Gabriel's fictional experience and response (a writer's material), or instead its subject (constituting the triangle in "The Dead" as autobiographical in the full rhetorical sense), reduces to choice in defining *autobiographical fiction:* to repeat the point made in the fourth chapter, either answer is a tautology. Hence, the question is moot.

What is germane is that Joyce created art out of his life by making not just functional but instrumental, in a story about a character very different from himself, his own deeply personal, private experience. How central to his conception of autobiographical art is the deeply personal will be discussed in the following pages. A reasonable inference here is that with the situation in which he placed the Dubliner Gabriel Conroy, he enabled himself to return to making fiction significantly out of himself.

The progression from a minor integration into successful fiction of his autobiographical motive (in "The Sisters" transformed), through his more ambitious integration of it some months later (in the eventual final story of *Dubliners*), points to the mature writer's successive full expressions of that motive in *A Portrait of the Artist as a Young Man, Ulysses,* and *Finnegans Wake.* His achievement in "The Dead" brought him to the initial development of his mature poetics of autobiography in the *Portrait;* perhaps it even gave him the confidence to reattempt, in the weeks after he completed "The Dead," the autobiographical novel that would embody the initial development of his mature poetics.

How far he developed that poetics is shown in the *Wake.* Its first full paragraph traces time back through events that had "not yet" occurred, among them an unnamed Jacob's tricking his blind father into giving him his brother Esau's birthright, and before that in time the rainbow following the flood, with a drunken Noah ("pa's malt") and two of his three sons, called "Jhem or Shen." Japheth is unmentioned; and Ham and Shem are invoked not with the cumulative *and* but the alternative *or*: the suggestion is that "Jhem" and "Shen" are two names for one individual. Moreover, this is a late development.[5] Joyce seems to have planted at the very beginning of the *Wake*, as it neared completion, explicit identification of himself with that one of the antagonistic twin sons of the Earwickers, brothers whom he presented the biblical Jacob (Heb. *Yaäcob*, Eng. *James*) and Jacob's gullible brother as anticipating.

The elaborately mutated opposition of Shem and Shaun in the *Wake* is akin to that of the satirized bohemian and bourgeois contraries in W. S. Gilbert's *Patience*, "ultra-poetical, super-aesthetical" and "steady and stolid-y, jolly Bank-holiday" young men, the disgraceful "fleshly" poet Bunthorne and respectable reformed poet Grosvenor; surprisingly, neither operetta nor characters is mentioned.[6] Both brothers' names are derivative. Sean the Post marries the title character in Dion Boucicault's *Arrah-na-Pogue* (Arrah is the Irish form of Nora). More interesting, and more central to the poetics of autobiography in the *Wake*, a white-collar criminal of the middle nineteenth century, a prodigious forger named James (Townsend Savard or Townshend Saward) was called "Jim the Penman"; and a play and novel of that title exist. The reference at the end of the fifth part of I to "that odious and still today insufficiently malestimated notesnatcher . . . Shem the Penman" (125.21–23) originally had "Jim the Penman" (*First-Draft Version*, p. 89).

A principal source for Shaun, especially in early drafts, seems to be the writer's brother, (John) Stanislaus. Two alternative views of the historical sources for Shaun actually complement each other as informed and helpful. The *Third Census* lists "various of Joyce's enemies," not including Stanislaus (p. 262), and has an extensive account of Wyndham Lewis's presence in Shaun and the reasons for it (pp. 166–68). In *Joyce-Again's Wake: An Analysis of "Finnegans Wake"* (1965; Westport: Greenwood, 1975), the late Bernard Benstock argues for the primacy of Stanislaus, pointing out in a note that analogues to the Earwicker children Shem, Shaun, and Issy correspond to the three Daedalus children in *Stephen Hero*, Stephen, Maurice, and Isabel (pp. 216–21). What is especially relevant here is that the respectable Post incorporates a number of historical figures and, in contrast, his antagonist brother the egregious Penman is identified with a single particular historical writer—who considered those historical figures antagonists (Stanislaus so largely as critical of his major works; see, for example, *James Joyce*, pp. 576–79).

The "shadow extensions" of the Earwicker children Benstock cites in making his astute connection with *Stephen Hero* are "Jerry-Kevin-Isabel."[7] As the final part of its introductory material, the *Third Census* has a thirteen-page chart of such "extensions" of the five Earwickers whose title makes the point: "(WHO IS WHO WHEN) EVERYBODY IS SOMEBODY ELSE." Every reader recognizes the prominence in the book of analogues, mutations, exchanged or combined identities, and assumed roles, of the two brothers. In *The Mime of Mick, Nick and the Maggies*, for example, Glugg and Chuff are said to be played by fictional characters Mr. Seumas McQuillad and Mr. Sean O'Mailey, and Saint Michael/Chuff is "the fine frank fairhaired fellow . . . who wrestles for tophole with the bold bad bleak boy Glugg" (220. 14–15). Old Nick comes off badly again and again: "Lord Chuffy's sky sheraph and Glugg's got to swing" (226. 19–20). And the archetypal *Wake* pattern implicates the Joyce brothers directly when the seven RAYNBOW girls utter a long paean to "dear sweet Stainusless" (237–39).

If Shaun has other historical sources than Stanislaus, Joyce put himself in other characters than Shem and his mutations, especially in Earwicker.[8] However, the set-piece portrayal of Shem, the seventh section of I, which Joyce first drafted during the year after he had completed *Ulysses* (*James Joyce*, p. 794), is the principal example of his poetics of autobiography in the *Wake*.

The pair of short names in the declaration that begins it, "Shem is as short for Shemus as Jem is joky for Jacob," recalls the suggestion of a single individual with two names he had interjected in the first paragraph of the book ("Jhem or Shen"). Jem is "jokily" altered from (the short form of the English equivalent of German) Jacob, both to suggest an "Irished" pronunciation of Jim (Flann O'Brien uses that spelling for characters' names) and to make the name assonate with the short form of Seamus. Moreover, the analogy between *short* and *joky* (in "is as short for . . . as . . . is joky for") is false (joky). And integrating and fulfilling both jokinesses, Joyce's word invokes the Latin *jocax* (*jocosus* would be joky), source of the particular Anglo-Norman form of *joyeux* (perhaps Old French *joios*?), from which his family name is derived: among other names, his college newspaper *St. Stephen's* called him "the mystic Joacax." And as James is—like Jacob—from the Latin Jacobus, which is from the Hebrew Yaäcob, so the Irish Seamus is from the English James: they are the same name, and Jem's last name is Jocax/Joios.

The reason why Joyce asserts and repeats the identification of J(h)em and She(n)m is that his own history and nature are not merely the subject of his character's—that is to say, Shem is not just an autobiographical representation of himself. Instead, the character Shem in no way is not also—that is to say, simultaneously—the author, Jim: Shemus (Seamus) is "Sameas" (483.4), the categorical limit of fiction breached.

In the seventh section of I, Shem is attacked and ridiculed for Joyce's ambition: "if reams stood to reason . . . he would wipe alley english spooker . . . off the face of the erse" (178. 5–7), and Joyce's artistic practice: "he . . . skrevened nameless shamelessness about everybody ever he met . . . while all over . . . this rancid Shem stuff the evilsmeller . . . used to stipple endlessly inartistic portraits of himself" (182. 13–19).

Although the treatment is unusual, Joyce's giving a character both his ambition and his practice could be within the bounds of autobiographical fiction. However, Shem also is attacked and ridiculed for Joyce's actual major works: "his usylessly unreadable Blue Book of Eccles" (179.26–27); and of the *Wake* itself and the glosses on passages he wrote to friends to gain its acceptance by them: "explaining . . . with a meticulosity bordering on the insane, the various meanings of all the different foreign parts of speech he misused . . . until there was not a snoozer among them but was utterly undeceived . . . by the recital of the rigmarole" (173. 33–174. 4).

The section also catalogues all Joyce's publications, naming (as critics have pointed out) the stories of *Dubliners* in a paragraph (86–87); mentions numerous significant events in Joyce's career; and incorporates Stephen Dedalus. The identity of author and character, Joyce's presence literally *in propria persona*, is insisted on in such things as the "ABORTISEMENT" which begins "Jymes wishes to hear from wearers of abandoned female costumes" (181. 27–33).

If Joyce did write the "Dear Mister Germ's Choice" letter of February 9, 1929 (*Letters* III, pp. 187–88), he could have included from it a variant of "Shem" that also names himself, "Shame's Voice," because of the ribald mockery of himself in the section. Extreme, the mockery also is almost—but not quite—unrelenting. For it is persistently equivocated.

A difficulty I have when reading the *Wake*, accompanying my constant certainty that I am missing a lot of the meanings packed into individual words, is my frequent uncertainty about the immediate source of those words. The "odious . . . notesnatcher . . . Shem the Penman" quoted above could be Shem characterizing attacks on him as a plagiarist (forger), since it may be Shem who is giving the account of the "mamafesta" of ALP that the reference to Shem concludes. And in this section devoted to him, the words could be those of the *Wake* general narrator until near the end. For example, the past tense is used, and the second paragraph begins "Shem's bodily getup, it seems." But when near the end Shaun speaks as JUSTIUS, he says "no longer will I follow you obliquelike through the inspired form of the third person singular" (187. 28–30). So the portrait of Shem is more likely by his brother-antagonist. And that complicates the persistent equivocation in it.

At the conclusion of his direct final attack on Shem, JUSTIUS "points the deathbone and the quick are still" (193. 29). MERCIUS "(of hisself)" responds with an appeal for tolerance which becomes praise of their "wonderful mummy," ends with the words "Anna Livia," and is followed by "He lifts the lifewand and the dumb speak" (193. 31–195. 5). The "Anna Livia Plurabelle" section follows, demonstrating the writer's power to create, make the still quick, the dumb speak.

This exchange favoring Shem at the end of the section is anticipated by one just before it begins, at the end of the sixth section, so that the pair of exchanges bracket the portrayal of Shem in the section. The eleventh numbered question in the sixth section resolves into "if the fain shinner pegged you to shave his immartial ... shoul ... would you?" (149. 7–10). Shaun's answer is "No," followed by a justification twenty pages long (149–68). The sixth section ends almost immediately after this eleventh answer, with the final question and answer:

12. *Sacer esto?*
Answer: *Semus sumus*!

The question follows the form of a ritual malediction ("Let him be accursed?"), the answer in the plural with exclamation mark seems to signify "What else is appropriate for Shem?" However, as Shaun's condemnation is subverted in the bracketing complement at the end of the section about to begin, it is subverted here—by the primary meaning of *sacer* and the pun on *summus*. These few words just before the Shem section begins provide a tonal key to its persistent equivocations.

A few examples must suffice. The second paragraph, leading to the assertion "Shem was a sham and a low sham" at the beginning of the third (170. 25), describes "Shem's bodily getup, it seems," then says young Shem asked his brothers and sisters "when is a man not a man?" and after their unsatisfactory answers (some punning on titles dear to Joyce), declared to them "when he is a—yours till the rending of the rocks,—Sham." Shem may be not mere sham, but shamrock. And the paragraph beginning "Sniffer of carrion," which declares "it never stphruck your mudhead's obtundity ... that the more carrots you chop, the more turnips ... [through potatoes, onions, beef, mutton and herbs] the fiercer the fire and the longer your spoon and the harder you gruel with more grease to your elbow the merrier fumes your new Irish stew" (189.28–190.9), embodies the equivocation in (grace: power) "to your elbow," "merrier," and "new Irish stew." Hence, "Shamman" invokes "shaman," and the root charge that Shem the Penman is a sham because he is a forger equivocates the indictment by also signifying one who forges artifacts out of material, as Stephen declared his intention to do with language "in the smithy of my soul" at the end of the *Portrait*.

In one place, mockery actually shades into unequivocal advocacy. Following the destruction of *Dubliners* (Joyce believed the books were burned) by Roberts of Maunsel and their printer Falconer ("Robber and Mumsell, the pulpic dictators . . . and . . . their pastor Father Flammeus Falconer"), Shem "winged away . . . across the kathartic ocean . . . . You ask, in Sam Hill, how?" he chose exile (185. 1–8). The answer invokes two related historical occurrences: "The Scandal of *Ulysses*" (advertised by a broadside), the notorious review of it as scandalous because it failed to be truly titillating (as a sham), in *The Sporting Times or the Pink 'Un*, the salacious London bookmaking paper; and the praise of that review by Alfred Noyes before the Royal Society of Literature. The passage is an indignant attack on "our sporting times" and the "Anglican ordinal" who "may ever behold the brand of scarlet on the brow of her of Babylon and feel not the pink one in his own damned cheek" (8–13).

The Latin paragraph that follows this unequivocal expression of Joyce's outrage begins as praise "(*Primum opifex, altus prosator*)" that puns on *primus* and embraces both meanings of *altus*, then describing Shem's making indelible ink of his excrement, translates the second of the opening phrases together with "*in manum suam evacuavit*," parenthetically: "(highly prosy, crap in his hand, sorry!)" (14–18). Shem is once again mocked—until the last word. Its equivocation is in the impossibility of determining to, against, or even by, whom the boisterous "sorry!" is addressed. And in the previous sentences on that page, it is the destroyers of the Maunsel *Dubliners* edition who are treated mockingly, and outrage at something that happened to *Ulysses* is expressed without equivocation.

Competitive brothers, Shem and Shaun appropriate traits from each other; and they are complementary. One pair of opposed analogues for them that runs through the *Wake* is the paired images of tree (Shem/stem) and stone (Shaun/Stan). Tree and stone are operative paradigms for the brothers, corresponding, as they do, to Blake's Energy and Constraint. But the traditional values that attach to the two images cannot be discounted: as at the end of the Shem section, the brothers often are associated respectively with life and death, to Shem's advantage. Also to Shem's advantage is Shaun's bigotry, for example, his calling Shem "semisemitic" ("serendipitist"—a good word for the author of the *Wake*), and "Europasianised Afferyank" (191. 2–4).

The equivocal portrayal of Shem, subverting the antagonistic view of him with subtle vindication, is Joyce's assertion of author-ity; for in it he exculpates not just a fiction representing himself, but simultaneously also literally himself. Of his project, *The Reader's Guide to "Finnegans Wake"* declares: "Joyce was always composing portraits of himself, but most of them . . . are distanced and controlled by irony or other device. . . . The . . . chapter on Shem is little more than the author's apology and his boast" (p. 131). The very different appraisal in *Joyce-Again's Wake* of Joyce's assertion of author-ity is more responsive to it: "Joyce's comic treatment of Shem the Penman . . . [is] the three-dimensional mirror in which he must view his juxtaposition to the panorama [of "life . . . around him"] with equal objectivity. This allows Joyce to write a parody of himself and his artistic process with a detachment that is twice-removed" (p. 121).

Following the Latin paragraph about Shem's ink-making, Shaun quotes Shem as giving Whitman's reason ("I embrace multitudes") for writing about himself: "thereby, he said, reflecting from his own individual personal life . . . a dividual chaos . . . common to allflesh" (186. 2–5); and this is a real if secondary reason for James Joyce's autobiographical fiction. But with Shem Joyce subverted the very concept, by dissolving the distinction between fictional character and living author. In *Finnegans Wake*, his poetics of autobiography reached the end of its evolution in implosion.[9]

Its final entropic turn in *Finnegans Wake* is anticipated playfully in the last pages of *Ulysses*, when Molly, complaining about her menstruation, exclaims "O Jamesy let me up out of this pooh" (18.1128–29/p. 633). But *Ulysses* embodies the fullest development of his poetics before that turn. Its almost transcendent apogee was his composing the whole novel to have Bloom function for Stephen on June 16, 1904, as Nora Barnacle had begun to do for him on that date. In the text, he made Stephen its limited exponent and its example as well. He made Stephen in *Ulysses* both the exponent and the example of his poetics of autobiography through two linked elements: the substance of Stephen's lecture on Shakespeare to the Dublin literary figures in the National Library; and Stephen's personal and social circumstances as he delivers it.

Stephen's elaborate thesis about the autobiographical origin of Shakespeare's plays is full of flaws, as he privately admits—although his declaration to his auditors at its end, that he does not "believe your own theory" (9.1065–67/p. 175), is belied by his thoughts throughout, especially his compulsive need to present it (see, for example, 846–49/p. 170).

The source both of that need to present his thesis, and of his private motive for formulating it, is Stephen's wishful claim that by creating his work the (male, like Shakespeare—and himself) artist achieves radical autonomy: "being no more a son [Shakespeare] was and felt himself the father of all his race" (868–69/p. 171). Mulligan's immediate response to the asserted claim, "Himself his own father," articulates Stephen's point. Alone among his auditors, Mulligan is aware that Stephen is speaking about himself as well as Shakespeare, and addressing himself as well as them. Mulligan's pronoun is ambiguous, echoing his ambiguous pronoun when, in the first chapter of the novel, he tells Haines Stephen "proves by algebra that Hamlet's grandson is Shakespeare's grandfather and that he himself is the ghost of his own father." Hence: "What? Haines said, beginning to point at Stephen. He himself?" (1.555–58/p. 15).

Although his proposal that Shakespeare achieved autonomy through his art expresses Stephen's apparent central motive for his disquisition, its central thesis remains that Shakespeare's plays are essentially autobiography. He believes, however, that they are subtly so: Joyce has caused him to oppose the simplistic practice ("bad habit"), then newly in vogue, of searching in Shakespeare's plays for hints about details of his life; and Stephen opposes above all the specific belief, espoused energetically in the room by Best and Eglinton, that Hamlet is a self-portrait.

Stephen asserts Shakespeare represented himself not in the prince but in the murdered king and supplanted husband—and in other betrayed and banished figures in the plays. He states his central thesis about "the creation [Shakespeare] has piled up to hide him from himself" (475/p. 162) briefly just before Mulligan announces his presence in the room, then repeats it in his peroration. The passage is familiar:

> the theme of the false or the usurping or the adulterous brother or all three in one is . . . always with him. The note of banishment . . . sounds uninterruptedly from *The Two Gentlemen of Verona* onward till Prospero breaks his staff. . . . It doubles itself in the middle of his life, reflects itself in another, repeats itself. . . . But it was the original sin [of his brothers Richard and Edmund with his wife Ann] that darkened his understanding. . . . It is in infinite variety everywhere in the world he has created. . . . He laughed to free his mind from his mind's bondage. (997–1016/p. 174)

Stephen's thesis that Shakespeare was driven to autobiography plainly is not disinterested academic scholarship. His involvement is with the theory informing it: that Shakespeare thereby achieved the radical autonomy he himself craves. The explanation Stephen offers, G. J. Watson describes succinctly as "the art grows out of the life, and reflects back directly on that life," and calls "The central general meaning of his theory."[10]

Stephen's insistence in *Ulysses* on the reciprocal effect of Shakespeare's (that is, the artist's) life experience and art significantly glosses his own two complementary poetic efforts in the *Portrait,* both flawed precisely because he suppressed his life experience in composing them. Correspondingly, his insistence in *Ulysses* on that reciprocity contrasts with his ignoring the generative and informing role of the artist's life experience in his expatiations about the literary art when a couple of years younger, both in the *Portrait* and in its precursor and partial source.

The weaknesses of his disquisition about art to Lynch near the end of the *Portrait* have been discussed extensively by critics. Those of his essay (as Stephen Daedalus) in *Stephen Hero*, written "to define his own position for himself" (p. 76), are greater. For example, the conventional Aristotelian taxonomy there of lyric, epic, and drama as "three distinct natural kinds" (p. 77) of literature is significantly less impressive than the modernist account a decade later in the *Portrait* (used by the author for metafiction as autobiography), of a work "progressing" through two earlier states (distinguished by mostly the same words as in *Stephen Hero*) toward "dramatic" autonomy. The later Stephen seems to have benefited intellectually from the passage of time; however, although the much younger Joyce does so more blatantly than in the *Portrait* a decade later, he also distances himself—and when only a couple of years older than his Shelleyan young Hero—from Stephen Daedalus on art, for example in "When the poetic phenomenon is signalled in the heavens, exclaimed this heaven-ascending essayist" (p. 80).

Both versions of the younger Stephen share with the Stephen of *Ulysses* an expressive orientation toward literature. Dedalus's subject is "the phenomena of artistic conception, artistic gestation and artistic reproduction" (p. 182). The earlier Daedalus's project is described as "to establish the relations which must subsist between the literary image, the work of art itself, and that energy which had imagined and fashioned it, that centre of conscious, reacting, particular life, the artist." And he is said to affirm that "the artist who could disentangle the subtle soul of the ["literary"] image from its mesh of defining circumstances most exactly and re-embody it in artistic circumstances chosen as the most exact for its new office, he was the supreme artist" (pp. 77–78).

Absent from these expressive formulations by the two younger Stephens is the radically expressive insistence of Stephen in the National Library that "the supreme artist" not only "disentangle[s]" and "re-embod[ies]"—selects and transmutes, a conventional idea—but does so with himself. Moreover, against the crude fashionable autobiographical conception of his plays as incorporating historical facts about Shakespeare, Stephen proposes autobiography that is of the artist's most intimate inner self: the plays express (betray) Shakespeare's consciousness and life experience.

Joyce's own mature art does not eschew but precisely incorporates historical facts about Joyce. His fiction combines a mimetic ground of people, places, and events in his life with adaptation (such as Stephen's temperament, so different from that of "Sunny Jim"), invention (such as Stephen's meagre productivity), and objectification (authorial separation—such as the ironic play on Icarus in the *Portrait*). He adapts, invents, and objectifies on a ground of history to create the vehicle for his autobiography of consciousness and intimate life experience expressed as Stephen in the *Portrait* and *Ulysses*. I shall try to show later why Joyce withheld from Stephen in the *Portrait* Stephen's doctrine in *Ulysses* that the created work of "the supreme artist" is radically intimate inner autobiography. No one I know of has proposed that in *Ulysses* his young facsimile is not speaking for Joyce himself.[11] The reality—inevitably with Joyce—is more complicated; but Stephen's doctrine seems to be a central part of that reality.

Stephen's wishful claim—overtly about Shakespeare—that the artist can achieve existential autonomy through his art, is distinct from his doctrine of art as inner autobiography. He does not postulate with that claim of achieved autonomy what is currently called self-fashioning, which results from an act of will; such control by the artist would contradict Stephen's portrayal of him as compelled by his consciousness to create out of his inner experience. Stephen does not even postulate the artist's achievement of knowledge.

What his claim—his theory—proposes is that the artist achieves autonomy as a happy consequence of creating as he is compelled to do, because his involuntary creation enables him to reconcile himself with the world. Attempting "to hide him from himself" by his creation, Shakespeare instead, in Stephen's last words on him, "found in the world without as actual what was in his world within as possible" (1041–42/p. 175); hence, "We walk through ourselves, meeting robbers, ghosts . . . [other people/characters], but always meeting ourselves" (1044–46).

Because the personal (autobiographical) compulsion of "the supreme artist" has that happy consequence, Stephen's personal motive for giving his disquisition on Shakespeare does not compromise, but complements, his theory about the happy result of autobiographical art: Stephen is driven to a virtuoso rhetorical creation asserting that Shakespeare achieved autonomy by making his plays about his essential self because Stephen himself craves ("his mind's bondage") to achieve the autonomy he claims is possible.

The mature author of *Ulysses* may not have believed what in 1904 his facsimile Stephen fervently claims Shakespeare's involuntary autobiographical creation achieved for him: Stephen is very troubled that mid-June midday. Nevertheless, as has been said, Stephen's doctrine that Shakespeare was ("the supreme artist" is) radically autobiographical—expresses in his creation his own consciousness and life experience—seems to be a fundamental element of the mature Joyce's poetics of autobiography. And when not much older than Stephen he had attempted in *Stephen Hero*, and abandoned as failed, autobiographical art. Stephen is not yet an artist in *Ulysses*, but Joyce portrays him as understanding the symbiosis of a writer's life and work the young man has not yet been able to realize in practice, and when younger ignored in theory.

In the chapter, Joyce makes Stephen not only the articulate exponent of that fundamental element of his poetics of autobiography, but also the example of the poetics as a whole. He does so by way of the rude snubbing Stephen is subjected to in the course of his Shakespeare lecture, which was discussed in the first chapter. By way of that incident, he demonstrates the limitation of Stephen's doctrine when compared to his own poetics. For Stephen's account of Shakespeare's practice as autobiographer is only a partial description of Joyce's own practice. The younger Stephen, even in *Stephen Hero*, defined "supreme" art in terms of the artist. Now Stephen says that "supreme artist" in fact takes for his subject his own intimate inner life. But Stephen disdains the historical details of that artist's (Shakespeare's) life; and Joyce embraces those details of his own life as part of his subject. What is missing from Stephen's doctrine, for Joyce, is Stephen himself.

A few minutes into Stephen's lecture, in rapid succession the party "at [George] Moore's" and the departing AE/Russell's volume "of our younger poets' verses," are mentioned (274, 291/pp. 157–58); and Stephen has thoughts expressing his sense of rejection, and enjoins himself to "See this. Remember" and to "Listen."

As was pointed out, Joyce renders his facsimile's situation judiciously. He portrays the literary men as critical of but eager to hear Stephen's ideas. Moreover, he portrays Stephen as contemptuous of Lyster (for example, the first thing he does in the chapter is to "sneer" a rejoinder to Lyster's comments on Hamlet: 16–17/p. 151); yet when Stephen is snubbed, "The quaker librarian [the senior among those remaining] came from the leavetakers. Blushing, his mask" compliments the young man on "your views" (326–28/p. 158).

Nevertheless, as "The Holy Office" documents, when Stephen's age his creator and subject—a much more prolific poet—himself experienced Stephen's sense of rejection and isolation. And in Joyce's concrete example of his poetics of autobiography in the chapter Stephen, feeling rejected and isolated, less likens himself to Shakespeare than constructs Shakespeare in his own image. The thesis of his lecture to those who snub him is that rejection and isolation ("The note of banishment") is the pervasive autobiographical element in Shakespeare's plays. Just before making the full statement of his thesis in his peroration, Stephen thinks "I am tired of my voice, the voice of Esau," though he urges himself "On" (981–82/p. 174). And his injunctions to himself to "See this," "Remember," and "Listen," join with a declaration Joyce has him make less than two pages later to signify the etiology, and so the exemplary nature as autobiography, of the portrayed experience of that character in that chapter of James Joyce's novel: "So in the future, the sister of the past, I may see myself as I sit here now but by reflection from that which then I shall be" (383–85/p. 160).

Following the next chapter, which Joyce called "an *Entr'acte* for *Ulysses* in middle of book after 9th episode" (*Letters* I, p. 149), the narrative strategies in his novel and the situation begin simultaneously the changes in both that will continue until it ends. In this last of the first half of its chapters, Joyce makes Stephen simultaneously: serve (by his experience) as illustrative example of his origin in both the historical life and the intimate inner self of his creator when his age; and expound (in his lecture) the latter, inner, aspect of the poetics of autobiography thus exemplified. For, to adapt Stephen's phrase when speaking of the autobiographical "world" Shakespeare "created," the author of *Ulysses* is everywhere in the novel he created.

A rich instance of Joyce's presence occurs when, in Bella Cohen's brothel in Nighttown, Bloom's painful fantasy of gratefully witnessing with permission Molly's and Boylan's copulation coincides with the whispers and amusement among his and Stephen's companions, until Lynch points to and "Stephen and Bloom gaze in the mirror," where they see Shakespeare's "beardless" face "crowned by the reflection of the reindeer antlered hatrack in the hall" (15.3722–3824/pp. 459–63). In this memorable incident in the novel, beardless Bloom and Stephen unite in the image of the suffering victim of sexual betrayal Stephen has expounded and Bloom has joined. But the author himself is implicated as well: an artist like the one with whom Stephen explicitly identifies, Joyce also is Stephen's original, and a husband (and father) the age of Bloom. Even his late invention, and retrospective incorporation throughout, of the clamorous pseudo-absence critics call The Arranger, asserts at every occurrence—from playful mock headlines to hand-made musical notation—James Joyce's agency. His phantom surrogate, it (he/she?) serves to augment the pervasive presence in *Ulysses* of its author, whose poetics of autobiography causes his consciousness and life experience to invest not only his facsimile character and memorable incidents, but the texture of the novel and even its very plot.

His fiction about his facsimile character had not begun well. In the second chapter I suggested the reason why at twenty-three the young Joyce abandoned *Stephen Hero,* and devoted himself to completing his non-autobiographical volume of stories, was because he determined that in *Stephen Hero* he was not solving the problem of making autobiographical fiction "dramatic," "impersonalis[ing]" it, in Stephen's words to Lynch in the *Portrait* (186)—mentioned a few pages back—about the process undergone by a successful work of "literature, the highest and most spiritual art," from its first to its third and most finished state ("form"). And Joyce used those words of Stephen's to effect his own elegant metafictional history of the "progressing" of his novel portraying his young facsimile—during the ten years specified on its last page—from its "lyrical" origin in 1904, through the intermediate (and so unsatisfactory) "epical" state of *Stephen Hero,* to its achieved "form," in which achievement Stephen is saying more than Stephen knows.

In 1917, while *Ulysses* was in progress and three years after the *Portrait,* T. S. Eliot declared "the more perfect the artist, the more completely separate in him will be the man who suffers and the mind which creates." Joyce's poetics of autobiography also enjoins the separateness, a dialectic between the impulse to autobiography of "the supreme artist," and his awareness of the need to make—about himself—effective art. And if *Ulysses* is the apogee of its realization, he previously celebrated near the end of the *Portrait* the success in that novel of his poetics: James Joyce's achievement—for the first time—of a work about himself.

He celebrated his success in the very paragraph that contains, beginning in the sentences that embody, his esoteric autobiographical account of the ten-year "progress" of its writing. The paragraph is the climactic final one of young Stephen's disquisition about art. Joyce's celebration in the latter sentences of it, of his achievement with the *Portrait,* is illuminated by two contexts. The first juxtaposes what Stephen declares in those sentences about a writer's *personality,* against Eliot's positing in a seminal essay the relations of personality and poetry.[12] The second illuminating context is a historical connection Joyce makes, by way of what Stephen declares in them about a writer's *invisibility.*

The third and final part of "Tradition and the Individual Talent" is a single paragraph following Eliot's ringing declaration that poetry "is not the expression of personality, but an escape from personality." The paragraph asserts "The emotion of art is impersonal"—"has its life in the poem and not in the history of the poet," who learns how to achieve the "escape" partly by being conscious of her or his relation to the tradition (the subject of the first part of the essay). The second part begins, "The other aspect [other than the tradition] of this Impersonal theory of poetry is the relation of the poem to its author." Its second paragraph contains the clause about the "separate" man and mind. First Eliot makes his analogy between a poet's mind and the catalyst for a chemical reaction: the mind causes ("operate[s] upon"), but does not participate. Then he declares, "The mind of the poet . . . may partly or exclusively operate upon the experience of the man himself; but, the more perfect the artist, the more completely separate . . ."

In Stephen's account of three "forms"—the final paragraph of his disquisition—in which he is saying more than he knows about the *Portrait* itself, Joyce has him also anticipate by three years Eliot's classic modernist point about how the artist must deal with himself as a person to achieve an autonomous—by modernist definition, a successful—work:

> The simplest epical form is seen emerging out of lyrical literature when the . . . personality of the artist passes into the narration itself. . . . The dramatic form is reached when the vitality which has flowed and eddied round each person fills every person with such vital force that he or she assumes . . . aesthetic life. The personality of the artist . . . finally refines itself out of existence, impersonalises itself, so to speak. The esthetic image in the dramatic form is life purified in and reprojected from the human imagination.

Eliot allows for autobiographical poetry ("the experience of the man himself") by "the mind which creates," and created it frequently, of course. In contrast to Eliot, and to his slightly older self in *Ulysses*, Stephen does not allow for autobiographical fiction. The personality of the writer "refines itself out of existence" in the work by creating (as his word "dramatic" suggests) "each person . . . every person" in it. In other words, Joyce has made Stephen fail to consider the possibility of achieving an autobiographical novel like that in which he is speaking.

Stephen's impressive modernist anticipation of Eliot, through which his creator also provides in the *Portrait* the history of the making of the *Portrait*, simultaneously begins, in a stunning compound autobiographical ventriloquy, Joyce's celebration of his achievement in the *Portrait*. And Stephen's ignoring autobiographical fiction is necessary to Joyce's celebration. For it, he confutes not only what Stephen says anticipating Eliot about the writer's personality, but also what Stephen goes on to say, in the famous conclusion of the paragraph and of his disquisition on art, about the writer's invisibility:

> . . . and reprojected from the human imagination. The mystery of aesthetic like that of material creation is accomplished. The artist, like the God of the creation, remains within or behind or beyond or above his handiwork, invisible, refined out of existence, indifferent, paring his fingernails.

The historical second illuminating context for Stephen's famous final words about art is the connection they invoke. Joyce has Stephen echo a well-known passage in a letter by the writer usually identified, with Ibsen, as one of Joyce's models. On March 18, 1857, Flaubert wrote about *Madame Bovary* to Mademoiselle Leroyer de Chantepie:

> It is a *totally fictitious* story; it contains none of my feelings and no details from my own life. The illusion of truth (if there is one) comes, on the contrary, from the book's impersonality [*de* l'impersonnalité *de l'oeuvre*]. It is one of my principles that a writer should not be his own theme [*qu'il ne faut pas* s'écrire]. An artist must be in his work like God in creation, invisible and all-powerful [*comme Dieu dans la création, invisible et tout-puissant*].[13]

Stephen follows Flaubert in invoking God and the creation not as casual simile (trope), but as precise analogy, as specifying the proper relation of writer and work: God is not the subject character of His creation. Stephen's Flaubertian conception of the writer's invisibility, "like the God of the creation," is expressed in his repeated phrase, "refines itself . . . refined out of existence" (in the writer's "handiwork").

Joyce's counterstatement through Stephen's words occurs in two elements of Stephen's assertion. One is his respective Flaubertian synonyms for the two variants of his repeated phrase. "Refines itself out of existence" is followed by "impersonalises itself" (*"l'impersonnalité"*); "refined . . ." is preceded by (Flaubert's) "invisible." Both Stephen's synonyms for the repeated phrase in this first element can be understood as congruent with it; but both subtly contradict it: an impersonalized—camouflaged or occulted—personality and especially an invisible one, strictly speaking, continue to exist in a writer's "handiwork." Hence, in the second element of Stephen's assertion Joyce confutes, his rhetorical flourish, "The artist . . . remains within or behind or beyond or above his handiwork," the first two alternatives signify something very different from the other two—signify immanence, presence, not transcendence. And of course the fact of the *Portrait* affirms the immanent Joyce's ventriloquy within Stephen's words.

Whatever Flaubert's general importance to Joyce, respecting autobiographical fiction he was Stephen's model only. Invoking Flaubert on the writer's proper relation to her or his work by having Stephen echo the French master's words, Joyce does so not merely to confute his young man, but to declare his triumph over the emphatic proscription by the great master. Thus does he celebrate his successful creation of his invisible presence as himself in the *Portrait*. The art his poetics of autobiography enacted in that novel only begins with the most overt manifestation of his poetics, young Stephen Dedalus. It includes the record of the earlier stages of the novel unknowingly articulated by that facsimile character. And the art achieved by his poetics is consummated by the declaration he made in the *Portrait* specifying his achievement by it of the autobiography proscribed by Flaubert.

The inversely chronological and brief sketch of the evolution of Joyce's poetics of autobiography that has occupied most of this final chapter began with its terminal entropy in *Finnegans Wake*. Its genesis, I proposed earlier in the chapter, was in Joyce's successful implanting of his own deeply private personal experience into "The Dead." The autobiographical material he implanted is almost precisely the kind he was to have his facsimile describe eleven years later (*James Joyce*, p. 442), in Stephen's lecture on Shakespeare. And that limited instance in which he made his fiction out of an intimate occurrence seems to have inaugurated James Joyce's successful, in Stephen's words, "walk through ourselves." It followed his having the boy of "The Sisters" gratuitously share with Stephen Dedalus, in his revision of the story, his own sensitivity to language. His equally early possible ghostly cameo appearance in "Grace" would be young Joyce playfully expressing his autobiographical impulse. Both these harbingers of his poetics of autobiography occurred less than two years after his liberating and empowering union with Nora Barnacle.

His transforming the boy of "The Sisters" from ineffectual witness in 1904 then 1905, to effective subject of the story in 1906, anticipated his transforming his autobiographical facsimile Stephen from ineffectual *picaro* of *Stephen Hero* in 1904–05, to effective subject of the *Portrait* in 1907–14. Between those strikingly similar transformations occurred only his confirmation of achieved maturity as a writer, "The Dead," the rich story into which he successfully incorporated for the first time his own consciousness and intimate life experience. The similarity of that pair of transformations—his transforming the story of a Dublin boy he wrote, and the autobiographical partial novel he started, when twenty-two—is significant. It bespeaks the connection between the earlier of them, his metamorphosis of "The Sisters" out of its mediocre predecessor in 1906, and what he began to develop immediately after that achieved metamorphosis. For with "The Dead," he began to develop the poetics that was a major component in the mature James Joyce's mastery of the making of literature—as the young writer's brother put it on the day he launched the enterprise in earnest, his twenty-second birthday—"about himself." And that poetics extended well beyond creating his facsimile Stephen Dedalus. Its manifestations include the elegant metafictional history, and metafictional celebration, of his achievement with the *Portrait*. And it pervades the texture and subsumes the very plot of *Ulysses*.

Finally, the point must be made that he transcended his impulse to autobiography. Stephen is not the subject of *Ulysses*, but its second person: the story in the novel of Stephen's delivery from his perilous condition, which Joyce compounds with elegant covert autobiography implanted in the plot, is only ancillary to the story in the novel of the man who is the agent of that delivery. And in *Finnegans Wake*, Shem/Jim is even less central. Having succeeded in making art about his life, Joyce went on to decenter himself in his art, to assert in a transcendent gesture of modesty the writer's relation to the world that is her or his subject.

# Appendix: Lawrence and Autobiography

The purpose of this appendix is to substantiate the point made about young Lawrence in the introduction: that the fictional practice he developed was the pragmatic exploiting of his life experience in his art.

\* \* \*

In his first work of fiction and first major artistic undertaking, the novel I called in the introduction the functional antecedent to *Sons and Lovers*, Lawrence's practice was precisely what has been generally assumed by critics as well as biographers about his life and art. He was painting, had written only a few poems and no stories, when he began *The White Peacock* in the spring of 1906 (Joyce began *Stephen Hero* when a year and a half older, at twenty-two). He finished the first draft a little over a year later, then did two more drafts and a final revision, with substantive changes in the plot and the portrayal of characters in all but the revision; he completed the novel and selected its title at the end of four years.[1]

In Lawrence's more precocious first novel, the autobiographical assertion is more muted than is Joyce's "Hero" in his. Cyril Beardsall witnesses and narrates the story of others, primarily of the deterioration of his boyhood friend, the vigorous and sensual George Saxton. The other two principal characters are Cyril's sister Lettie and George's sister Emily. In the revised novel: George loses Lettie to the mine-owner's son and marries another; the intellectual and romantic relationship between Cyril and Emily declines and she marries another. Educated, cosmopolitan, and jejune, Cyril lives in London and marries no one.

*The White Peacock* almost totally ignores in its idyllic setting both the physical and social reality of Lawrence's mining town; and in the relationship of Cyril with Emily it ignores his psychological reality: true erotic love for his mother imposing on any ostensible romantic attachment. But its verisimilitude includes a number of incidents reported by Jessie Chambers, and extends even to the retained names of people on whom a number of characters are based.[2] In a series of letters about the novel to a friend, Blanche Jennings, Lawrence called Cyril "a young fool . . . and a frightful bore" (*Letters* I, p. 61), and wrote "I hate the fellow. . . . I *will* leave out Cyril" (p. 69); nevertheless, its personal verisimilitude—Cyril—survived.

George and the others may be Cyril's subject, but in an important sense *The White Peacock* is about the experience of its people and places by its narrator and center of consciousness. And abundant evidence exists of how simply autobiographical Lawrence was in his first work of fiction. In the first letter to Jennings cited above, he called himself a mutual friend's "own real actual Cyril"; in another, he wrote "I . . . have married Lettie [to] Leslie and George [to] Meg, and Emily to a stranger and myself to nobody" (p. 141). Jessie Chambers, whom he calls "Emily" in a letter cited (p. 68), though he cautions she is "not like" Emily, reports that to her complaint about an added character, the mature sensual gamekeeper Annable, whose relationship with Cyril is slight but analogous to that of George, Lawrence "shook his head decisively, and said: 'He *has* to be there. Don't you see why? He makes a sort of balance. Otherwise it's too much one thing, too much *me*,' and grinned" (*Personal Record*, p. 117).

A striking instance of the naive literalism of young Lawrence's autobiographical practice is a twelve-word sentence Chambers reports he wrote to her as the major revision of "Nethermere" was nearing completion; it is conjecturally dated July 1909: "Do you mind if, *in the novel*, I make Emily marry Tom?"[3] More significant of his practice than the question, which actually poses a departure from autobiography, is his emphasis. And that simultaneously invokes the decade-long relationship between them, portrayed in *The White Peacock*, exfoliated in *Sons and Lovers*, anatomized in her *D. H. Lawrence: A Personal Record*, and discussed in scores of letters he wrote to her (surviving only in passages quoted in her book) and to others, and in many of the memoir-biographies and every one of the formal biographies of him.

Chambers writes that Lawrence did the "rounding-off of the story" to which she attributes his twelve-word question "during our brief moment of harmony" (*Personal Record*, p. 119). "Moment" is a reasonable metaphor for a few months in a decade, around the summer of 1909. The nature of the disharmony that followed is an element of Lawrence's life of special relevance to his fictional practice; and the following five paragraphs (with summary documentation) recapitulate it, in its context.

On January 29, 1908, her twenty-first birthday, Chambers received from Lawrence a letter declaring that he loves "the deep spirit within" her: "Look, you are a nun, I give you what I would give a holy nun. So you must let me marry a woman I can kiss and embrace and make the mother of my children" (I, pp. 42–43). He left home to begin teaching in Croydon, nine miles south of London, in October. During the following summer of "harmony," she urged him to send his poems to Ford Madox Hueffer's *English Review,* which he, she, and her family all read and admired. He refused, but invited her to "Send whatever you like"; Hueffer accepted them promptly (and later helped him place the just-completed *White Peacock,* still as "Nethermere"). He wrote in an "Autobiographical Sketch" the year before he died, "The girl had launched me . . . on my literary career." On November 27, she visited him at Croydon; he was to take her the next day to lunch with Hueffer and Violet Hunt. According to her account of the night of her arrival, he kept her into the early morning discussing his personal life. He had no money and could not marry, so "I think I shall ask some girl if she will give me . . . [sic] that . . . [sic] without marriage." In response to his question, she replied she would not consider it "wrong": "But it would be very difficult." He then declared "Well, I think I shall ask *her.*"[4]

*She* was a colleague with whom he was romantically involved, and whom he took Chambers to meet, Agnes Holt. (Biographers infer reasonably from the evidence that Holt declined his request.) Less than a month later, on Christmas Eve, he visited Chambers at her home, Haggs Farm, walked with her and, according to a more explicit account than the one she published, declared that "he had found out—he had really loved me all along and not realised it. He had told Agnes Holt that he belonged to me, everything was over between them." They kissed and embraced for a while, then he asked her to become his lover, told her that marriage "for the moment is inexpedient" unless they were unable to avoid her becoming pregnant. Worthen describes the event in *The Early Years* and comments, "Only Jessie's devotion to him could ever have brought her to accept him." A month later, on January 28, 1910, in a long letter to Jennings, Lawrence denigrated Holt and wrote of himself and Chambers: "We have fine, mad little scenes . . . so strange, after ten years, and I had hardly kissed her all that time. . . . She is coming to me for a week-end soon. . . . What would my people and hers say? . . . they will not know." He then asked her to burn the letter, asked "Do *you* think I am wrong?" and in the final paragraph mentioned "a new girl [Helen Corke]—a girl who *interests* me." He did not mention Louisa Burrows, a fellow college student, with whom he had been corresponding for years, and to whom he would become engaged on December 3, six days before his mother's death (December 9, 1910).[5]

The relationship Lawrence imposed on Chambers Christmas Eve, 1909, presumably the cause of their lost brief "harmony," produced by her account fewer than five assignations, and at least one letter to her (in March 1910), declaring "You have done me great good, my dear," and expressing the desire "to touch and to hold" her. He ended their affair on September 1, the day after announcing his intention and his distress about it in a letter to Corke, his current love interest; to another correspondent, he had five weeks before called himself "a bit of a pig" because of his treatment (use) of Chambers. Thereafter, he attempted with some success to restore the old intellectual relationship with her; her mother and sister May (Holbrook) also remained friendly, but her father, she reports, "managed to convey a sense of forfeited regard that Lawrence felt acutely." "Lawrence passed the manuscript to me as he wrote" his work in progress ("Paul Morel," before he responded to a "skit" his future wife wrote about the novel entitled "Paul Morel, or His Mother's Darling," with the more descriptive title *Sons and Lovers*). And Chambers saw him, although infrequently, during 1911, a year that ended with his life-threatening pneumonia, and during which he was engaged to Louisa Burrows. (He broke the engagement on February 4, 1912, and eloped with Frieda May 3.)[6]

When Lawrence resolved the relationship between his facsimile Paul Morel and Miriam Leivers in the last half-dozen pages of *Sons and Lovers* almost two years after he broke with Chambers: Miriam proposes they marry; Paul declines "to give life to her by denying his own," but asks her to become his lover again, as she had been for a short time (in Chapter VII, "The Test on Miriam"); and she calmly and decisively refuses: it is one instance of her difference from Chambers, which some critics have noted. The construction by "E.T." (Chambers's pseudonym is the initials of the protagonist of an eponymous novel she wrote) of her relationship with Lawrence makes no distinction between Paul Morel and his creator "in the treatment of Miriam": "[Lawrence's] mother had to be supreme, and for the sake of that supremacy every disloyalty was permissible." In her memoir-biography, Helen Corke adopts Chambers's view that Miriam was "her image as reflected in the distorting mirror of Mrs. Lawrence's mind."[7]

But even Chambers's history itself, against which she persistently measures Lawrence's fiction, is not without its (understandable) bias. Her sister May's extensive account of the relationship differs from hers in some respects. (Sagar observes "Often it is nearer to Lawrence's [he means in *Sons and Lovers*] than to Jessie's.") She wrote of Burrows as attracting Lawrence only physically, yet they exchanged criticism and collaborated as writers: Lawrence's first fiction published in the *English Review* was the story satirizing the propertied class, "Goose Fair," his rewriting of one of Burrows's stories; they shared the payment for it. Chambers's assertion "He wrote to me almost every week from Croydon" is believable (it cannot be confirmed, since she destroyed his letters); but he wrote many personal letters from there, almost all to women. Her feeling for him made her victim to his normal—that is, youthfully frenetic—erotic drive. His for her seems to have shared the common denominator of all those for women (other than his mother) articulated in the letter in which he announced to Jennings that he had "married . . . myself to nobody": "I do *not* believe in love: mon Dieu, I don't, not for me: I never could believe in anything I cannot experience or, which is the equivalent[,] 'imagine.'" His experience was to change. He had had affairs with one or more married women; but he labored with intense conviction to persuade his lover Frieda Weekley to leave her children for elopement into exile with him.[8]

My reason for recounting these details of young Lawrence's life is the different ways they are manifested in his fiction. Those different manifestations document his developing conception of the relationship of a writer's life and art. A sequence of five details of his life is most important. The first is his epistolary question, believed to date from July 1909 because he saw her in early August (when she told him the *English Review* had accepted his poems), did Chambers "mind if *in the novel,* I make Emily marry Tom?" The second is his November 1 letter to Jennings announcing his sending "up to Mr Hueffer" the third draft of "Nethermere," in which "I have married . . . Emily to a stranger and myself to nobody." The third is his conversation with Chambers during the early hours of November 28 about seeking "that." The central fourth in the sequence is his December 24 visit to the Chambers family home, Haggs Farm, during which he privately proclaimed to Chambers his love for her and extracted her agreement to sexual intercourse with contraception, without marriage. The last is his break with her on August 1, 1910, following seven months of occasional assignations.

※　※　※

The story pattern described briefly in the introduction, and said there to be embodied in "A Modern Lover" and "The Soiled Rose"/"The Shades of Spring," implicates the five central details of Lawrence's involvement with Chambers set out above, beginning with his question did she "mind" if he turned Emily in his first novel from Cyril, to "marry Tom."

The scene that introduces the "stranger" Tom Renshaw to *The White Peacock* occurs in the next-to-last of its short chapters. In the final chapter, "after a bad attack of delirium tremens, George had been sent . . . to stay with Emily" at her and her farmer husband Tom's home; there Cyril, newly returned from France and apprised of George's condition, visits his old friend from London; and he finds Emily happy in marriage and "six months gone with child" (pp. 402–3, 406). When he visits George from London two years earlier, in the previous chapter, first "I wandered around Nethermere, which had now forgotten me," though "I had fondly believed it cherished me in memory." Then, at George's house, the maid tells him his bibulous friend is still in bed and the family at church; "But Miss Saxton is in," though "She's engaged":

> I found my old sweetheart sitting in a low chair by the fire, a man standing on the hearthrug pulling his mustache. . . .
> "Let me introduce you. Mr Renshaw, Cyril. Tom, you know who it is. . . . I am going to marry Tom in three weeks' time," she said, laughing. . . .
> "Why didn't you tell me?" I asked.
> "Why didn't you ask me?" she retorted, arching her brows. . . .
> "It is such a joke," she said. "To think you should feel cross, now, when it is—how long is it ago—?"
> "I will not count up," said I.

Then Emily says "I am a thousand years older than he," laughing, "Just as you are centuries older than I," and compares the two men ("'And I was never gentle, was I?' I said") (pp. 387–91).

The story pattern combines this invented episode at the end of *The White Peacock*, of the London intellectual being confronted by the young woman and her "stranger," with the central detail of the enumerated five in Lawrence's own life experience, which occurred two months after he had sent off the completed manuscript of the novel: his visiting the model for Emily at the Chambers farm on Christmas Eve 1909, and persuading her to accept an alteration which was distinctly not a reversal of what he had done "*in the novel.*" In that story pattern, a young man who has moved himself from a lower to a higher class, and from rural circumstances to London or Oxbridge, returns after years away to the place of his early life, in order to visit at her family's farm home the young woman with whom he had had an intense celibate emotional involvement, in which he more than she had influenced the other's cultural and intellectual development. Although he is more developed than she ("older than I"), like him she is far more so than her new man, parents, and brothers (she is the only female child). He is confronted by her new man, eager to marry her; she is confronted by him, her former soul-mate, attempting to reassert his hold over her.

It is clear from Lawrence's mature work that the story pattern he initiated as late invention for his first novel enabled him, when young, to begin embodying in fiction one aspect of the increasingly complex (and sometimes contradictory) "unitary inner vision" of the mature "hedgehog" as "artist-philosopher": D. H. Lawrence's dualistic metaphysics/cosmology ("The Infinite is two-fold") as it concerns the individual person. His pattern confronts an (educated, middle-class) embodiment of mind/spirit with one (often rural) of body/sense; its two men are precursors of the dozens of juxtaposed characters in his fiction, each embodying in extreme form either "blood-consciousness" or "ego-consciousness."[9]

Elements of the pattern crop up in his fiction. Three instances already mentioned are: the story "Second Best," cited by Harry T. Moore, which omits the confronting London intellectual; Paul's failed proposition to Miriam at the end of *Sons and Lovers*, which occurs at a chance meeting, and lacks a rival; and the story "The Horse-Dealer's Daughter," which also echoes the Mayhews of *The White Peacock*, children of a bankrupt and dead horse-dealer, with the sister keeping house for her coarse brothers. Lawrence's story has the plebeian brothers and the visiting intellectual (the local doctor, friend to one brother); but Mabel is no more sophisticated than her brothers, and farmwoman and intellectual come together.

But it is the sequence of stories fully delineating the pattern, "A Modern Lover" and the two versions he made of a story with a gamekeeper, "The Soiled Rose" and its successor "The Shades of Spring," that documents Lawrence's development as a creator of fiction out of his personal history. Minor details the stories share from Lawrence's life experience are a specific upholstered chair in the Chambers's parlor, the intellectual's having painted when young, and his active correspondence with the young woman; and they share other details, such as the rival men's walking alone together. However, their most important shared element, the pattern itself, in fact functions inversely.

The story pattern has the effect of distinguishing the whole sequence radically both from its origin in the introjection to the end of *The White Peacock* of a "stranger," and from its other source, the historical relationship of Lawrence and Chambers; for the stories involve three characters introduced in rapid succession, to create and resolve a single situation. Moreover, the pattern enables each sequent story to be itself distinct. The dynamics of the evolving relationship, as they confront one another, of different, invented characters in each, causes the stories to differ as the characters do.

In the first sequent story, "A Modern Lover," Mersham's consciousness asserts its centrality after the first fourteen words: "The old, wide way, forsaken and grown over with grass, used not to be so bad. The farm traffic from Coney Grey must have cut it up" (*Stories*, p. 1). And the ironic treatment of him begins in the opening paragraphs, by portraying the character trait Lawrence reproved in later fiction, and radically typified in "The Lovely Lady." Mersham is an emotional and vital parasite, who likens himself romantically to a bird that in fact is, in large measure, a scavenger:

> his soul had moved among the faces ["in the large city in the south"] ... flying low over the faces of the multitude like a sea-gull over the waters, stooping now and again, and taking a fragment of life ... to feed upon. Of many people, his friends, he had asked that they would kindle again the smouldering embers of their experience; he had blown the low fires gently with his breath, and had leaned his face towards their glow. ...
>
> Surely, surely somebody could give him enough of the philtre of life to stop the craving which tortured him. (p. 2)

His snobbery is presented early, but as a vehicle for the portrayal of nasty rudeness as a "react[ion]" to awkwardness. The farm family has invited him to dinner:

> The conversation went haltingly.... Then there grew an acute, fine feeling of discord. Mersham, particularly sensitive, reacted.... He used English that was exquisitely accurate, pronounced with the Southern accent, very different from the heavily-sounded speech of the home folk. His nicety contrasted the more with their rough, country habit. They became shy and awkward.... He kept up all the time a brilliant tea-talk that they failed to appreciate. (p. 5)

His egotism ("particularly sensitive," "exquisitely accurate," "brilliant") is reinforced in the parlor, not only by his observation that Vickers seemed in his photo "a bit of a clown beside the radiant, subtle photos of himself," but also because after "He guessed they had kept up the holly and mistletoe for him," Muriel's first words when she joins him are "Why didn't you tell me you were coming?" Lawrence's juxtaposition here of Mersham's presumption and its refutation points to the most significant character flaw for the story of this egotistical, snobbish, emotionally and vitally parasitic, modern lover: the London intellectual's ignorance. It is an ignorance about life and about love, which he reveals in the course of the story, both toward the other human being he believes he understands profoundly and—most dramatically—respecting himself.

His ignorance with Muriel is a lack of elementary human awareness. As Lawrence himself did, he has visited the farm during the Christmas season to induce his partner in a long celibate relationship to make it erotic. He begins his suit by saying "you have something to give me" and "We've got to begin again—you and me—living together, see? Not speculating and poetising together—see?" She has difficulty understanding "the change in you," and he explains, "I used to shrink from the thought of having to [*sic*] kiss you, didn't I? . . . Well—I don't, now" (his claim contradicts "He had not kissed her" when he arrived; p. 3). He continues by professing "with slow, brutal candour" his ignorance of what love is, "but—I think you're beautiful—and we know each other so well," when Tom Vickers is heard arriving (pp. 9–10). The section of the story ends with his question before Vickers joins them, "And how firmly is he fixed?" (p. 11); and the next section (IV) answers it in his favor. As that section is about to end, he uses the phrase "my virgin modesty":

> Tom gave a guffaw at the notion of Mersham's virgin modesty. Muriel's brow wrinkled with irritation, and she turned from her sweetheart to look in the fire.

### V

> Mersham . . . was sure that Vickers would not count seriously in Muriel's movement towards himself. (p. 15)

His certainty seems confirmed when, "talking well," he declares with Vickers present, "you are washed with the whitest fire of life—when you take a woman you love—and understand." His effect on her follows: "Perhaps Mersham did not know what he was doing. Yet his whole talk lifted Muriel as in a net . . . and placed her in his arms, to breathe his thin, rare atmosphere. She . . . believed implicitly he could not do wrong" (p. 17). The sympathetic portrayal of Muriel's vulnerability to Mersham functions in the plot, of course; it also expands the story beyond satire of that "modern" lover.

Having bested Vickers in what appears to Muriel a true love triangle, Mersham outwaits him. When Vickers departs, "Muriel did not kiss him goodbye" or accompany him to the barn for his bicycle; Mersham does accompany him and see him off. Then he returns to the house and asks her to "come a little way with me": "She answered him with her eyes.... She smiled brightly at her lover, like a child, as she pinned on her hat" (p. 19). This is the situation between them when, in the dark, he resumes his suit with a kiss and talk about her body. He says "we would marry tomorrow—but I can't keep myself," and asks her to "come to me"; they embrace and kiss again, and then she has a revelation about her "lover" who "could not do wrong" which Lawrence discloses as much by her silence and subsequent very "quiet" speech as by what she says:

> For a while they stood ... clasped together. Then he heard her voice, muffled in his shoulder, saying:
> "But—but you know—it's much harder for the woman—it means something so different for a woman."

The intellectual understands Muriel's point about sexual intercourse without emotional commitment to be a reference to the danger of pregnancy, and thereby causes the revelation marked by her silence:

> "One can be wise," he answered slowly and gently. "One need not blunder into calamities."
> She was silent for a time. Then she spoke again.
> "Yes, but—if it should be—you see—I couldn't bear it."
> He let her go, and they drew apart....
> "If—if!" he exclaimed sharply, so that she shrank with a little fear. "There need be no ifs—need there?"
> "I don't know," she replied reproachfully, very quietly.
> "If I say so—" he said, angry with her mistrust....
> "But you *do* know," he exclaimed. "I have given you books—"
> "Yes, but—"
> "But what?" He was getting really angry.

And she ceases to humor him by discussing his subject, contraception, returns to her original point: "It's so different for a woman—you don't know" (p. 21). Her last phrase resonates. His exploitative project, his bullying, his unjustified indignation, all pale in egregiousness beside this superior being's failure of comprehension. It is extreme enough to have an element of pathos.

Muriel promptly concludes the exchange by supplementing her repeated objection with a new impediment to an affair: the need for secrecy, "creeping together in the dark." For "It was as if she had tipped over the fine vessel that held the wine of his desire, and had emptied him of all his vitality. He had played a difficult, deeply-moving part all night, and now . . . there was left only weariness" (pp. 21–22). And "A Modern Lover" ends shortly with Mersham's imperative "you'll write to me. Good-bye" and Muriel's failure to respond.

The autobiographical materials in the story are apparent. Muriel has been given Chambers's point about women that was made in the early hours of November 28, 1909, when Lawrence announced to her his intention of asking "*her*" for "that." Mersham has been given Lawrence's exploitative December 24 suit to Chambers. If the story revealed no more about him, he could be called an autobiographical character as a projection—nastier, stupider, less erotically vigorous, and so forth than his creator. The psychologically oriented could use the story as a projective test that reveals, through Lawrence's exaggerations of them, tendencies in himself he found disturbing. But the question whether or not a character so flawed can be "his autobiographical hero Cyril Mersham" (*Early Years*, p. 210) is obviated decisively by the nature of the other ignorance Lawrence gave that character—ignorance respecting himself—about life and love. The quoted passage of his having "played a . . . part all night" (recalling "having to kiss you") and "the fine vessel that held the wine of his desire" indicates that ignorance.

Early in Mersham's exchange with Muriel, she looks at his (single) "photo, which had been called the portrait of an intellectual prig, but which was really that of a sensitive, alert, exquisite boy" (p. 8); and the third epithet in the series surprises, even in her idealizing. Moreover, although "modesty" scarcely suits him, he is "virgin": "He had looked for many women to wake his love, but he had been always disappointed. So he had kept himself virtuous, and waited. Now he would wait no longer" (p. 11). An incident early in the story, insignificant by itself especially in view of its final comparison, is a harbinger. He is observing the washing-up of Muriel's miner brothers, "two well-built lads" (p. 3): "Now they stood wiping themselves, the fire-light bright and rosy on their fine torsos, their heavy arms swelling and sinking with life. . . . Benjamin, the younger, leaned his breast to the warmth, and threw back his head, showing his teeth in a voluptuous little smile. Mersham watched them, as he had watched the peewits and the sunset" (p. 5).

The revelation about Mersham's sexual preference, so crucial to understanding him and the story, occurs when he accompanies Vickers to the barn. As they enter it, Vickers guides him past an overhead beam, then lights his bicycle lamp and pumps up a tire:

> "Thanks," said [Mersham] gratefully. He knew the position of the beam to an inch . . . but he allowed Vickers to guide him past it. He rather enjoyed being taken into Tom's protection.
>
> Vickers carefully struck a match, bowing over the ruddy core of light and illuminating himself like some beautiful lantern in the midst of the high darkness of the barn. . . . his face, gathering all the light on its ruddy beauty, seemed luminous and wonderful. . . .
>
> "After all," said Mersham, "he's very beautiful; she's a fool to give him up."
>
> Tom shut the lamp with a snap, and carefully crushed the match under his foot. Then he took the pump from the bicycle, and crouched on his heels in the dimness, inflating the tyre. The swift, unerring, untiring stroke of the pump, the light balance and the fine elastic adjustment of the man's body to his movements pleased Mersham.
>
> "She could have," he was saying to himself, "some glorious hours with this man—yet she'd rather have me, because I can make her sad and set her wondering." (p. 18)

In Vickers's using the cylindrical bicycle pump Lawrence has created as blatant an image as the repeated stroking of the thick tail of the dead fox by March, the robust woman in "The Fox." But Mersham is conspicuously oblivious to what his response to that and Vickers as a whole signifies about him, just as he is with the washing young miners. An earlier title for the story, "The Virtuous" (*Letters* I, p. 275 n. 5), does not just play ironically on the mildly vicious Mersham's having "kept himself virtuous," but also points to his ignorance about himself.

When Vickers departs, "'*Sic transit*,' he murmured—meaning Tom Vickers, and beautiful lustihood that is unconscious like a blossom"; and walking with Muriel he angers her by talking about the *gloria mundi* with no more self-awareness:

> "Think how splendid and fierce he'd be—"
>
> "Why do you talk about him?" she said.
>
> "Because I want you to know what you're losing—and you won't till you see him in my terms. He is very desirable—I should choose him in preference to me—for myself." (pp. 19–20)

Cyril Mersham's ignorance of his sexual preference is only the most striking of the many negative traits Lawrence gave the subject character of his story "A Modern Lover." Had he created in Mersham one of the ostensible "versions of Lawrence's continual rewriting of his autobiography," his calumny against himself would have included, as was said in the introduction, charging himself with unawareness of things about himself he points out.

John Adderley Syson, the London intellectual of Lawrence's story pattern in "The Soiled Rose" and "The Shades of Spring," is a totally different character from the miscreant Cyril Mersham. Syson also is—as Mersham is—very different from Lawrence himself. Lawrence's extrapolation from his own life experience in such different directions when creating Mersham and Syson exemplifies his pragmatic use of it as he wrote each of the sequent stories. Being a less singular character than Mersham, Syson less discourages psychologically oriented treatment of him as expressing Lawrence's concern about tendencies in, or aspects of, himself. But for the reasons given in Mersham's case, such treatment would be beside the point, which is that once again Lawrence is using his life experience pragmatically as material for a fictional character very unlike himself, not invoking it to make himself the implicit subject of a fictional facsimile.

He is using the life experience of a self significantly younger than when he wrote its first version, "The Soiled Rose"; that youthful Lawrence provides the attitude—which is central in the story—of the mature Cambridge-educated London gentleman toward the woman on the farm to whom Syson is returning almost a decade after he left home. While Mersham propositions the woman of his past celibate relationship, just as Lawrence did, Syson's design on Hilda Millership is in "The Soiled Rose" primarily, and in "The Shades of Spring" totally, platonic: his attitude toward her is that Lawrence expressed three years before he wrote "The Soiled Rose," in his birthday letter to Chambers declaring (in her rendition), "Look, you are a nun. I give you what I would give a holy nun"; Chambers may have recalled Lawrence's precise word, for it occurs at a key point in the story. According to her, young "Lawrence... insisted with equal force that he and I must never marry and also that we must never part" (*Personal Record*, p. 141).

Lawrence begins his story which treats Syson's—his own youthful—conception of his partner in the long celibate relationship, by confronting him with the gamekeeper, Arthur Pilbeam, who declares his fully romantic and committed involvement with Millership, and who is confounded when Syson reveals he is married. For Syson is a married man, which also distinguishes him significantly from the Lawrence who drafted the story in December 1911; he had ended his liaison with Chambers, would end his engagement to Burrows shortly after leaving his sickbed, and had not met his future wife.

The story portrays Syson's learning he no longer can perpetuate his association with Millership, and that it was based on his misconception of her. Its four titles, "The Harassed Angel" (briefly "Rose"), "The Soiled Rose," "The Dead Rose," and "The Shades of Spring," reflect changes while Lawrence was writing and revising in what he called its "philosophy." "Harassed" describes objectively Syson's confronting the intimately involved Millership with his expectation. "Soiled" is turned to Syson, expressing his new understanding of a Millership who has chosen erotic love. "Dead," temporarily given the revised story, shifts the reference of "Rose" from Millership herself to Syson's debunked idealization of a woman who actually is full-blooded and, in the revision, independent and powerful. The eventual title exploits the evocative descriptions of nature in the spring throughout the story, as well as punningly signifying its twenty-nine-year-old principals.

An effective addition to "The Shades of Spring" both invokes its penultimate, and connects the two referents of its eventual, title. Unlike Mersham, and of course unlike Lawrence, who had no rival and who left Chambers, Syson experiences a grievous loss when Millership—at first regretfully and in the revision resolutely—supplants their celibate relationship with her new erotic one. Suffering near the end of the story, he thinks of a mortally wounded knight in a poem by William Morris, lying in a chapel "while day after day the coloured sunlight dipped from the painted window across the chancel" (*Stories* I, p. 210): the brightly colored window behind a chancel would be a rose window. Hence, the next sentence is "He knew now it had never been true, that which was between him and her, not for a moment."

But most of the alterations between the first published version of "The Soiled Rose" (*Forum* 43 [1913], 324–40) and the finished "The Shades of Spring" are to the two principals themselves, especially Millership. The nature descriptions and other expository passages were given slight stylistic revisions. Pilbeam was dignified; aside from dropped class markers, for example, his "almost feminine" mouth became "rather soft," and Syson's observation, "The man was certainly a bully," was dropped (325). The class divide in the farm family's reference to "dinner" and Syson's to "lunch" was made more explicit: "'You call it lunch, don't you?' asked the eldest son, almost ironical. He had once been an intimate friend of this young man" (p. 201), replaced a "sneered" exclamation in response to Syson's word (329). Regarding the principals themselves: complications in Syson's celibate attitude toward Millership (331–32) were eliminated; and on almost every page she was made more dignified, independent, and impressive.

For example, a paragraph that follows his erotic impulses toward her in the original version, when she is showing him apple buds, continues, "Watching his face, she laughed. He was dumb and stupid, and at bottom afraid. If he were going to fall in love with this old lover . . . then it would be a love that would invade many lives and lay them waste" (331–32). In the revision, in which throughout no erotic feeling for her is aroused in him, and she has absolutely no desire for him or even regret at losing him, the passage reads:

> Watching his face, her eyes went hard. She saw the scales were fallen from him, and at last he was going to see her as she was. It was the thing she had most dreaded in the past, and most needed, for her soul's sake. Now he was going to see her as she was. He would not love her, and he would know he never could have loved her. The old illusion gone, they were strangers, crude and entire. But he would give her her due—she would have her due from him. (p. 204)

Astutely, Sagar quotes this passage to illustrate the change marriage had made in Lawrence, and comments, "This is prose . . . which became possible for Lawrence only as, with Frieda's help, he learned . . . to understand and respect 'the living, striving *she*' in a woman" (*Life into Art*, p. 26; Sagar quotes from *Letters* II, p. 151).

A writer's development is a biographical fact; but it is not autobiographical fiction. Syson does not share Lawrence's personal development; and Lawrence's alteration of Millership in his revision of "A Soiled Rose," reasonably attributed to his experience of marriage, is even more significant of the remoteness of Syson and Syson's situation from any form of autobiographical projection than is (either the original or revised) Syson himself. At the end of "The Shades of Spring": she is indifferent to the departing Syson; she puts Pilbeam off about marriage ("What more would you have, by being married?"); when Pilbeam leaves her she looks "over the sunny country," her domain; and regarding corresponding, she and Syson have had an exchange:

"We drop our correspondence, Hilda?"
"Why need we?" she asked.
The two men stood at a loss.
"*Is* there no need?" said Syson.
"It is as you will," she said.

That exchange, and her remark that follows, chiding him about "*our* wild oats—we never sowed any," causes Syson to be "startled to see his young love, his nun, his Botticelli angel, so revealed" (pp. 209–11).

The change in Millership from the end of "The Soiled Rose" is clear. There: Syson mentions corresponding not with her but, correctly, with Pilbeam, if at all; she laments losing him; she tells Pilbeam "indulgent, but slightly bitter" they will marry ("He has gone quite out of my life—I don't know what I should do without you"); yet when Pilbeam leaves her she looks neither over the country nor even after Pilbeam, but "south . . . toward London, far away" (339–40).

In his revision of "The Soiled Rose," Lawrence made Millership its most impressive character and its dominant figure, and so increased the remoteness of his story about Syson from his own life experience involving Chambers. But even before he did so, Syson was too great an extrapolation from himself to exemplify anything but Lawrence's pragmatic use, as material, of his life experience.

The characterized differences between the shallow egotist and the morally sensitive idealist are apparent; a principal related difference is that the thoughtful Syson learns in the course of his story that he has been deluding himself, and the arrogant Mersham remains ignorant at the end of his. Lawrence used the same autobiographical material in creating their differences. Moreover, the ways he used it illustrate his attitude toward a writer's life experience and fiction.

Where Mersham treats the farm family at table with contempt, Syson realizes they believe he considers himself "too refined" to accept the invitation to eat with them, and "winced at the imputation" (p. 201). In the farmhouse parlor, Mersham regards "the little gilt-blazed water-colours that he hated so much because he had done them in his 'teens, and nothing is so hateful as the self one has left" (p. 6). Syson's "youthful water-colours on the wall no longer made him grin; he remembered how fervently he had tried to paint for her, twelve years before" (p. 203). Syson's attitude toward his youthful paintings is more normal than Mersham's and so, in the absence of specific evidence, one who chooses might surmise a greater similarity between it and Lawrence's own: the surmised connection to a writer who painted all his life would be insignificant, even if true. And of course, the relations of both men with the farm family are totally unlike Lawrence's with the Chamberses.

Another differently treated similarity between the characters may have originated not in Lawrence's life experience, but with his writing "A Modern Lover." To an admiring Muriel, Mersham says, "No, if you pull your flowers to pieces, and find how they pollinate, and where are the ovaries, you don't go in blind ecstasies over to them. But they mean more to you" (p. 20). And when Syson, shown her bower in the keeper's hut, asks Millership:

> "You think we might"—he glanced at the hut—"have been like this—you and I?"
> She shook her head.
> "You! No; never! You plucked a thing and looked at it till you found out all you wanted to know about it, then you threw it away," she said. (p. 207)

A boast by "the Lawrentian hero" admiringly received by the woman in one story is a great reproach made by the woman to "the Lawrentian hero" in the other. This differently repeated, apparently invented element in the sequence of stories has the same status as the repeated invented other man ("stranger") in the story pattern itself, and the same status as Lawrence's repeated use, radically extrapolated in different directions, of elements of his own life experience: as material for the making not of autobiographical fiction, but of fiction whose subject is other than a surrogate of the author.

Two points about the story pattern Lawrence used for his very different stories about very different characters should be made. The first concerns its formal nature, the other its historical verisimilitude. Superficially, the pattern is an instance of probably one of the oldest story types in human culture, the love triangle. Lawrence used the triangle frequently in his fiction. To cite two of his most well-known stories: the title character in "The Prussian Officer" is driven to the abuse that moves the plot because of the orderly's love for his fiancée; in "The Fox," the young man kills the small woman who keeps house and so secures her robust mate for himself. Both stories oppose homosexual and heterosexual love, and thereby embody the author's comment on the alternatives. The love triangle is an excellent vehicle (exploited even by Hollywood) for confronting the individual at its apex with choices of value, culture, ideology, and so forth: it was an obvious resource for so ideological and homiletic a writer as Lawrence. However, the story pattern Lawrence used resembles a love triangle only superficially. Even the novels and stories that only partly adhere to it share with the sequent stories that embody it, the fact that the woman does not have (as she has in, for example, *Chatterley*) the power to choose between two men. Hence, Syson in "The Soiled Rose" and "The Shades of Spring" is married; and Mersham in "A Modern Lover" will not be.

As the situation in the story pattern derives partly from Lawrence's experience, so both intellectual young men derive partly from Lawrence himself. I hope I have shown how much the excessive weight given to his having been the historical source of those characters occludes reading the stories. But he made other significant departures from historical verisimilitude. Probably the most obvious is that pointed to in his summer 1909 question to Chambers: there was no other man in her life. Almost as striking is the disparity between the plebeian farm families in the stories and the Chamberses of The Haggs. Their literary interest has been mentioned; a number of the children were Lawrence's peers culturally, members of his intellectual circle. Jessie herself, also a teacher, and the writer of stories—one of which Garnett saw and recommended to the *English Review* (*Croydon Years,* pp. 31–32)—and a novel, is not readily distinguishable from the writing teacher in a London suburb. Worthen entitles a brief discussion of Lawrence's alteration of the reality "The Haggs as Myth" (*Early Years,* pp. 246–48).

Correspondingly, Lawrence's relationship with the farm family, as was mentioned earlier, was wholly unlike that of the men in the stories. His association with the Chamberses was continuous and intimate, except for Mr. Chambers's disaffection. Not only did he see Chambers herself repeatedly, even when resident at Croydon and after their physical intimacy, but he visited the family often and corresponded and vacationed with some of them. While seeking a teaching post after finishing at the University of Nottingham, he "spent much of his time at the farm, helping with the work," May Holbrook writes. "He endeared himself to all my family" (*Composite Biography* III, pp. 610, 602). And (like Mersham's in "A Modern Lover") his photograph "occupied the place of honor" in the Chambers parlor (*Early Years,* p. 227). A little over a year before his death, he wrote to the youngest Chambers, David, a member of the faculty at Nottingham, about his visits to the family farm, declaring in part, "Whatever I forget, I shall never forget The Haggs—I loved it so. I loved to come to you all.... Tell your mother I never forget, no matter where life carries us.... Oh I'd love to be nineteen again, and coming up through the Warren and catching the first glimpse of the buildings," and concluding,

"I am somewhere still the same Bert who rushed with such joy to the Haggs" (*Letters* VII, p. 618). The "myth" he wrought in his story pattern, respecting both the Chambers family and his attitude toward them, is one more instance of his creation of true fiction out of personal history. The sequent stories themselves show how thorough was his subversion of autobiography.

\* \* \*

The first of the sequent stories was not published until a posthumous volume of early fiction given its name, *A Modern Lover* (London: Secker, 1934). Apparently in response to one of a series of questions about Lawrence's early stories, Chambers wrote to Delavenay "*A Modern Lover* D.H.L. showed me in December 1909" (*L'homme* II, p. 694). However, Delavenay comments on Chambers's account of the Christmas Eve meeting, "*Cette discussion se reflète, déformé*" in the story (*L'homme* II, p. 703; also I, p. 97); and its composition is dated January 1910 in *Early Years* (p. 473). Whether Cyril Mersham's proposition to Muriel (no last name) anticipates or "*reflète*" Lawrence's to Chambers has more interest than importance; that is not the case with the original state of "A Modern Lover." For if the title character in the published story was created almost half a year before Lawrence began work on the lost first draft of "Paul Morel," his pragmatic use of his life experience began that early.

Critics have speculated that the extant version is a revision. In the passage quoted from above, Delavenay writes parenthetically, "*Semble avoir été récrit en 1911.*" And in a long note in *The Short Fiction of D. H. Lawrence,* Janice Hubbard Harris refers to Delavenay's point about the Christmas Eve meeting, and writes:

> No manuscripts of the 1909 version are known to exist.... Identical to the published text, [an extant holograph manuscript] is probably Lawrence's 1912 revision. That it is not Lawrence's original 1909 story is clear from Jessie Chambers's remarks: "'A Modern Lover' D.H.L. showed me in December 1909. That was the first and quite different version; I'm sure he never intended it to be published" (Ibid., 694). Lawrence does not mention the tale in gathering and revising his tales in 1913 and 1914. (p. 262 n. 17)

Harris's assertion during her discussion of the story, "Lawrence revised it in 1912 with the intention of publishing it" (p. 38), seems to contradict the final sentence of her long note. And the letter she cites as evidence of "Lawrence's 1912 revision" supports her sentence more than her surmise.

Written to Garnett about "The Soiled Rose" on "8th March 1912," it contains a paragraph that declares, "I enclose a story I wrote three [sic] years back, and had forgotten. It is on the same theme . . .—it is really curious. But before it was ever submitted to a publisher, I would like thoroughly to revise it" (*Letters* I, pp. 372–73).

Finally, Chambers's assertion about a "first and quite different version" also does not indicate he ever revised "A Modern Lover," since her second version is "The Soiled Rose." The passage quoted by Delavenay continues after the excerpt in Harris's note, "The 'Rose' business is rather puzzling. . . . The theme [of an earlier poem] was a rose (though not soiled) and was obviously a reference to me."

Although it is always possible Lawrence revised the story he wrote the winter of 1909–10 and never published, there is no evidence he did so; and the last sentence quoted from his letter to Garnett indicates he did not publish because he did not revise. Moreover, internal evidence suggests he did not; for example, two photos of Mersham on the mantelpiece become a single photo a page later (*Stories* I, pp. 7, 8). His achievement in the coolly pragmatic use of his life experience for art in "A Modern Lover" is impressive if it dates from 1912. But it is more so if his "curious" story dates, as the evidence indicates, from the time of that experience, more than two years earlier in his development.

The history of "The Soiled Rose" and its successor is well documented. He drafted the story almost exactly two years after "A Modern Lover," during the latter part of December 1911, while still "in bed" from his double pneumonia (I, pp. 343, 553), probably as "The Harassed Angel" (see *Early Years*, p. 475). He fixed on "The Soiled Rose" before publication in March 1912 in the *Forum* (New York, with London distribution). In May, his publisher Secker's *Blue Review* printed a version that eliminated class markers (such as the dropped *g*) from the dialogue of the gamekeeper and improved clarity, among other light revisions. He revised the story into "The Shades of Spring" with the initial title "The Dead Rose" more than two years later, in July 1914, for his volume *The Prussian Officer*, and in October made final revisions in proof (*Calendar*, pp. 52, 53, 54–55). Hence, "A Modern Lover," "The Soiled Rose" and "The Shades of Spring" all are separated by two years or more.

Until recent decades, critics tended to ignore this sequence of stories using the same pattern; the introduction mentioned that Moore relates "The Shades of Spring" to "*White Peacock* and *Sons and Lovers* material," but cites "A Modern Lover" only later, in passing (*Life and Works*, pp. 97–98, 105). Recent critics who do discuss the sequent stories tend to treat them as a group "explor[ing] Lawrence's relationship with Jessie Chambers" (*Short Fiction*, p. 36), and even as one story, "A Modern Lover" having been "completely rewr[itten]," then revised (*Life into Art*, p. 18; *History, Ideology, and Fiction*, p. 16). It seems evident that the stories are neither connected nor autobiographical: they do not share a single implicit subject, the author's own life experience. Instead, Lawrence wrote two fundamentally different stories, in which he extrapolated the strikingly different central character of each from himself, then significantly changed the second story.

Aspects of an author's life may be said roughly to include, in order of diminishing possibility of verification: circumstances (environment); overt acts; experiences; temperament (personality); character; consciousness. It is not like simplistic biographical surmises to consider that Mersham and Syson may well not just draw on Lawrence's circumstances, acts, and experiences, but also embody *his perception of* tendencies in his character. Moreover, any (different) tendencies he perceived and drew on for Mersham and Syson (respectively) probably would have existed. In that case, both his perception and the tendencies are autobiographical material for his fictional characters. But the probable existence—and/or use by Lawrence for his characters—of those different tendencies does not affect my contention; for it does not make the fictional men embodying them implicit representations of their creator. Because they are radical extrapolations, of different tendencies in Lawrence, Mersham and Syson exemplify not an autobiographical project but a method for making fiction.

Writers who use autobiographical material almost always extrapolate from it, of course. The crux of critical disagreement is the extent here—hence, the result here—of extrapolation: the status of Lawrence's life in these stories related to it. Beginning with the earliest recent critic already cited, Delavenay (1969) compares the stories as *"un 'cycle de Jessie,'"* in which he identifies Lawrence and Chambers as Syson and Mersham, Miriam and Hilda. Hence, "*Syson (Lawrence) cite pour Hilda (Miriam)*" and, after he has discussed "A Modern Lover," "*Ici* [in "The Soiled Rose"] *Lawrence s'appelle* Syson, *Jessie devient* Hilda"; moreover, both men are examples of Lawrence's own "*snobisme*" toward "*ses amis d'autrefois*" (*L'homme* I, pp. 143, 70 n. 26, 109; see also pp. 78, 97–99, 108, 144, 158, 160, 178).

Holderness (1982) relates Lawrence to "the specific cultural movement of the 1890s," and declares: "A single illustration will suffice here to make the connection, to show how significant Aestheticism was for Lawrence. . . . *A Modern Lover* . . . is an earlier version of the story *The Shades of*

*Spring*, published in 1913 [*sic*]. The story in both versions is obviously based on personal experience.... The young man, Cyril ... is evidently in the full flower of an aesthetic phase" (*History, Ideology, and Fiction*, pp. 15–16).

After presenting evidence for Mersham's aestheticism as manifest proof of (the implicit subject) Lawrence's, he turns to "The later story, [which] though much altered, retains the same structure of feeling" (p. 18).

Harris (1984) names as "the Jessie Chambers stories" "'A Modern Lover,' 'Second Best,' and 'The Soiled Rose'/'The Shades of Spring.'" She then makes, although she qualifies it, an observation that significantly distinguishes her reading of the stories from the previously cited recent ones: "In the ... trio, the intellectual hero is occasionally viewed with irony, but in none of the early versions is that irony consistent." She writes perceptively of "the Lawrentian character" in "A Modern Lover":

> Cyril Mersham, the tale's hero, is frequently designated by himself and the narrator as sensitive, passionate, intelligent....
>
> The scenes, however, imply a less complimentary view of Cyril and his relationship to Muriel. Told that he has a wonderful nonchalance, we see him fairly humming with tension. His inability to imagine Muriel's feelings demonstrates little intelligence or sensitivity. If he is passionate, it is a theoretical passion. Never does Cyril touch Muriel [*sic*], want her. Also, Cyril sees her new friend Vickers in the most condescending of terms. ... one sees little of [Vickers] apart from Cyril's view and thus has a hard time judging. However, this may be conscious irony on Lawrence's part. Sagar notes the juxtaposition of Cyril's looking up at Orion as he wades through the mud in the opening scene. Cyril's last name, Mersham (mere sham), may be a tip-off. (*Short Fiction*, pp. 36–38)

Harris's discussion of the two versions of the other story delineates an imputed progressive "gain in perspective over 'A Modern Lover'" (pp. 41–43). But it seems reasonable to infer that her complaint of Lawrence's insufficient "perspective" especially on "Cyril's view" of Vickers, following her sound perceptions about other aspects of his complex portrayal of Mersham, illustrates the hermeneutic grid created by the popular critical assumption about the relation between his life and his art expressed in her phrase "the Lawrentian character."

Her reference to "Sagar" is to an essay published before the three recent books surveyed, "'The Best I Have Known': D. H. Lawrence's 'A Modern

Lover' and 'The Shades of Spring'" (*Studies in Short Fiction* 4 [1966–67], 143–51). The phrase in its title is from a letter Lawrence wrote to Helen Corke a year after his elopement with Frieda, in which he criticizes "the philosophy which is in *The Soiled Rose*" as inadequate: "You see, I have been married for this last year" (*Letters* I, p. 553). Sagar's interest in Lawrence's Life is not just as the source of, but also as the cause of development in, his Art. And he uses the letter as a context in autobiography for the change marriage had made, to explain—as mentioned above—the differences he shows Lawrence crafted when revising the story into "The Shades of Spring." Incorporated with modifications into *Life into Art* (1985), his discussion of the sequent stories associated with "the difficulties of [Lawrence's] relationship with Chambers" (*Life into Art,* p. 16), is the most comprehensive known to me, and also seems the most valuable, especially in its treatment of "The Soiled Rose"/"The Shades of Spring." It begins by identifying the fictional source of the story pattern, and declaring an interest in the pattern similar to mine, then promptly initiates a comparison of its instances as different versions of the same creative endeavor:

> Towards the end of *The White Peacock* there occurs an episode which Lawrence was later to use as a short story, 'A Modern Lover.' . . . In December 1911, he completely rewrote it as 'The Soiled Rose'; and in July 1914 revised it and changed the title to 'The Shades of Spring.' These four versions of essentially the same material provide a paradigm of Lawrence's remarkable development over those five years. . . .
> . . . What the episode [of Cyril confronted by Emily and her suitor Tom] cries out for is irony, but irony is stylistically impossible within the restricted personal focus, the self-consciousness, that Lawrence's first person narrative involves. . . .
> In 'A Modern Lover' . . . the young man, still called Cyril but now in the third person, returns to a winter landscape. . . .
> The very title . . . prepares us for the controlling ironic tone which enables Lawrence to distance himself from Cyril and his sentimental egotism. But Cyril is far from being a merely comic figure. We feel that his vitality has been drained from him partly by Muriel's cowardice, her fear of love. . . . The strongest presence in the story is the landscape, which provides . . . sanctions which Lawrence himself does not sufficiently understand to be able to embody them in human relationships. (pp. 18–22)

Sagar is more sympathetic to the "sentimental egotis[t]" Mersham, partly the victim of Muriel's "fear of love," than is Harris to the "condescending" (to Vickers) figure lacking in "sensitivity," "intelligence," and "passion." But both fault the young author of "A Modern Lover" for not yet having developed to, respectively, "sufficiently understand" his material, and have sufficient "perspective" on it. My purpose has been to show that neither of these generally perceptive critics is being just to young Lawrence. The sequence of stories does not record a sequence of his self-projections: Syson of "The Soiled Rose" is not his more-adequately-understood-than-Mersham facsimile of himself, refined through a further gain in perspective in "The Shades of Spring."

The two Sysons differ as characters do in original and revised stories; and neither Syson is much like either Mersham or their common author. He derived these characters not from stages in his development, but from the different ways he used his life experience in making each story. My principal case in point is "A Modern Lover." As the two critics specify, it treats Mersham ironically; but the ostensible inadequately conceived autobiographical projection so treated is instead a created character, made free-standing by the very extent of the difference from himself the creator's irony created.

* * *

That Lawrence persisted in the pragmatic use of his personal history strictly as material for fiction cannot be shown in the scope of this appendix. But it can be indicated briefly by reference to three prominent examples, dating from different points in his career.

In the fall of 1911 he sent Chambers an unfinished draft of *Sons and Lovers*, his novel in which he was the acknowledged subject. She criticized its lack of verisimilitude, on the grounds that "what had really happened was much more poignant and interesting than the situations he had invented," and suggested he "keep it true to life." She reports, "He fell in absolutely with my suggestion and asked me to write what I could remember of our early days, because, as he truthfully said, my recollection of those days was so much clearer than his."

Using her "recollection[s]," he rewrote the novel. But both his historically inaccurate unfinished novel about an ostensible facsimile of himself, and his motive for transforming it into the "true to life" published novel, further confirm his newly developed pragmatic attitude to the relations of a writer's life and art.[10]

In 1920 he began his unfinished *Mr Noon*, "a sort of comic novel" (*Letters* III, p. 639) in two parts. Gilbert Noon's sexually predatory nature "and adventures in Part I are loosely based on those of . . . [a] boyhood friend." In Part II, Noon meets the daughter of a German baron, married and a mother, who like Frieda Lawrence has a "wide mouth" and is "full-bosomed." After that first meeting Gilbert Noon's experiences with Johanna correspond to those of Lawrence with Frieda in the early phase of their union. Drawing on Lawrence's letters and Frieda's autobiography, the explanatory notes to *Mr Noon* make elaborate connections between their life and his novel. And Mark Kinkead-Weekes, in *D. H. Lawrence: Triumph to Exile, 1912–1922*, the second volume of the recent "Cambridge Biography," uses the novel as a source, although he cautions against considering it "reliable biographical evidence" (pp. 18–19).

The self-referential, wholly external narrator of *Mr Noon* declares about the love affair, "Dear Gilbert, he had found his mate and his match"; that flippant and brittle entity complicates the relationship between the author and his novel. The narrator's blatant externality includes self-distancing from a protagonist who in Part II of *Mr Noon* suddenly begins to have, with a new character strikingly like Frieda, experiences strikingly like Lawrence's with Frieda. This sudden endowing a character treated ironically by his narrator with his own life experience, an extension of the strictly pragmatic use that is his usual practice, constitutes not an autobiographical project, but an example of a point made earlier: Lawrence's casual use of autobiographical material in some of his fiction.[11]

The minor element complicating the relationship between the author and his novel is Lawrence's gratuitous hyper-Victorian identification of the external and flippantly obtrusive narrator as himself. But the major source of complication is his blatant and totally irrelevant self-referentiality. For example, in two places half a page apart, the narrator comments on reviews of Lawrence's novel *The Lost Girl* (1920) as its author: "Now my critic in the *Observer* of December 1920 says I am . . ."; "How a *Times* critic dropped on me for . . ." (p. 118; documentation on p. 313). To summarize Lawrence's practice in *Mr Noon*: the character of Noon is based on a friend; his own life experience suddenly is imposed on Noon; the narrator treats Noon ironically throughout; the narrator asserts his identity with the author; and that external narrator/Lawrence turns from the novel he is narrating to discuss his own recent life experience *in propria persona*. In *Finnegans Wake*, Joyce turned his poetics of autobiography to terminal entropy by not only giving Shem minute particulars of his own recent life experience, but naming himself as Shem. In *Mr Noon*, Lawrence went to an analogous extreme of possible relationships between an author's life and his fiction: having objectified Noon with irony even as he gave Noon his experience, he turned from the fiction in which he coolly used himself, to talk as narrator about the narrator as himself.

Richard Lovat Somers in *Kangaroo* (1923) both has a history strikingly like that of David Herbert Lawrence and shares his creator's elaborately worked out cosmology. Yet Somers is not an implicit autobiographical facsimile of the author. He is a well-known political thinker and writer, not what Lawrence himself most essentially was, the prolific creator of fiction, poetry, and plays (and paintings). The author's political intellectual who speaks for him about politics and society has his ideas and even his language: passage after passage of Somers's doctrinal assertions is indistinguishable from the language of Lawrence's doctrinal essays. And Lawrence pragmatically used elements of his own life experience to provide a history and domestic life for the spokesman for his political and social philosophy. But again, Lawrence's ideological spokesman is not his facsimile: a writer fashioning a character to represent himself as the character's implicit subject does not deny the character his most essential defining identity.[12]

These three very different examples of it indicate that the deliberate use of his life experience D. H. Lawrence developed when young persisted in his fictional practice throughout a distinguished if truncated writing life.

# Notes

## Introduction

1. Paul Delany, "'A Would-Be-Dirty Mind': D. H. Lawrence as an Enemy of Joyce," *Joyce in the Hibernian Metropolis: Essays,* ed. Morris Beja and David Norris, pp. 76–82, 77.

2. *Letters* I, p. 69; Leavis, pp. 306, 306n; Graham Holderness, *D. H. Lawrence: History, Ideology and Fiction,* p. 76; Ford Madox Ford, *Return to Yesterday,* pp. 376, 377; and *D. H. Lawrence: Interviews and Recollections,* ed. Norman Page (Totowa: Barnes, 1981), vol. 1, p. 64. Page questions Hueffer's reliability (l.c.); and John Worthen's *D. H. Lawrence: The Early Years, 1885–1912* proposes that his account actually derived from Lawrence (p. 171).

3. Jessie Chambers ("E.T."), *D. H. Lawrence: A Personal Record,* p. 184. Jessie Chambers's sister, May Chambers Holbrook, a good friend, reports that when he told her of his disappointment because his dying mother "didn't like" his just-published first novel, *The White Peacock,* she asked, "What *did* she want?"; and in response, "'Me,' he said softly. 'Just me.'" Edward Nehls, *Composite Biography* vol. 3, p. 618.

4. Richard Ellmann emphasizes Joyce's relationship with his mother in *James Joyce,* pp. 122–23, 128–30, 292–95. Peter Costello, in *Years of Growth,* gives as the cause of death the doctor's original diagnosis of cirrhosis of the liver (p. 210).

5. In this case, Joyce's was shorter: a year and two months. May Joyce died August 13, 1903, and her son left Ireland October 9, 1904. Lydia Lawrence died December 9, 1910, and her son left England May 3, 1912. Joyce later visited Ireland; Lawrence spent periods, including the war years, in England.

6. *Hibernian Metropolis,* pp. 76, 77. Others have reviewed the details of their hostility. See, for example, Monroe Engel, "Contrived Lives: Joyce and Lawrence," *Modernism Reconsidered,* ed. Robert Kiely (Cambridge, Mass.: Harvard University Press, 1983), pp. 65–80, 66, 66 n. 2.

7. *Letters* I, pp. 294, 309.

8. *Calendar,* p. 127. Extensive similarity between the two novels is argued by Zack Bowen in "*Lady Chatterley's Lover* and *Ulysses,*" in *D. H. Lawrence's "Lady": A New Look at Lady Chatterley's Lover,* ed. Michael Squires and Dennis Jackson (Athens: University of Georgia Press, 1985), pp. 116–35.

9. A recent brief review of important literary figures hostile to Joyce's work reveals the frequent opposition of Lawrence to Joyce. See Morris Beja, "Approaching Joyce with an Attitude," in *Hibernian Metropolis,* pp. 71–75.

10. Thus, a cause of "the grosser stupidities of our intellectual *élite* at Lawrence's expense" (p. 21), in an extended exposition of them, is that "he had

against him . . . the major personal influence in the climate of literary opinion: that of T. S. Eliot" (p. 22). Earlier, Leavis complains of "a long battle to win recognition for Lawrence, and to kill the currency of the grosser misconceptions and prejudices. . . . A number . . . came from T. S. Eliot" (pp. 11–12).

11. For a discussion of their common social and cultural treatment of Lawrence, see *History, Ideology, and Fiction,* pp. 20–21, 40–47.

12. A sympathetic recent juxtaposition is on pp. 126–32 of the chapter "Structures of Modernism," in Tony Pinkney, *D. H. Lawrence and Modernism* (Iowa City: University of Iowa Press, 1990). For earlier modified praise of both, without juxtaposition, see "Frank O'Connor on Joyce and Lawrence: An Uncollected Text," *Journal of Modern Literature* 12 (1985): pp. 215–20.

13. Joyce, quoted in *Portraits of the Artist in Exile: Recollections of James Joyce by Europeans,* ed. Willard Potts (Dublin: Wolfhound, 1979), 87. On the meeting, proposed by Harry Crosby, see *Hibernian Metropolis,* p. 77.

14. This juxtaposition is very different from opposing Lawrence, commendably writing a "bright book of life," to a popular characterization of mature Joyce as poststructurally engaged in "verbal play that destabilizes meaning" at the expense of "a world outside the text." See H. M. Daleski, "Life as a Four-Letter Word: A Contemporary View of Lawrence and Joyce," *D. H. Lawrence in the Modern World,* ed. Peter Preston and Peter Hoare (Cambridge: Cambridge University Press, 1989), pp. 90–103, 91–92.

15. Actual series of such novels taking the character well into adulthood include, in chronological order: Dorothy Richardson's eight under the collective title *Pilgrimage,* begun at that time (1915); Thomas Wolfe's of four; and Anthony Powell's of twelve, under the collective title *A Dance to the Music of Time.*

16. In a diary entry while she was working on the novel, Woolf wrote: "to have father's character done complete in it; and mother['[s; & St Ives [locale of the family summer home on the Cornish coast]; & childhood." *The Diary of Virginia Woolf* (New York: Harcourt, 1977–84), III, p. 18. For similar reflections, see pp. 6 and 208.

17. Of course, Paul Morel's parents are prominent in *Sons and Lovers,* and their relationship is an important secondary subject. The complexities and subtleties of Lawrence's novel deserve, and have received, detailed careful study not possible in this introduction; and so references to it will be limited to the greatest extent possible.

18. It is printed in his volume *Let Your Mind Alone* (1937; New York: Harper, 1976).

19. The appendix describes Lawrence's fictionalizing in the early drafts of his ostensible *Künstlerroman.* The undoubted confessional and other intimate personal elements in *Sons and Lovers* are corollaries of his eventual pragmatic decision to adhere closely to his life experience.

1.

1. *Portrait*, ed. Chester G. Anderson, pp. 20, 43; subsequent references are to this edition.
2. *Ulysses*, 4.287–90/p. 51. For Vance's valentine, see *James Joyce*, pp. 31–32.
3. Stanislaus misunderstood or misremembered his brother's attitude to Vance, judging from the valentine incident, and from the likelihood that Vance and not "Dante" had threatened the child Joyce's eyes with eagles; see the first "Epiphany" in, for example, *Workshop of Daedalus*, p. 11. The most recent of the many printings of Joyce's "Epiphanies" is in *James Joyce: Poems and Shorter Writings*, ed. Richard Ellmann, A. Walton Litz, and John Whittier-Ferguson (London: Faber, 1991).
4. A medieval archbishop named Turpin appears in some *chansons de geste*, including the *Chanson de Roland*, no known ballads. But in modern times ballads, including a "Turpin Hero," were written about the highwayman Dick Turpin (1703–1739), to whom Joyce refers in *Finnegans Wake* (457.12). See, for example, *Turpin Hero: 30 Folk Songs for Voice and Guitar* (London: Oxford University Press, 1974).
5. Two recent examples are: Galya Diment, in *The Autobiographical Novel of Co-Consciousness: Goncharov, Woolf and Joyce* (Gainesville: University Press of Florida, 1994), pp. 111–42; and Suzanne Nalbantian, in *Aesthetic Autobiography: From Life to Art in Marcel Proust, James Joyce, Virginia Woolf, and Anais Nin* (New York: St. Martin's, 1994), pp. 57, 130–33, 161. Nalbantian proposes that "The association of Bloom with Joyce is provocative precisely because the exterior parallel[s] between Bloom and Joyce appear nil" (p. 131).
6. For documentation and a fuller discussion of these and other apparent sources for Stephen Dedalus, see *Argument*, pp. 190–99. See also, for example, *James Joyce*, p. 148.
7. The absence of Yeats from a group that included, aside from his close collaborator and friend Russell, an early mentor (T. W. Lyster) and a schoolfellow (W. K. Magee/John Eglinton), is conspicuous. The reason may have been only verisimilitude, Yeats having left Dublin for his home in London on April 16; or Joyce may have been expressing respect. See Yeats's letters of April 15 and 16, *Collected Letters of W. B. Yeats*, ed. John Kelly and Ronald Schuchard (Oxford: Oxford University Press, 1994), III, pp. 580–83.
8. The publication day of the likely sample story Russell sent with it, July 2, has recently been proposed as the date of his invitation. See chapter 3, n. 6, below.
9. *New Songs* was published by O'Donoghue and Company; A. H. Bullen published it in London later in the year. It was reviewed by *Dana* in May (and so in the first number), according to Don Gifford and Robert J. Seidman, *Notes for Joyce: An Annotation of James Joyce's "Ulysses"* (New York: Dutton, 1974), p. 171. For Russell's praise, see *James Joyce*, pp. 100, 134, 760.
10. *Letters* II, p. 7; and *My Brother's Keeper*, pp. 74, 82, 100–101, 104–106, 151. See also *James Joyce*, pp. 50, 76, 78, 83, 154, 178.

11. He drafted "The Holy Office" only weeks after if not before June 16: in *James Joyce Remembered* (New York: Oxford University Press, 1968), his friend Constantine (C.P.) Curran prints the letter sent on August 8 rejecting the poem, "sent me in answer to my demands for copy for *St. Stephen's*, which I was then editing" (pp. 46–47). Of *New Songs* Joyce wrote to Stanislaus "What is wrong with all these Irish writers—what the blazes are they always snivelling about?" (*Letters* II, p. 78). Four of its eight poets were men, all of whom he knew: Padraic Colum, Thomas Keohler (T. G. Keller), Seumas O'Sullivan (James S. Starkey), and George Roberts. All but Keller were members of Russell's (and Yeats's) Dublin literary set in 1904, and those three (even his friend Starkey) Joyce satirized in "The Holy Office." Eight years later, Roberts would be the speaker and main subject of "Gas from a Burner" for his egregious treatment of *Dubliners*.

12. "Most of the entries in [the notebook] seem to have been made between 1907 ... and 1909," *Workshop of Daedalus*, p. 92; the entries are on p. 104. The Nighttown chapter was begun in June 1920 (*James Joyce*, p. 442).

13. See, for example, Paul John Eakin, *Fictions in Autobiography: Studies in the Art of Self-Invention* (Princeton: Princeton University Press, 1985). Making the point that departure from historical fact can be either conscious or unintended, Eakin quotes Mary McCarthy's observation at one point (p. 124) in *Memories of a Catholic Girlhood* (New York: Harcourt, 1957): "This story is so true ... that I find it almost impossible to sort out the guessed-at and the half-remembered from the undeniably real" (p. 12). For a recent critical review of theoretical studies, see chapter 2 (pp. 26–42) in "Theories of Autobiography," in Nalbantian, *Aesthetic Autobiography*.

14. Who "paid the rent" has been debated, and is not a trivial question; see *Eliot, Joyce and Company*, pp. 274–75.

15. See Frank Budgen, *James Joyce and the Making of "Ulysses"* (London: Grayson, 1934), p. 52.

16. J. F. Byrne, *Silent Years: An Autobiography with Memoirs of James Joyce and Our Ireland* (New York: Farrar, 1953), pp. 35–37. In *Time of Apprenticeship*, Marvin Magalaner makes a detailed comparison of Joyce's two uses of Byrne's experience (pp. 110–14).

17. Documents that became available after publication of *Argument* have made possible exploring more fully here a point first proposed in its conclusion (pp. 463–66).

18. Quoted from *Workshop of Daedalus*, pp. 163–64.

19. Brenda Maddox, *Nora: The Real Life of Molly Bloom* (Boston: Houghton, 1988), p. 27. For Joyce's venereal infection, see *James Joyce*, p. 150, *Selected Letters*, p. 177, and Kathleen Ferris, *James Joyce and the Burden of Disease* (Lexington: University Press of Kentucky, 1995), pp. 26–28, 32–33. Ellmann's placing the first experience with a prostitute at fourteen (see pp. 47–48), which in David Pierce's *James Joyce's Ireland* (New Haven: Yale University Press, 1992) becomes "by the age of fourteen Joyce was frequenting brothels" (p. 28), has been refuted

by Costello in *Years of Growth* on good external evidence: Stanislaus's assertion that the experience occurred after Joyce's attendance at the play *Sweet Briar,* generally accepted, dates it "In the second week of August" 1898, when the play was first staged in Dublin (pp. 150–51).

20. *Selected Letters,* p. 159. The parenthetical page numbers that follow are to this volume.

21. Hence, on December 16:
I have come now and the foolery is over. Now for your questions!
   We [the cinema] are not open yet. (p. 191)
See also pp. 184, 186, 190, 192.

His first letter in the series and an unknown number of possible others are missing; ten are extant, of eleven letters he sent her during the period. He received the first of her complementary letters after his of December 6 (pp. 183–84) and before his of December 8 (pp. 184–85). A letter he sent during his first Dublin visit may have anticipated these (see p. 166).

22. His description of it specifies that she "slid your hand down down [*sic*] inside my trousers" (p. 182), so that she may have only partly "unbuttoned me" (p. 183). Probably they were obliged to remain clothed in that field at that time of evening.

23. Both a letter in the *New York Review of Books* (May 12, 1994) taking issue with Denis Donoghue's article cited on the first page of the next chapter and Donoghue's response (pp. 56–57) reiterate what is an unsubstantiated recent assumption (successfully both prurient and romantic) shared by Costello (p. 225) and Edna O'Brien (in her biography *James Joyce* [London: Weidenfeld and Nicholson, 1999], p. 39), as well as Maddox. In *The Consciousness of Joyce* (New York: Oxford University Press, 1977), Ellmann alleges that Nora and Joyce "touched each other's bodies" their first evening (p. 23); but he did not add even that limited surmise to the revised edition (1982) of *James Joyce.*

24. *Years of Growth* describes his prior experience as limited to "the trade in sex . . . from the prostitutes" and "delusive virginal posturing" by the girls and young women of his circle (p. 226). In *Stephen Hero,* Stephen Daedalus remarks of Emma Clery, "by her code of honour she was obliged to insist on the forbearance of the male and to despise him for forbearing" (p. 68).

25. I am indebted for this point to a conversation with Professor Stephen Whittaker of the University of Scranton.

26. *Letters* II, p. 19. Lady Gregory had suggested Yeats's solicitude "if you can get up early enough"; he wrote to her about the day on December 4. See Elizabeth Coxhead, *Lady Gregory* (London: Secker, 1966), p. 124; R. F. Foster, *W. B. Yeats: A Life, I: The Apprentice Mage 1865–1914* (New York: Oxford University Press, 1997), p. 277; and *Collected Letters of Yeats,* III, p. 268. For his efforts on Joyce's behalf, see also, for example, pp. 272–73, 276. His December 18 letter to Joyce is on p. 281.

## 2.

1. Denis Donoghue, "Joyce's Many Lives," *New York Review of Books*, October 21, 1993, pp. 28, 31–35, 28.

2. His letter of May 5, 1906, about "the centre of paralysis" designates its "aspects," treated by the twelve stories, "childhood, adolescence, maturity and public life" (*Letters* II, p. 134).

3. *Ulysses* (London: Allen, 1980), p. 171; his specific subject is Ellmann's *James Joyce*. Ellsworth Mason (Ellmann's friend and a consultant on *James Joyce*) warned against early manifestations of the "habit" in private correspondence in March 1955, and criticized its persistence in the finished manuscript in 1958; see Joseph Kelly, *Our Joyce* (Austin: University of Texas Press, 1998), pp. 152, 153–54, 247. Morris Beja's concise recent biography declares, "few artists have drawn so heavily . . . on the fabric of their own lives in weaving their fictions," then warns "Fiction must not be confused with reality"; but this latter sentence concludes, "yet the more we have come to learn about the smallest details of Joyce's life, the more we have come to see correspondences between that life and his art" (*Literary Life*, p. ix).

4. Only more important dates are documented. The chronology of his writing is drawn principally from volumes I and II of the *Letters*. *The Complete Dublin Diary of Stanislaus Joyce*, ed. George H. Healey (Ithaca: Cornell University Press, 1971), *James Joyce, Joyce Annotated*, and Gabler, "Introduction," which have only minor disagreements, also were consulted. Of the two 1992 biographies, *Literary Life* follows this chronology, but *Years of Growth* does not always: for example, despite the evidence, Costello claims that Joyce continued work on *Stephen Hero* "until August 1905" (p. 220).

5. Gabler, "Introduction," p. 3 n. 5. See also Wolfhard Steppe, "The Merry Greeks (with a Farewell to Epicleti)," *James Joyce Quarterly* 32 (1995), 597–617, esp. 603–605.

6. Heinemann may already have rejected the manuscript; see *Letters* II, p. 109 n. 1.

7. Apparently, the printer began setting it up first: the only extant proof pages, numbered 12 and 13, are from it (and are discontinuous); 13 has the marginal notation "we cannot print this" and the printer's initials. See *In Search of James Joyce*, p. 18.

8. For example, "it began at a railway station like most college stories," and Stephen Daedalus became temporarily Stephen Daly (Stanislaus, quoted in *James Joyce*, p. 264). On August 10, 1909, Joyce wrote Stanislaus in Trieste from Dublin asking to be sent "the new version of my novel"; this may have been no more than the first three chapters. He sent Ezra Pound the finally revised first chapter about the beginning of 1914; serial publication began in the *Egoist* on his birthday, February 2. It is not known when he completed writing and/or revising the remainder of the book; see R. W. Owen, *James Joyce and the Beginnings of "Ulysses"*

(Ann Arbor: UMI Research Press, 1983), pp. 41–60, for different views of the chronology of composition.

9. One of these caused Theodore Spencer to create a new chapter a few pages into chapter XVIII, to make the total twenty-six; see his edition, p. 75, and Hans Walter Gabler's preface to his edition of the *Portrait* and the *Stephen Hero* fragment (New York: Garland, 1978), p. xi.

## 3.

1. *Dubliners* (ed. Robert Scholes and A. Walton Litz), p. 29. The parenthetical page references for stories are to this edition.

2. In *James Joyce's Dublin Houses and Nora Barnacle's Galway* (London: Mandarin, 1990), Vivien Igoe declares that they stayed "three full years" beginning in late 1894 or early 1895, had moved by "the autumn of 1898" (pp. 56, 50). *Ulysses* has the Dedalus family there as late as December 3, 1898 (17.143–44/pp. 547–48). See also *James Joyce*, p. 42; *Years of Growth*, p. 134; *Letters* II, p. lv; and *Finnegans Wake*, p. 420. That "perhaps superstition" caused Joyce to alter the address from No. 13 (*James Joyce's "Dubliners,"* p. 27) is unlikely, since the *Wake* list includes "13 Fitzgibbets," which is given as 14 (*sic*) Fitzgibbon Street in *Letters* II, p. lv.

3. The bazaar ran from May 14 to 22, 1894. An extensive description of it is given in Torchiana, pp. 56–60.

4. See Torchiana, p. 60; and Heyward Ehrlich, "Joyce's 'Araby' and the 'Splendid Bazaar' of 1894," *James Joyce Literary Supplement* 7 (spring 1993), pp. 18–20, 19.

5. *James Joyce*, p. 13. *Years of Growth* is less certain: see pp. 39–40; a note on the latter page says that Ellmann confused Joyce's great-uncle with an unrelated Father Cornelius O'Connell.

6. For the evidence identifying that story, in the July 2 issue of *The Irish Homestead*, as the one Russell sent, see Danis Rose and John O'Hanlon, "The Origin of *Dubliners*: A Source," *Joyce Studies Annual 1993*, ed. Thomas F. Staley (Austin: University of Texas Press, 1993), pp. 178–80, and Gabler's introduction to *Dubliners*, pp. 1–2; Rose and O'Hanlon print the text of "The Old Watchman" after their essay, on pp. 181–84.

7. In his intelligent discussion of the story in *Joyce's "Dubliners": Substance, Vision, and Art*, Warren Beck calls the boy "the generic adolescent smitten by first love," and comments, "It is everyman's puberty rite" (pp. 102, 97).

## 4.

1. Two years later, in "The Dead," he posed the obligation of nationalism in a colonized country in the exchange between Miss Ivors and Gabriel Conroy. In the two novels that followed, he made (especially nationalist) politics a prominent part of the boy and student Stephen's experience, and political conditions and attitudes are ubiquitous in *Ulysses*.

2. For recent discussions of it, see the introductory material and apparatus in Gabler's edition, and pp. 17–51 of *In Search of James Joyce*. The details that follow are taken from Gabler, "Introduction," pp. 19, 8, 5–6.

3. Whether acting intuitively or deliberately, Polly must be aware of her future life if unmarried. The story carefully reveals that mother and daughter are not colluding, although Mrs. Mooney compares herself favorably to mothers unable to get their daughters married.

4. For a detailed account of the role of culture and class in "An Encounter," see *Joyce, Bakhtin, and Popular Literature*, pp. 31–46.

5. For documentation and a fuller discussion, see *Eliot, Joyce, and Company*, p. 277.

6. See *Argument*, pp. 272–73.

7. Fallon reports that when he told Joyce in 1931 that Joe Wilkins, with whom and his younger brother Joyce's apparent classmate Leo (*Years of Growth*, p. 139) "he had played Red Indians . . . had later become a priest," "Joyce seemed surprised at" what his narrator knew about Joe Dillon in 1905: "'I never thought Joe would make a priest' was his comment" (*The Joyce We Knew*, p. 57; see also p. 47). Jackson and McGinley simply declare that Dillon "was actually Joe Wilkins," in *James Joyce's "Dubliners,"* p. 12. The biographical traps, beginning with Joyce's reported declaration, are apparent.

8. Denis Donoghue, "Is There a Case against *Ulysses?*" in *Joyce in Context*, ed. Vincent J. Cheng and Timothy Martin (Cambridge: Cambridge University Press, 1992), pp. 19–39, 23.

9. For the latter he draws on a chapter in Gilles Deleuze and Félix Guattari, *A Thousand Plateaus: Capitalism and Schizophrenia*, tr. Brian Massumi (London: Athlone, 1988), which states that "an impersonal collective assemblage" determines all enunciation ("The social character of enunciation"), and "It is for this reason that indirect discourse, *especially 'free' indirect discourse*, is of exemplary value" (quoted from p. 25; emphasis in original).

10. "Benstock Principle," pp. 10–21, 18, 19.

11. An extensive recent study of free indirect discourse is Monica Fludernik's *The Fictions of Language and the Languages of Fiction: The Linguistic Representation of Speech and Consciousness* (New York: Routledge, 1993); see, especially, pp. 3–7, 72–109, 398–408. "A Comprehensive [fifty-nine-page] Bibliography" is on pp. 465–523. Other recent studies include: Roy Pascal, *The Dual Voice*; and Dorrit Cohn, *Transparent Minds: Narrative Modes of Presenting Consciousness in Fiction* (Princeton: Princeton University Press, 1978).

12. This is most obvious in passages depicting strong emotion. Erich Auerbach writes in *Mimesis* that in contrast to Stendhal and Balzac, Flaubert "expresses no opinion and makes no comment." But he points out that in "a paragraph [which] is the climax of the portrayal of her despair" (in Première Partie, IX), although "directly, [the reader] sees only Emma's inner state" ("we are first given Emma and then the situation through her"), "it is not Emma who speaks but the writer. . . .

Flaubert . . . bestow[s] the power of mature expression upon the material which she affords, in its complete subjectivity." *Mimesis*, pp. 429, 428, 426–27. *The Dual Voice* includes *Madame Bovary* in its examples; but Pascal criticizes Flaubert for "usurpation": using his own discourse to render Emma's consciousness (pp. 104–111).

13. Jane Austen, *Emma* (London: Nelson, n.d.), p. 232; *The Man with a Nose and the Other Uncollected Short Stories of H. G. Wells*, ed. J. R. Hammond (London: Athlone, 1984), p. 11; Joseph Conrad, *Tales of the East*, ed. Morton Dauwen Zabel (New York: Anchor, 1961), p. 89. Zabel's introduction says "Conrad mistakenly called" "The Lagoon" his first story when it was his second (p. 13, n 1).

## 5.

1. Roughly midway between the early comparisons of the three versions of the story and today, Florence L. Walzl published "Joyce's 'The Sisters': A Development," a long and widely ranging discussion of changes through "surviving manuscripts, proof sheets, and published versions" that focuses on "the Homestead version" and a generalized "later" or "published version" (pp. 375, 389, 387). Her first note is a useful selective bibliography of criticism of the story to 1970 (pp. 417–18).

2. Gabler, *Dubliners*, p. 126. Subsequent references to the first holograph *Dubliners* (1905) text in Gabler's synoptic printing of the story will use parenthetical numbers preceded by G. As above, numbers in parentheses are page references to the Scholes and Litz edition of *Dubliners*.

3. Walzl's study notes: "Joyce eliminated from the late versions [sic] of 'The Sisters' virtually all material dealing with Father Flynn as a mental case" (pp. 392–93).

4. The critical thesis that Flynn is suffering from paresis ("general paralysis of the insane"), a syphilitic brain disorder, which in effect endorses the judgment of Cotter and Eliza, not only ignores the series of strokes Joyce gave Flynn, but also subverts his having precisely put Flynn's mental condition in question.

5. Critics have noted a similarity with "An Encounter," in each boy's awareness of an appeal to him for understanding; the analogy does not require likening Flynn to the old pederast of that story.

6. More extravagant than the attribution of paresis to an old person explicitly suffering the common affliction of recurring strokes, and more so than speculations about sado-masochism, is the assertion that the relationship between the boy and the palsied, physically grotesque old man is actively sexual, and Flynn's simony, abuse of his religious pupil. The tangible grounds proposed are: the Victorian slang term sister (origin of sissie); the consonance of the word simony with sodomy; and the references to Flynn by both Cotter and Eliza as "queer" ("An Encounter" is invoked). Only the last point warrants attention: a historical dictionary will confirm that *queer* as slang for male homosexual originated in the United States decades after the story was written.

My intention in mentioning this ingenuity is to forestall a consensus like the long-held (usually enraged) former one about Molly Bloom that she is (portrayed as) extremely promiscuous. Both kinds of surmise, and as well the rage directed at a fictional character in Molly's case, are matters for cultural studies, because each signifies more about a culture of criticism than about the literature it addresses.

7. According to an Irish-American Catholic undertaker friend, and a Dublin professor and priest, to bury a priest with a chalice is unusual but does not controvert canon law.

8. In "Joyce's 'The Sisters': A Pennyworth of Snuff" (*College English* 27 [1965]: pp. 189–95), Thomas E. Connolly explains in detail why the altar boy cannot have been at fault without "perform[ing] some . . . outlandish action" (p. 193).

9. When Stephen is reflecting on the invitation of the director to join the Jesuit order in chapter IV of the *Portrait*, "idly" and "idle" are used in both senses in successive sentences, followed by "He would never [become a] priest" (p. 144). *Joyce's "Dubliners"* directed me to the recurrence of the words (p. 74).

10. The short letter to his friend Curran mentioned in my opening pages, undated but written between initial composition of "The Sisters" and of "Eveline," announces his plans for "a series of epicleti [-clets?]" and continues, "I call the series Dubliners to betray the soul of that hemiplegia or paralysis which many consider a city" (*Letters* I, p. 55).

11. Phillip Herring makes this point in "Structure and Meaning in Joyce's 'The Sisters,'" in *The Seventh of Joyce*, ed. Bernard Benstock (Bloomington: Indiana University Press, 1982), pp. 131–44, pp. 133–34.

## 6.

1. "Tom Kernan that drunken little barrelly man that bit his tongue off falling down the mens WC drunk in some place or other and Martin Cunningham . . . and Fanny MCoys husband . . . and . . . Jack Power" (18.1264–72/p. 636).

2. Quoted in *Joyce Annotated*, p. 101. As Torchiana interprets "actual grace," he is its agent: "Actual grace ['temporary, an assist from God'] arrives in the person of the 'young man in the cycling suit'" (Torchiana, pp. 209, 206).

3. The assumption he is not divine but a human cyclist ("because he is a traveler") leads one recent critic to designate him the only example of the "masculine" "engendered trope" in the volume after the three boys of its initial stories. See Earl G. Ingersoll, *Engendered Trope in Joyce's "Dubliners"* (Carbondale: Southern Illinois University Press, 1996), p. 107.

4. Loose jacket, trousers gathered at the knee (usually a Norfolk jacket and knickers), long socks, and a cricket or golf cap; he could not have afforded to buy one. For a description of variant cycling suits during the last two decades of the nineteenth century, see Phyllis Cunnington, "Cycling," chapter 13 (pp. 225–45) in Phyllis Cunnington and Alan Mansfield, *English Costume for Sports and Outdoor Recreation from the Sixteenth to the Nineteenth Centuries* (London: Black, 1969), pp. 232–35.

5. The phrase was originally "Shem or Som." In draft: "Shem" became "Hem," "or" became "and," and "Som" became "Son"; "Hem" became "Jhem," "and" became "or" again, and "Son" became "Sen." "Sen" eventually was made "Shen," closer to "Shem." See *First-Draft Version*, pp. 9, 46.

6. The word "patience" occurs, of course. Also, Gilbert and Sullivan are mentioned, as are *H.M.S. Pinafore*, *Trial by Jury*, and an operetta about twins with book not by Gilbert, *Cox and Box*. I rely for this and similar information not on memory, but on James S. Atherton, *The Books at the Wake: A Study of Literary Allusions in James Joyce's "Finnegans Wake"* (1959; Carbondale: Southern Illinois University Press, 1974); Clive Hart, *A Concordance to "Finnegans Wake"* (Minneapolis: University of Minnesota Press, 1963); William York Tindall, *A Reader's Guide to "Finnegans Wake"* (New York: Farrar, 1969); and especially Adaline Glasheen's cumulative *Third Census*.

7. The phrase is from the intrepid early study by Joseph Campbell and Henry Morton Robinson, *A Skeleton Key to "Finnegans Wake"* (New York: Harcourt, 1944), p. 27.

8. For a discussion of this see, for example, *Joyce-Again's Wake*, pp. 229–39.

9. For an analogous development in Lawrence's practice, see the Appendix, pp. 179–80.

10. *Irish Identity and the Literary Revival*, p. 209. Watson's inference that Stephen is saying the artist consequently achieves knowledge ("through his art . . . the artist . . . understand[s] himself . . . and hence . . . his relationship with the world") is unwarranted, as I will show.

11. In *The Classical Temper: A Study of James Joyce's "Ulysses"* (London: Chatto, 1961), S. L. Goldberg writes of Stephen's "new theory": "Here, if anywhere, is something like a mature aesthetic of [Joyce's] own" (p. 66). Watson quotes the sentence approvingly in *Irish Identity and the Literary Revival* (p. 209). See also, for example, Dolf Sörensen, *James Joyce's Aesthetic Theory: Its Development and Application* (Amsterdam: Rodopi, 1977), p. 58; and Hélène Cixous, *The Exile of James Joyce* (New York: Lewis, 1972), pp. 587–88.

12. For both Joyce's Stephen and young Eliot, the word seems to have the common meaning of temperament, identifying nature: the personness of the expressing writer; in one place Eliot specifies "the man, the personality." *Selected Essays*, p. 9. The other quotations are on pp. 7–8, 10, 11, 7–8.

13. *The Selected Letters of Gustave Flaubert*, tr. Francis Steegmuller (New York: Farrar, 1953), p. 195; Flaubert, *Correspondance* 2, ed. Jean Bruneau (Paris: Gallimard, 1980), p. 691. All emphases are in the original. Flaubert had made the analogy of the writer with God, present everywhere and visible nowhere, in a letter to Louise Colet on December 9, 1852, addressing not autobiography, but the author's comments in *Uncle Tom's Cabin*. See *Correspondance* 2, p. 204. In *Flaubert and Joyce: The Rite of Fiction* (Princeton: Princeton University Press, 1971), Richard K. Cross takes the contrary position to mine respecting Joyce's relation to Flaubert's attitude; see pp. 176–83.

## Appendix

1. The second draft was completed in April 1908, the third in October 1909; the first two were entitled "Laetitia," the third "Nethermere." See, for example, *Calendar,* pp. 4, 6, 8, 11, 12, 15.

2. See, for example: the first three notes to chapter I (p. 414) of part 1; n. 5 to chapter I (p. 421) and n. 1 to chapter VII (p. 423) of part 2; and the first two notes to chapter I (p. 424) of part 3.

3. *Letters* I, p. 131. It should be kept in mind that Chambers destroyed Lawrence's letters to her when young. The texts of them transcribed in the *Letters* in fact are her memorial reconstructions published two decades later; see *Letters* I, p. 22 n. 2.

4. *Personal Record,* pp. 157, 167–68; *Phoenix II: Uncollected, Unpublished, and Other Prose Works by D. H. Lawrence,* ed. Warren Roberts and Harry T. Moore (New York: Viking, 1968), p. 593; *Early Years,* pp. 218–19; and Harry T. Moore, *The Priest of Love: A Life of D. H. Lawrence* (1954; rev. ed. New York: Farrar, 1974), pp. 108–109.

5. *Early Years,* pp. 250, 291; *Letters* I, p. 154. Chambers's account is quoted and summarized from a narrative and letters she sent the author, then destroyed, in *L'homme* II, pp. 701–702; the English translation, *D. H. Lawrence, the Man and His Work; the Formative Years: 1885–1919* tr. Katharine M. Delavenay (Carbondale: Southern Illinois University Press, 1972) lacks this material.

6. *L'homme* II, p. 704; *Letters* I, pp. 157, 173, 166; *Personal Record,* pp. 199, 197; *Life into Art,* p. 91; *Early Years,* pp. xxviii–xxix, 327–28.

7. *Personal Record,* pp. 201, 152; Helen Corke, *D. H. Lawrence: The Croydon Years,* p. 33.

8. *Composite Biography* III, pp. 552–620; *Life into Art,* p. 86; *Early Years,* pp. 242, 276, 289, 383–84; *Letters* I, p. 141.

9. Of course, he believed that both "the Soul" and "the Spirit" (as he took to calling the contraries), in "polarity" (a term he used often), should abide in each person. His cosmology, with its four centers of consciousness and three sets of circuits, is easy to ridicule; but his metaphysical dualism has a long and distinguished history.

10. *Personal Record,* pp. 190, 192, 193. *Life into Art,* p. 84. On his use of her material, see "The Genesis of Sons and Lovers *as revealed in the Miriam Papers,*" *Life and Works,* pp. 285–305.

11. For a time, he projected a third part (*Letters* III, p. 667). *Mr Noon,* ed. Lindeth Vasey (Cambridge: Cambridge University Press, 1984), pp. xl, 123, 186, 118 (documentation on p. 313); for a chronology of composition, see pp. xx–xxvi.

12. *Triumph to Exile,* pp. 293–94, 346–47. *Letters* II, p. 618. *Kangaroo* (New York: Compass, 1960), pp. 199, 205.

# Bibliography

Auerbach, Erich. *Mimesis: The Representation of Reality in Western Literature.* Trans. Willard Trask. New York: Anchor, 1957.
Beck, Warren. *Joyce's "Dubliners": Substance, Vision, and Art.* Durham: Duke University Press, 1969.
Beja, Morris. *James Joyce: A Literary Life.* Columbus: Ohio State University Press, 1992.
Benstock, Bernard. *Joyce-Again's Wake: An Analysis of "Finnegan's Wake."* 1965. Reprint, Westport: Greenwood, 1975.
Benstock, Shari, and Bernard Benstock. "The Benstock Principle." In *The Seventh of Joyce*, ed. Bernard Benstock, pp. 10–21. Bloomington: Indiana University Press, 1982.
Berlin, Isaiah. *The Hedgehog and the Fox: An Essay on Tolstoy's View of History.* New York: Mentor, 1957.
Chambers, Jessie ("E.T."). *D. H. Lawrence: A Personal Record.* 1935. Reprint, Cambridge: Cambridge University Press, 1980.
Corke, Helen. *D. H. Lawrence: The Croydon Years.* Austin: University of Texas Press, 1965.
Costello, Peter. *James Joyce: The Years of Growth, 1882–1915.* New York: Pantheon, 1992.
Delany, Paul. "'A Would-Be-Dirty Mind': D. H. Lawrence as an Enemy of Joyce." In *Joyce in the Hibernian Metropolis: Essays*, eds. Morris Beja and David Norris, pp. 76–82. Columbus: Ohio State University Press.
Delavenay, Emile. *D. H. Lawrence: L'homme et la genè se de son oeuvre.* 2 vols. Paris: Klincksieck, 1969.
Eliot, T. S. *After Strange Gods.* New York: Harcourt, 1934.
———. *Selected Essays: 1917–1932.* New York: Harcourt, 1932.
Ellmann, Richard. *James Joyce.* 1959. Rev. ed., New York: Oxford University Press, 1982.
———. *The Consciousness of Joyce.* New York: Oxford University Press, 1977.
Ford, Ford Madox. *Return to Yesterday.* New York: Liveright, 1932.
Gabler, Hans Walter, ed. *A Portrait of the Artist as a Young Man.* New York: Garland, 1978.
Gabler, Hans Walter, and Walter Hettche, eds. *Dubliners.* New York: Garland, 1993.
Gifford, Don. *Joyce Annotated.* Berkeley: University of California Press, 1982.
Glasheen, Adaline. *Third Census of "Finnegans Wake."* Berkeley: University of California Press, 1977.
Harris, Janice Hubbard. *The Short Fiction of D. H. Lawrence.* New Brunswick: Rutgers University Press, 1984.

Hayman, David. *A First-Draft Version of "Finnegans Wake."* Austin: University of Texas Press, 1963.

Holderness, Graham. *D. H. Lawrence: History, Ideology and Fiction.* Dublin: Gill, 1982.

Jackson, John Wyse, and Bernard McGinley, eds. *James Joyce's "Dubliners:" An Annotated Edition.* London: Sinclair, 1993.

Joyce, James. *Dubliners.* Ed. Robert Scholes and A. Walton Litz. New York: Viking, 1969.

——. *Finnegans Wake.* New ed. London: Faber, 1960.

——. *Letters of James Joyce.* 3 vols. Ed. Stuart Gilbert and Richard Ellmann. New York: Viking, 1957, 1966.

——. *Poems and Shorter Writings.* Ed. Richard Ellmann, A. Walton Litz, and John Whittier-Ferguson. London: Faber, 1991.

——. *A Portrait of the Artist as a Young Man.* Ed. Chester G. Anderson. Boston: St. Martin's, 1993.

——. *Selected Letters of James Joyce.* Ed. Richard Ellmann. New York: Viking, 1966.

——. *Stephen Hero.* Ed. Theodore Spencer. New York: New Directions, 1944.

——. *Ulysses: The Corrected Text.* Ed. Hans Walter Gabler. New York: Vintage, 1986.

Joyce, Stanislaus. *My Brother's Keeper.* London: Faber, 1958.

Kenner, Hugh. *Dublin's Joyce.* London: Chatto, 1955.

——. *Joyce's Voices.* Berkeley: University of California Press, 1978.

Kershner, R. B. *Joyce, Bakhtin, and Popular Literature: Chronicles of Disorder.* Chapel Hill: University of North Carolina Press, 1989.

Kinkead-Weekes, Mark. *D. H. Lawrence: Triumph to Exile, 1912–1922.* Cambridge: Cambridge University Press, 1996.

Lawrence, D. H. *The Complete Short Stories of D. H. Lawrence.* Vol. 1. New York: Viking, 1961.

——. *Kangaroo.* New York: Compass, 1960.

——. *Mr Noon.* Ed. Lindeth Vasey. Cambridge: Cambridge University Press, 1984.

——. *The Letters of D. H. Lawrence.* 7 vols. Cambridge: Cambridge University Press, 1979–93.

——. "The Soiled Rose." *Forum* 43 (1913): pp. 324–40.

——. *The White Peacock.* Ed. Alan Newton. 1911. Reprint, Hammondsworth: Penguin, 1982.

Leavis, F. R. *D. H. Lawrence: Novelist.* 1955. Reprint, New York: Clarion, 1969.

Magalaner, Marvin. *Time of Apprenticeship: The Fiction of Young James Joyce.* London: Abelard, 1959.

Moore, Harry T. *D. H. Lawrence: His Life and Works.* 1951. Rev. ed., New York: Twayne, 1964.

Nehls, Edward, ed. *D. H. Lawrence: A Composite Biography.* Vol. 3. Madison: University of Wisconsin Press, 1957–59.

O'Connor, Ulick, ed. *The Joyce We Knew.* Cork: Mercier, 1967.
Pascal, Roy. *The Dual Voice.* Manchester: Manchester University Press, 1977.
Sagar, Keith. *D. H. Lawrence: Life into Art.* New York: Viking, 1985.
———. *D. H. Lawrence: A Calendar of His Works.* Manchester: Manchester University Press, 1979.
Scholes, Robert. *In Search of James Joyce.* Urbana: University of Illinois Press, 1992.
Scholes, Robert, and Richard M. Kain, eds. *The Workshop of Daedalus: James Joyce and the Raw Materials for "A Portrait of the Artist as a Young Man."* Evanston: Northwestern University Press, 1965.
Shaw, George Bernard. *Man and Superman.* 1903. Reprint, Baltimore: Penguin, 1952.
Sultan, Stanley. *The Argument of "Ulysses."* 1964. Middletown: Wesleyan University Press, 1987.
———. *Eliot, Joyce, and Company.* New York: Oxford University Press, 1987.
Tindall, William York. *A Reader's Guide to "Finnegans Wake."* New York: Farrar, 1969.
Torchiana, Donald T. *Backgrounds for Joyce's "Dubliners."* Boston: Allen, 1986.
Walzl, Florence L. "Joyce's 'The Sisters': A Development." *James Joyce Quarterly* 10 (1973): pp. 375–421.
Watson, G. J. *Irish Identity and the Literary Revival: Synge, Yeats, Joyce, and O'Casey.* London: Croom Helm, 1979.
Worthen, John. *D. H. Lawrence: The Early Years, 1885–1912.* Cambridge: Cambridge University Press, 1991.

# Index

AE. *See* Russell, George
"After the Race," 44, 87
Anti-autobiography: "Araby" as, 55–57, 60, 61, 83, 130, 131; "An Encounter" as, 42, 55, 60, 61, 70, 130, 131; *Finnegans Wake* as, 143; Joyce and, 48, 49, 60, 62, 149; Lawrence and, 8–9, 11–13, 48, 155–80; "A Painful Case" as, 130; "The Sisters" as, 57, 58–60, 61, 130, 132
"Araby," 41, 42, 44, 64, 70–74, 81–83, 85, 89, 117, 119, 133; *The Abbot* (Scott) in, 52; as anti-autobiography, 55–57, 60, 61, 83, 130, 131; Araby Bazaar date, 49, 54, 56, 98, 187n.3; boy's difference from other protagonists in *Dubliners*, 130; boy's difference from Stephen in *Portrait*, 63; boy's difference from those in "An Encounter" and "The Sisters," 98; boy's similarity to boy in "An Encounter" and Duffy in "A Painful Case," 130; boy's similarity to Stephen in *Portrait*, 63, 130; *The Devout Communicant* in, 53–54, 71; Mangan, 54, 71; Mangan's sister, 53, 71, 72, 74, 90; *Memoirs of Vidocq* in, 52; Mrs. Mercer, 94; minor revisions from original manuscript, 66, 68; narrator's difference from those of "An Encounter" and "The Sisters," 50, 54–55, 60; narrator's similarities to that of "An Encounter," 76, 79; North Richmond Street in, 47, 48, 49, 60, 71; religion in, 70–72, 74, 120, 130, 131; sexuality in, 70–72, 73, 74, 120, 128, 130; the story's similarities to "An Encounter" and "The Sisters," 51–53, 129; Westland Row in, 51
Aristotle, 19; Berlin on, 5; Aristotelian taxonomy in *Stephen Hero*, 145
Ascot Heath, 39
Auerbach, Erich: *Mimesis*, 188n.12

Austen, Jane: *Emma*, 85
Autobiography, 20; "An Encounter" as, 55, 60; *A Portrait of the Artist as a Young Man* as, 131, 150; element in "Grace," 133, 153; Joyce and, 1, 13, 47, 49, 61, 132, 133, 136; Joyce's autobiography of consciousness and life experience in *Portrait* and *Ulysses*, 146–53; Joyce's poetics of autobiography, 43, 45, 136, 137–38, 143, 147, 148, 149–53; Lawrence and, 1, 10, 13, 156; Stephen (in *Ulysses*) as expounder of, 147, 148; *Stephen Hero* as, 147; Woolf's and Faulkner's "historical autobiography," 8; Worthen on Lawrence's, 10
Autobiographical fiction, 182n.15; "An Encounter" as, 42, 130; *A Portrait of the Artist as a Young Man* as, 14–19, 21–22, 27–39, 40; "Araby" as, 130; *Finnegans Wake* as, 140, 143, 153; Joyce and, 6–7, 8, 13, 14–40, 48, 49, 55, 60, 62, 130, 136, 140, 143, 146, 149–53; in Joyce's early fiction, 41–46; Lawrence and, 8, 13, 15; Stephen Dedalus (in *Ulysses*) on, 146–47; "The Dead" as, 62, 137, 153; "The Sisters" as, 132–33; *Ulysses* as, 16–20, 22–27, 38, 39–40, 148, 153. *See also* Anti-autobiography; *Bildungsroman*; *Künstlerroman*

Balzac, Honoré de, 188n.12
Barnacle, Nora, 23, 27, 29, 39, 40, 44; as analogue for Bloom, 40; tribute to, in plot of *Ulysses*, 23–40
Beck, Warren: *Joyce's "Dubliners": Substance, Vision, and Art*, 122, 130, 187n.7, 190n.9
Beja, Morris: "Approaching Joyce with an Attitude," 181n.9; *James Joyce: A Literary Life*, 18, 20, 56, 186nn.3, 4

Benstock, Bernard: "The Benstock Principle," 84, 85; *Joyce-Again's Wake: An Analysis of "Finnegans Wake,"* 138, 143

Berlin, Isaiah: *The Hedgehog and the Fox: An Essay on Tolstoy's View of History,* 5, 13

*Bildungsroman: A Portrait of the Artist as a Young Man* as, 6–7, 47, 131; Joyce and, 6–7; Lawrence and, 6; *Sons and Lovers* as, 6–7. See also Künstlerroman

Blackrock, Ireland: Joyce family's move from, 63; in *A Portrait of the Artist as a Young Man,* 63

Blake, William: Energy and Constraint, 142; Shaw on, 5

"Boarding House, A," 44; Bob Doran, 86; Bob Doran's seduction in, 67, 93; Jack Mooney, 86; Mrs. Mooney, 86, 188n.3; Polly Mooney, 67, 93, 188n.3; revisions from earlier manuscript, 67, 86

Boucicault, Dion: *Arrah-na-Pogue,* 138; Sean the Post, 138

Bowen, Zack: "*Lady Chatterley's Lover* and *Ulysses,*" 181n.8

"Brilliant Career, A," 32

Brontë, Charlotte: and autobiographical fiction, 1

Budgen, Frank, 20, 21; *James Joyce and the Making of "Ulysses,"* 26

Bunyan, John: Shaw on, 5

Burrows, Louisa: Lawrence's engagement to, 157, 158, 168

Byrne, J. F.: encounter of, with Father Darlington in *Stephen Hero* and in *Portrait,* 21–22, 48

Callanan, Ellen, 57–58
Callanan, Mary Ellen (daughter), 57
Campbell, Berkeley: "The Old Watchman" as influence on "The Sisters," 59, 187n.6
Carr, Henry: as Private Carr (*Ulysses*), 17
Catholicism, 62; in "An Encounter," 69–70, 71, 76, 80, 120, 130, 131; in "A Painful Case," 130; in "Araby," 54, 70–72, 74, 76, 130; in "Grace," 133, 134–35; in *Portrait* (Annunciation as metaphor, 33–34; Eucharist as metaphor, 36, 37; Gabriel, 34); Stephen's analogy of God's creation and artists' creation (in *Ulysses*) and, 151; in "The Sisters," 53–54, 76, 98, 101, 102, 104–5, 106, 107–8, 109, 114, 117, 118, 122, 123, 124, 125–29, 133; Virgin Mary (Madonna), 33–34. See also Roman Catholic Church

Cézanne, Paul, 38

*Chamber Music,* 19, 31

Chambers, David: Lawrence writing to, 172

Chambers, Jessie, 11, 12, 155, 159, 168, 170, 171, 173, 174, 192nn.3, 5, 10; *D. H. Lawrence: A Personal Record,* 2, 156, 167, as "E.T," 158; and her father's disaffection from Lawrence, 172; Lawrence sending unfinished draft of *Sons and Lovers* to, 178; and recommendation for publication of story of, in *English Review,* 172; relationship of, with Lawrence, 156, 157, 158, 161, 175

Cheng, Vincent J., and Timothy Martin: *Joyce in Context,* 188n.8

Cixous, Hélène: *The Exile of James Joyce,* 191n.11

"Clay," 86

Colum, Padraic, 2, 41, 47, 184n.11

Connolly, Thomas E.: "Joyce's 'The Sisters': A Pennyworth of Snuff," 190n.8

Conrad, Joseph: "The Lagoon," 86, 189n.13

Corke, Helen, 157, 158, 177; *D. H. Lawrence: The Croydon Years,* 172

Cosgrave, Vincent, 17; alleged romance of, with Nora Barnacle, 23, 24, 40

Costello, Peter, 185n.23; *James Joyce: The Years of Growth, 1882–1915,* 17, 18, 49, 56, 57, 58, 59, 181n.4, 185nn.19, 24, 186n.4

"Counterparts," 44, 45; sexual references in, 69

Cousins, Margaret (Gretta) and James, 18, 22–23

Croyden, England: Lawrence in, 156–57, 172

Cummins, Maria S.: *The Lamplighter,* 78

Cunnington, Phyllis, and Alan Mansfield:

*English Costume for Sports and Outdoor Recreation from the Sixteenth to the Nineteenth Century*, 190n.4
Curran, Constantine, 44, 190n.10

Daleski, H. M.: "Life as a Four Letter Word: A Contemporary View of Lawrence and Joyce," 182n.14
*Dana* (literary magazine), 43, 183n.9
D'Annunzio, Gabriele, 31
Dante Alighieri: Berlin on, 5
"Dead, The," 45, 46, 65, 66, 67, 84, 88, 119, 129, 133, 134, 135, 152–53; Gabriel Conroy, 16, 58, 62, 136–37; Gretta Conroy, 62, 136, 137; feminism in, 136; Misses Flynn, 58; Michael Furey, 136; Molly Ivors, 136; juxtaposed with "The Shadow in the Rose Garden," 4; Misses Morkan, 57, 136; Pope Leo X in, 136
Dedalus, Stephen, 3, 11, 15, 22, 25, 27–38, 38–40, 43, 46, 47, 48, 49, 54, 55, 56, 60, 63–64, 74, 78, 142, 149, 190n.9; artistic doctrine of, 146–48; autobiographical protagonist of *Stephen Hero* as antecedent for, 7, 21, 153; and difference between Stephen in *Stephen Hero*, in *Portrait*, and in *Ulysses*, 146; and difference from boys in "An Encounter," "Araby," and "The Sisters," 63; and differences from Joyce, 16, 21, 146; disquistion of, about art, 150–53; as expounder of Joyce's poetics of autobiography, 147, 148; and his Flaubertian conception of a writer's invisibility and Joyce's counterstatement, 151–52; lecture of, on Shakespeare, 143–45, 146, 147–48, 152; and his "Parable of the Plums," 122; and similarity between Stephen in *Stephen Hero*, in *Portrait*, and in *Ulysses*, 145; similarity of, to boy in "The Sisters," 130, 153; similarity of, to boys in "An Encounter" and "Araby," 63, 131; similarity of, to Joyce, 14, 16, 17, 18–19, 20, 27, 28–29, 32, 63, 131; Stanislaus as model for, 21; as Stephen Daly, 186n.8
Delany, Paul: "A Would-Be Dirty Mind: D. H. Lawrence as an Enemy of Joyce," 3
Delavenay, Emile, 174, 175; *D. H. Lawrence: L'homme et la genèse de son oeuvre*, 173, 192n.5
Deleuze, Gilles, and Féliz Guattari: *A Thousand Plateaus: Capitalism and Schizophrenia*, 188n.9
Dempsey, George, 56
Dickens, Charles: Shaw on, 6
*Différance*, 62
Diment, Galya: *The Autobiographical Novel of Co-Consciousness: Goncharov, Woolf, and Joyce*, 183n.5
Dodder River, 24
Donoghue, Denis, 43, 185n.23; "Is there a case against *Ulysses*?" 84
Drumcondra, Ireland: the Joyce family's move from, 49–50
Dublin, 20, 42, 130; in Joyce's fiction, 16, 17, 18, 27, 28, 47, 50, 61, 63–64, 70, 72, 74, 105, 120, 122, 125, 126, 132, 134, 135, 136, 143; Joyce's self-exile from, 2, 181n.5; Joyce's visits to, 23, 24, 25, 185n.21
*Dubliners*, 19, 41, 42, 44, 45, 46, 47, 48, 51, 56, 59, 60, 61, 62, 63, 64, 68, 73, 74, 79, 91, 92, 97, 106, 108, 119, 123, 125, 128, 132, 133, 135, 136, 184n.11, 187n.1, 190n.10; in *Irish Homestead*, 26, 65, 84, 86, 87, 88; and Maunsel and Company's contract with Joyce to publish, 66–67; mentioned in *Finnegans Wake*, 140, 142

Eakin, Paul John: *Fictions in Autobiography: Studies in the Art of Self-Invention*, 184n.13
Eglinton, John (W. K. Magee), 183n.7; as editor of *Dana*, 18, 183n.9. *See also Ulysses*
*Egoist, The*, 186n.8
Eliot, T. S., 19, 149, 151; as admirer of *Ulysses*, 4, 181n.10; *After Strange Gods*, 4; as a critic of Lawrence, 4, 181n.10; juxtaposing "The Shadow in the Rose Garden" and "The Dead," 4; "Tradition and the Individual Talent," 150, 191n.12

Ellmann, Richard, 187n.5; *The Consciousness of Joyce*, 185n.23; *James Joyce*, 16, 17, 18, 20, 23, 33, 37, 40, 43, 44, 45, 46, 49, 57, 58, 62, 63, 136, 137, 138, 139, 152, 181n.4, 183nn.2, 6, 184nn.12, 19, 185n.23, 186nn.3, 8
"Encounter, An," 41, 44, 64, 74–76, 81, 82; as anti autobiography, 42, 55, 60, 61, 70, 130, 131; and boy's difference from other protagonists in *Dubliners*, 130; and boy's difference from Stephen in *Portrait*, 63; and boy's difference from those in "Araby" and "The Sisters," 98; and boy's experience as autobiography, 55; and boy's similarity to boy in "Araby" and Duffy in "A Painful Case," 130; and boy's similarity to boy in "The Sisters," 189n.5; and boy's similarity to Stephen in *Portrait*, 63, 130; Father Butler, 68, 97; the Canal (Newcomen) Bridge in, 50; class bias in, 68, 70, 75, 120; Joe Dillon, 69, 70, 80, 188n.7; Mrs. Dillon, 80; few revisions from original version of, 66–67, 68; Mahony, 48, 52, 68, 69; Mahony as foil for narrator in, 75–76; and Mahony's difference from Stanislaus, 70; narrator's difference in, from those of "Araby" and "The Sisters," 50, 54–55, 60, 74; narrator's similarities in, to that in "Araby," 76, 79; North Richmond Street in, 55; the Pigeon House in, 51, 70; religion in, 69, 70, 71, 76, 80, 120, 130, 131; sexuality in, 68, 69, 70, 71, 120, 130, 131; similarities in, to "Araby" and "The Sisters," 51–53, 129; violence in, 68, 69, 70, 80, 120, 128
Engel, Monroe: "Contrived Lives: Joyce and Lawrence," 181n.6
*English Review, The*: Jessie Chambers encourages Lawrence to send his poems to, 157, 159; Garnett recommends one of Chambers's stories to, 172; Lawrence's first publication in, 158–59
*Ens* and *idea*, 26, 27, 28, 29, 37, 39
"Eveline," 44, 84, 86, 87, 119, 190n.10; Eveline (character), 72; Nora's situation compared to, 26
"Exiles": Richard Rowan, 16

Fairview: the Joyce family living in, 50
Fallon, William G., 55, 56, 188n.7
Faulkner, William, 7; *The Reivers*, 8
Ferris, Kathleen, *James Joyce and the Burden of Disease*, 184n.19
*Finnegans Wake*, 49, 126, 131, 152, 183n.4, 187n.2; *A First Draft Version of "Finnegans Wake,"* 138; "Anna Livia Plurabelle" section of, 141; as autobiographical fiction, 139, 143, 153; Chuff (as Mr Sean O'Mailey), 139; as complementary to Shaun, 142; Stephen Dedalus incorporated in, 140; destruction of *Dubliners* in, 142; H. C. Earwicker, 16 (Joyce as source for, 139); and Earwicker children corresponding to Dedalus children in *Stephen Hero*, 138; Glugg (as Mr. Seamas McQuillad), 139; Jacob (biblical reference), 137; Jhem/Shem, 138, 139, 140; "Jim the Penman," 138; Joyce brothers implicated in, 139; "The Mime of Mick, Nick and the Maggies" section of, 139; poetics of autobiography in, 137, 143; the "scandal" of *Ulysses* in, 142; Shaun the Post, 143 (as complementary to Shem, 142; speaking as JUSTIUS, 141; Stanislaus as source for, 138, 139); Shem and Shaun in, 138; Shem the Penman, 43, 138, 140, 142, 153 (as autobiographical character, 15, 139, 179–80; quoting Whitman, 143; speaking as MERCIUS, 141)
Flaubert, Gustave, 188n.12; and analogy of God's creation and artists' creation, 152; *Madame Bovary*, 85 (comments on, 151); on *Uncle Tom's Cabin*, 191n.13
Ford (Hueffer), Ford Maddox, 2, 157, 159; *Return to Yesterday*, 181n.2
Free Indirect Discourse: in Joyce's fiction, 31, 83, 84, 85, 86, 87, 93–94, 188n.9

*Freeman's Journal, The,* 57; and Nannie then Eliza Flynn's solecism in "The Sisters," 111

Gabler, Hans Walter: edition of *Dubliners,* 88; introduction to *Dubliners,* 26, 45, 51, 52, 60, 66, 86, 133, 136, 186n.4
"Gas from a Burner," 184n.11
Gauguin, Paul, 38
Gay, John: *The Beggar's Opera,* 128
Gifford, Don: *Joyce Annotated,* 31, 54, 102, 186n.4
Gilbert, W. S.: Bunthorne, Grosvenor, *Patience,* 138
Gissing, George Robert, 42
Glasheen, Adaline: *Third Census of "Finnegans Wake,"* 138, 139
Goethe, Johann Wolfgang von: Shaw on, 5
Gogarty, Oliver St. John, 2
Goldberg, S. L.: *The Classical Temper: A Study of James Joyce's "Ulysses,"* 191n.11
Gorman, Herbert: *James Joyce: A Definitive Biography,* 42
"Grace," 44, 67; autobiographical possibility in, 133, 135, 153; the constable, 134, 135; Martin Cunningham, 133, 134; Fogarty, 134; Mrs. Kernan, 134; Tom Kernan, 133, 134, 135; "Charley" M'Coy, 133; Jack Power, 133, 134, 135; Father Purdon, 97, 133, 135; religion in, 133, 135–36; similarity to *Ulysses,* 133–34; as thematic complement to "The Sisters," 133; young man in cycling suit, 133, 134–35, 153, 190n.3
Guattari, Féliz. *See* Deleuze, Gilles

Haggs Farm (Jessie Chambers's home), 157, 159, 160
"Hallow Eve" ("[The] Clay"), 44
Hardy, Keir, 2
Harris, Janice Hubbard: *The Short Fiction of D. H. Lawrence,* 173, 174, 175, 176, 178
Hauptmann, Gerhard: James Duffy's translation of *Michael Kramer* in "A Painful Case," 48, 130; *Michael Kramer,* 16

Hayman, David: *"Ulysses": The Mechanics of Meaning,* 77
Heinemann, William, Ltd. (publisher), 186n.6
Herodotus: Berlin on, 5
Herring, Phillip: "Structure and Meaning in Joyce's 'The Sisters,'" 190n.11
Hitler, Adolf, 17
Holbrook, May, 158, 172, 181n.3
Holderness, Graham: *D. H. Lawrence: History, Ideology and Fiction,* 175–76, 181n.2, 182n.11
Holloway, Joseph (journal), 22
Holt, Agnes: and Lawrence's proposal, 157
"Holy Office, The," 19, 148, 184n.11
Hopkin, "Willie" and "Sallie," 2
Hueffer, Ford Maddox. *See* Ford (Hueffer), Ford Maddox
Hunt, Violet, 157
Husserl, Edmund, 106

Ibsen, Henrik, 16, 151; influence of, on Joyce's work, 19, 32
*Idea* and *ens,* 26, 27, 28, 29, 37, 39
Igoe, Vivien: *James Joyce's Dublin Houses and Nora Barnacle's Galway,* 187n.2
Ingersoll, Earl G.: *Engendered Trope in Joyce's "Dubliners,"* 190n.3
*Irish Homestead, The,* 19, 26, 44, 48, 59, 60, 65, 84, 86, 87, 187n.6
"Ivy Day in the Committee Room," 44, 67, 134; Hynes's elegy to Parnell in, 32; Father Keon, 97; politics in, 64

Jackson, John Wyse, and Bernard McGinley: *James Joyce's "Dubliners": An Annotated Edition,* 114, 187n.2, 188n.7
James, Henry, "The Art of Fiction," 88, 90
Jennings, Blanche, 155, 156, 159
Joyce, James: Berlin on, 5; as Berlin's "fox," 5, 13; and the *Bildungsroman,* 6–7; contrariety of art of Lawrence and, 5, 40; and critics' emphasis on autobiography, 13; development of, as a fiction writer, 74, 77, 87, 132, 133, 136, 137, 149–53; hostility of, to Lawrence's fiction, 1, 3,

Joyce, James—*continued*
4, 5; on *Lady Chatterley's Lover*, 3, 6; Leavis on, 4–5; on London meeting with Yeats, 37; misreading of Lawrence by, 4; pragmatism in fiction of, 48; productivity of, 13; refusal of, to meet Lawrence, 5; as second most written about English author, 9; similarities of, to Lawrence (democratic socialism, 1–2; first publication, 2; mother's death, 2, 3, 23, 27, 181n.5; opposition to World War I, 1; religion, 1; self-exile, 2, 3; teaching, 1); six modes of disclosure in mature fiction of, 77–83, 89, 90, 120; venereal disease and, 184n.19. *See also individual works*

Joyce, John, 58; as Simon Dedalus, 20

Joyce, Mary Jane (May), 58

Joyce, Stanislaus, 17, 43, 45, 46, 47, 57, 61, 66, 67, 86, 130, 132, 136, 138, 183n.3, 184n.19, 186n.8; *The Complete Dublin Diary of Stanislaus Joyce*, 44, 186n.4; and critiques of drafts of *Dubliners*, 42, 44, 65; difference of, from Mahony in "An Encounter," 70; as model for Stephen Dedalus in *Portrait*, 21; *My Brother's Keeper*, 14, 20, 21, 32, 41, 48, 49, 55, 59, 62 (Eliot's preface to, 19); similarity of, to James Duffy in "A Painful Case," 48

Keats, John: "La Belle Dame sans Merci," 34

Kelly, Joseph: *Our Joyce*, 186n.3

Kenner, Hugh, 43, 77, 84–86, 119; *Dublin's Joyce*, 89, 90, 91; *Joyce's Voices*, 84; and "The Uncle Charles Principle," 84

Keohler, Thomas (T. G. Keller), 184n.11

Kershner, R. B.: *Joyce, Bakhtin, and Popular Literature: Chronicles of Disorder*, 93

Kinkead-Weekes, Mark: *D. H. Lawrence: Triumph to Exile, 1912–1922*, 179

Künstlerroman, 8, 46, 48; *A Dance to the Music of Time* (Anthony Powell) as, 182n.15; *A Portrait of the Artist as a Young Man* as, 7; *Pilgrimage* (Dorothy Richardson) as, 182n.15; *Sons and Lovers* as, 7, 13; Wolfe and, 182n.15. *See also Bildungsroman*

Lady Gregory, 185n.26

Lansdowne Road, 56; in "Araby," 57

Larbaud, Valery: as advocate of *Ulysses*, 4

Lawrence, D. H.: and anti-autobiography, 155–80; and autobiography, 1, 10, 13, 156, 171; as Berlin's "hedgehog," 5, 13, 161; contrariety of art of Joyce and art of, 5, 40; Eliot on, 4; elopement of, with Frieda, 158; engagement of, to Louisa Burrows, 157, 158, 168; extensive productivity of, 13; first publication of, in *English Review*, 158–59; hostility of, to Joyce's fiction, 1, 3, 4, 5; Joyce's refusal to meet, 5; Leavis on, 4–5; metaphysical/cosmological duality of, 161, 192n.9; misreading of Joyce by, 4; and "mother poems," 3; relationship with Jessie Chambers, 156, 157, 158, 161, 175; similarities to Joyce (democratic socialism, 1–2; first publication, 2; mother's death, 2, 3, 157, 181n.5; opposition to World War I, 1; religion, 1; self-exile, 2, 3, 181n.5; teaching, 1); on *Ulysses*, 3

Lawrence, D. H., works of:
—"Autobiographical Sketch," 157
—"Fox, The": love triangle in, 171; March, 166
—"Goose Fair": first publication in *English Review*, 158–59
—"Horse-Dealer's Daughter, The," 161
—*Kangaroo*, 180
—*Lady Chatterley's Lover*, 3, 172
—*Letters of D. H. Lawrence, The*, 3–4, 6, 156, 166, 173, 174, 177, 179, 181n.2
—*Lost Girl, The*, 179
—"Lovely Lady, The," 13, 162
—"Modern Lover, A," 159, 161–67; as anti-autobiography, 165–67; autobiographical elements of, 163, 165; biographical writings about, 9, 10; Cyril Mersham, 11, 12, 13, 162, 163, 164, 165, 166, 167, 171, 172, 173, 174, 175, 176, 177, 178; Muriel, 10, 162,

163, 164, 165, 167, 171, 173, 174, 176, 177, 178; Tom Vickers, 162, 163, 164, 166, 176, 177, 178; "The Virtuous" (earlier title), 166
—*Mr Noon*, 179–80, 192n.11
—"Nethermere" (*The White Peacock*), 156, 157, 159
—*Prussian Officer, The* (volume of stories), 174
—"Prussian Officer, The," 13; love triangle in, 171
—"Second Best," 161, 176
—"Shades of Spring, The," 159, 161, 176; as anti-autobiography, 170, 171; autobiographical element of, 167; four titles of, 168, 174; Hilda Millership, 12, 167, 168–70, 171, 177; Moore on, 10, 174; Arthur Pilbeam, 167, 168, 169, 170; revision of, 168; John Adderly Syson, 11, 12, 167, 168, 169, 170, 171, 172, 175, 178; Worthen on, 10
—"Shadow in the Rose Garden, The": juxtaposed with "The Dead," 4
—"Soiled Rose, The," 12, 159, 161, 167, 168, 169, 174, 176, 177. See also "Shades of Spring" *above*
—*Sons and Lovers*, 10, 11, 155, 156, 178, 192n.10; difference of, from *To the Lighthouse* and *The Reivers*, 8; Miriam Leivers, 158, 161; Paul Morel, 3, 158, 161, 173; Morel's parents, 182n.17
—*Studies in Classic American Literature*, 6; "Surgery for the Novel—or a Bomb," 4; on *Ulysses*, 4
—*White Peacock, The*, 10, 11, 157, 181n.3, 192n.1; Annable, 156; as antiautobiography, 155, 156, 160; as autobiography, 156; Cyril Beardsall, 7, 155, 156, 160; Lawrence on, 155–56; Lettie Beardsall, 155, 156; the Mayhews, 161; Tom Renshaw, 156, 159, 160; revision of, 155; Emily Saxton, 155, 156, 159, 160, 177; George Saxton, 155, 156, 160
Lawrence, Frieda (Weekley), 158, 159
Leavis, F. R., 2; *D. H. Lawrence: Novelist*, 4, 181n.2; on Eliot's negative criticism of Lawrence, 5, 181n.10; juxtaposing Lawrence and Joyce, 4–5
Léon, Paul, 46
*Letters of James Joyce*, 18, 24, 41, 42, 44, 46, 48, 50, 59, 61, 69, 136, 140, 148, 184n.11, 185n.26, 186n.4, 187n.2, 190n.10
Lewis, Wyndham: presence of, in Shaun of *Finnegans Wake*, 138
*Licensed Victuallers' Gazette, The*: in *Ulysses*, 20
Liffey (River): in "The Sisters" and "An Encounter," 51
"Little Cloud, A," 45, 86; Chandler, 130
London: Joyce meeting Yeats in, 37; in Lawrence's fiction, 155, 160, 163, 167
Long, John (publisher), 66
Lubbock, Percy: *The Craft of Fiction*, 120
Lyons, Julia Clare, 57
Lyster, T. W., 183n.7

MacDonald, Ramsay, 2
Maddox, Brenda: *Nora: The Real Life of Molly Bloom*, 184n.19
Magalaner, Marvin, 119; *Time of Apprenticeship: The Fiction of Young James Joyce*, 89, 90, 91, 123, 184n.16
Mangan, James Clarence: "Fragment of an Unpublished Autobiography," 16–17
Mansfield, Alan. *See* Cunnington, Phyllis, and Alan Mansfield
Martello tower (at Sandycove), 21
Martin, Timothy. *See* Cheng, Vincent J., and Timothy Martin
Marvell, Andrew: "To His Coy Mistress," 8
Mason, Ellsworth, 186n.3
Matisse, Henri, 38
Maunsel and Company: and contract with Joyce to publish *Dubliners*, 66–68. *See also* Roberts, George
McCarthy, Mary: *Memories of a Catholic Girlhood*, 184n.13
McGinley, Bernard. *See* Jackson, John Wyse, and Bernard McGinley
Melville, Herman, 1
Mexico: Lawrence in, 9
Moore, George: mentioned in *Ulysses*, 18, 147–48

Moore, Harry T., 11, 161; *D. H. Lawrence: His Life and Works*, 10, 174, 192n.10; on "Shades of Spring," 10, 174
Morrison, Arthur, 42
"Mother, A," 41, 44, 67, 79, 87
Murray, John, 59
Murray, Josephine, 42
Murray, Margaret Theresa (Flynn), 57, 59

Nalbantian, Suzanne: *Aesthetic Autobiography: From Life to Art in Marcel Proust, James Joyce, Virginia Woolf and Anaïs Nin*, 183n.5, 184n.13
Nehls, Edward: *D. H. Lawrence: A Composite Biography*, 172, 181n.3
New Mexico: Lawrence in, 9
*New Songs: A Lyric Selection. See* Russell, George
Nietzsche, Friedrich, 48
North Circular Road, 50
North Richmond Street: in "An Encounter," 55; in "Araby," 47, 48, 49, 50, 60, 71
Nottingham, University of: Lawrence seeking a teaching post at, 172
Noyes, Alfred: praises insulting review of *Ulysses*, 142

Ockham, William of ("Occam's Razor"), 105
O'Connor, Ulick: *The Joyce We Knew*, 56
O'Hanlon, John. *See* Rose, Danis, and John O'Hanlon
O'Sullivan, Seamus, 2, 184n.11

Page, Norman: *D. H. Lawrence: Interviews and Recollections*, 181n.2
"Painful Case, A," 44, 67, 119; anti-autobiography in, 130; "Bile Beans," 48; extensive revision of, 119; James Duffy, 62 (and difference from Joyce, 130, 137; similarity of, to boys in "Araby" and "An Encounter," 130; similarity of, to Joyce, 48, 130; similarity of, to Stanislaus, 48); religion in, 130; sexuality in, 130
Pankhurst, Emmeline, 2
Paris: Joyce's visit to, 37
Parnell Street, 94
Pascal, Roy: *The Dual Voice*, 188nn.11, 12
Pater, Walter, 31
Pierce, David: *James Joyce's Ireland*, 184n.19
Pigeon House: in "An Encounter," 51, 70
Pinkney, Tony: *D. H. Lawrence and Modernism*, 182n.12
*Poems and Shorter Writings* (ed. Ellmann et al.), 183n.3
*Pomes Penyeach*, 31
*Portrait of the Artist as a Young Man, A*, 13, 16, 27–38, 40, 43, 45, 48, 60, 63, 64, 65, 77, 84, 88, 129, 142, 190n.9; as autobiographical fiction, 6, 47, 131; as autobiography, 131; as *Bildungsroman*, 6–7; Byrne's encounter with Father Darlington ("Butt") altered in, 21; difference of, from *To the Lighthouse* and *The Reivers*, 8; E(mma) C(lery), 29, 30, 32, 33, 34, 35, 36, 37, 46; Heron, 56; Lynch, 15, 33, 145, 149 (Vincent Cosgrave as, 17); on the novel's title, 38–39; poetics of autobiography in, 137, 149–53; Mrs. "Dante" Riordan, 131 (Mrs. ["Dante" Hearn] Conway as model for, 14); and Stephen's artistic doctrine in *Ulysses* (withheld in *Portrait*), 146–49; Stephen's disquisition about art in, 150–53; Stephen's Flaubertian conception of a writer's invisibility and Joyce's counterstatement in, 151–52; Stephen's uncle Charles in, based on William O'Connell, 58; Stephen's villanelle in, 33–38; Eileen Vance, 14–15, 18, 29; Vance family in, 14, 18, 131, 132. *See also* Dedalus, Stephen
Pound, Ezra, 186n.8; as advocate of *Ulysses*, 4
Powell, Anthony: *A Dance to the Music of Time* as *Künstlerroman*, 182n.15
"Prayer, A," 31

Richards, Grant, 19, 43, 45, 61, 64, 65, 69, 87, 125; rejection of *Dubliners* by, 66–67, 68

Richardson, Dorothy: *Pilgrimage* as Künstlerroman, 182n.15
Roberts, George, 66, 142, 184n.11
Roman Catholic Church, 65; in Joyce's fiction, 102, 104, 105, 106, 108, 114, 118, 125, 127, 128, 129, 134, 136. *See also* Catholicism
Rose, Danis, and John O'Hanlon: "The Origin of *Dubliners*: A Source," 187n.6
Rousseau, Henri, 38
Royal Canal, 50
Rumbold, Sir Horace: as H. Rumbold, Master Barber in *Ulysses*, 17
Russell, George (AE), 43, 59; character in *Ulysses*, 17, 18, 19, 147, 183nn.7, 8, 184n.11; *New Songs: A Lyric Selection*, 19, 183n.9, 184n.11

Sagar, Keith, 10, 158; *D. H. Lawrence: A Calendar of His Works*, 11, 174; *D. H. Lawrence: Life into Art*, 11, 169, 175, 177, 178; Harris on, 176–77; *The Life of D. H. Lawrence*, 11; "'The Best I Have Known': D. H. Lawrence's 'A Modern Lover' and 'The Shades of Spring,'" 176–77
St. Patrick's Cathedral, 59
St. Stephen's (University College student newspaper), 22, 139
Savard (Saward), James Townsend (Townshend) ("Jim the Penman"), 138
Scholes, Robert: *In Search of James Joyce*, 31, 66, 84, 186n.7; "Semiotic Approaches to Joyce's 'Eveline,'" 84; *The Workshop of Daedalus: James Joyce and the Raw Materials for "A Portrait of the Artist as a Young Man,"* 55
*Selected Letters of James Joyce*, 17, 24, 25, 185n.21, 185n.22
Shakespeare, William, 1; Berlin on, 5; marriage of, to Ann Hathaway, 3; as the most written-about English author, 9; Shaw on, 6; Stephen's lecture on, 143–45, 146, 147–48, 152; "The expense of spirit" sonnet, 77
Shaw, George Bernard: comparing his own work with Shakespeare's, 5; dichotomizing writers, 5–6, 13; *Man and Superman*, 5
Shelley, Percy Bysshe, 6; Shaw on, 5
"Silhouettes," 62
"Sisters, The," 41, 43, 44, 46, 48, 54, 60, 63, 64–65, 74, 87, 88–129, 134, 136; as anti-autobiography, 57, 58–59, 61; boy's difference in, from those in "Araby" and "An Encounter," 98; and boy's difference from other protagonists in *Dubliners*, 130; and boy's difference from Stephen in *Portrait*, 63; boy's similarity in, to that in "An Encounter," 189n.5; and boy's similarity to Joyce, 133; and boy's similarity to Stephen in *Portrait*, 130, 153; and boy's similarity to Stephen in *Portrait* and Joyce created in revision, 131, 132; class difference without bias in, 68; Cotter, 52, 65, 89, 90, 91, 92, 93, 94, 95, 96, 97, 98, 101, 103, 107, 109, 120, 121, 123, 124, 126, 127, 189n.4, 189n.6; Eliza Flynn, 52, 58, 65, 68, 89, 91, 92, 93, 96, 97, 103, 107, 109, 111, 112, 113, 114, 115, 116, 117, 118, 122, 124, 125, 126, 128, 189n.4, 189n.6 (her more prominent role after revision of, 110, 121); Father James Flynn, 45, 51, 53, 58, 59, 64, 65, 89, 91, 92, 93, 94, 95, 96, 97, 99, 106, 107, 108, 109, 110, 111, 112, 113, 114, 115, 116, 117, 118, 120, 121, 122, 123, 124, 125, 126, 127, 128, 189n.4 (attendance of, at Irish College, 101, 103–4, 105; changes to character of, 100–103; date of death of, 49, 54, 98, 119); Nannie Flynn, 65, 68, 89, 90, 91, 98, 100, 108, 110, 111, 114, 116, 119, 122, 126; Irishtown in, 51, 58, 104, 113; Joyce's radical transformation of, 66, 67, 68, 79, 88–129, 131, 133, 137, 153; the Liffey in, 51; and Monahan sisters as models for Flynns, 58, 59; narrator's difference in, from those in "Araby" and "An Encounter," 50, 54–55, 60, 79; Father O'Rourke, 112, 114, 116, 118; "The Old Watchman" (Campbell) as influence on, 59, 187n.6; religion in, 53,

"Sisters, The"—*continued*
76, 98, 101, 102, 104, 105, 106, 107, 108, 109, 114, 115, 117, 118, 122, 123, 124, 125–29, 133; similarities in, to "Araby" and "An Encounter," 51–53, 129; as thematic complement to "Grace," 133; transformation of the Flynn sisters in, 110

Sörensen, Dolf: *James Joyce's Aesthetic Theory, Its Development and Application*, 191n.11

Spencer, Theodore (as editor of *Stephen Hero*), 46, 187n.9

*Sporting Times or the Pink 'Un, The*: review of *Ulysses* in, 142

Stendhal (Marie-Henri Beyle), 188n.12

*Stephen Hero*, 11, 15, 32–40, 42, 44, 45, 46, 48, 60, 63, 132, 145, 149, 155, 185n.24, 186n.4, 187n.9; as autobiographical art, 147; autobiographical protagonist of, as antecedent to protagonist of *Portrait*, 7, 21, 153; Byrne's encounter with Father Darlington rendered in, 21; Cranly, 32; and Daedalus children corresponding to Earwicker children in *Finnegans Wake*, 138; Maurice, 21; "Villanelle of the Temptress" ("Shine and Dark"), 32

Strindberg, August: *A Dream Play (Ett Drömspel)*, 29–30

Sultan, Stanley: *The Argument of "Ulysses*," 184n.17; *Eliot, Joyce and Company*, 185n.5

Thomas, Dylan: "Do Not Go Gentle into That Good Night," 37

Thurber, James: "My Memories of D. H. Lawrence," 10

Tindall, William York: *A Reader's Guide to "Finnegans Wake*," 143

Tolka River, 30

Torchiana, Donald T.: *Backgrounds for Joyce's "Dubliners*," 190n.2

"Two Gallants," 45, 86

*Ulysses*, 3, 8, 9, 13, 21, 26, 31, 32, 43, 60, 77, 79, 85, 87, 125, 126, 132, 137, 139, 142, 187n.2; as autobiographical fiction, 16–20, 22–27, 38, 39–40, 148, 153; Alf Bergan, 17; Leopold Bloom, 15, 20, 27, 39, 54, 78, 84, 134, 148 (as analogue for Nora, 40; connection of, to Joyce, 16, 149; difference of, from Joyce, 16; function of, for Stephen, 143); Milly Bloom, 15; Molly Bloom, 40, 134, 143, 148, 189n.6 (soliloquy of, 42, 78); "Bloomsday," 22, 23–40; Bella Cohen, 20, 148; Martin Cunningham, 133, 190n.1; Reuben J. Dodd, 133; John Eglinton/W. K. Magee, 18, 183n.7; Eliot on, 4; (Joseph) Haines, 18, 38, 144; Tom Kernan, 133, 134, 190n.1; Barney Kiernan's pub in, 78; Lynch, 17, 149; Lyster the librarian, 18, 148; Gerty MacDowell, 78; man in the macintosh, 133, 134–35, 190n.3; McCann (MacCann), 18; McKernan family, 18; (Charles) M'Coy, 134, 190n.1; Julia Morkan, 58; Kate Morkan, 57–58; Buck Mulligan, 17, 18, 38, 51, 144; Jack Power, 133, 134, 190n.1; Bob Reynolds, 18; George Russell ("AE" [character]), 17, 18, 19, 147, 183n.7, 184n.11; similarity of, to "Grace," 133–34; Stephen's artistic doctrine in (withheld from Stephen in *Portrait*), 146–49; Stephen's lecture on Shakespeare in, 144–45, 146, 147–48, 152; Stephen's "Parable of the Plums" in, 122

van Gogh, Vincent, 38

Verlaine, Paul: Joyce as translator of, 32

"Villanelle of the Temptress, The" ("Shine and Dark"), 32

Walzl, Florence L.: "Joyce's 'The Sisters': A Development," 189nn.1, 3

Webb, Beatrice and Sidney, 2

Wells, H. G.: "A Perfect Gentleman on Wheels," 86

Westland Road: in "Araby," 51

Whistler, James, 38

Whittaker, Stephen, 185n.25

Wilkins, Joe and Leo, 188n.7

Wolfe, Thomas: and *Künstlerroman*, 182n.15
Woolf, Virginia: *The Diary of Virginia Woolf*, 182n.16; "Modern Fiction," 4; *To the Lighthouse*, 7–8
Worthen, John: *D. H. Lawrence: The Early Years, 1885–1912*, 10, 157, 165, 172, 173, 174, 181n.2; "The Haggs as Myth" in, 172

Yeats, W. B., 31, 33, 183n.7, 184n.11, 185n.26; "Among School Children," 53, 72; *The Countess Cathleen*, 17; "Is" and "Ought" (or reality and justice) of, 26, 40; on Joyce's poetry (Stephen's villanelle in *Portrait*), 37; London meeting of, with Joyce, 37

Zabel, Morton Dauwen, 189n.13

Stanley Sultan is professor of English at Clark University. He is author of several books, including *The Argument of Ulysses* (1964) and *Eliot, Joyce, and Company* (1987).

**OHIO UNIVERSITY LIBRARY**
Please return this book as soon as you have finished with it. In order to avoid a fine it must be returned by the latest date stamped below. All books are subject to recall after tw